CHINA TRIALS

CHINA
TRIALS

The Quest for Liver Failure Therapy

TERRY WINTERS, PhD

China Trials: The Quest for Liver Failure Therapy

Published by
Munn Avenue Press
300 Main Street, Ste 21
Madison, NJ 07940
MunnAvenuePress.com

MUNN
AVENUE
PRESS

Paperback ISBN: 978-1-960299-18-5
Hard Cover ISBN: 978-1-960299-19-2

Printed in the United States of America

CONTENTS

Prologue 1

Chapter 1:   Hepatix Stumbles and Is Reborn 5

Chapter 2:   Technology and Start-Up of Hepatix...................................7

Chapter 3:   First Clinical Trials and EU Adventures......................... 14

Chapter 4:   Second Bankruptcy: What Have We Bought? 22

Chapter 5:   The Pivot to China.. 32

Chapter 6:   CHINA!.. 44

Chapter 7:   The China Decision 50

Chapter 8:   Fundraising for the China Trials.................................... 57

Chapter 9:   Preparing for the China Trials 66

Chapter 10:   The Surprising First Trial Patient 77

Chapter 11:   The Trial Starts 80

Chapter 12:   Slow Progress.. 86

Chapter 13:   Filing for SFDA Marketing Approval.............................93

Chapter 14:   Preparing for ELAD Market Launch 100

Chapter 15:   The Execution 105

Chapter 16:   Venture Capital Financing 107

Chapter 17:   Seeking China Approval 114

Chapter 18: US Trials and Compassionate Use 121

Chapter 19: China Stalemate 127

Chapter 20: Singapore Compassionate Use 131

Chapter 21: The Middle East 137

Chapter 22: Kameron Delivers 143

Chapter 23: Funding and Continuing China Stalemate 148

Chapter 24: US/EU Trials 153

Chapter 25: Aodong 160

Chapter 26: Negotiating the Agreement 166

Chapter 27: Chairman Li Directs the SFDA Program 172

Chapter 28: Swan Song in China 180

Chapter 29: Return to the US: Bankruptcy Avoided 194

Chapter 30: Rebuilding 199

Chapter 31: IPO! 208

Chapter 32: Disappointment 214

Chapter 33: Designing a New Trial 220

Chapter 34: Irrational Exuberance 230

Chapter 35: Disaster! 234

Figures 246

Epilogue 251

Glossary 253

Dedicated to the physicians, hospital staffs, and severe acute liver failure patients who participated in our clinical trials and compassionate use programs in China, US, England, Scotland, Ireland, Australia, Germany, Austria, Spain, Singapore, UAE, and Saudi Arabia.

They are still waiting for a cure!

Vist china-trials.com for more information and a photo gallery of some of the events.

BY THE SAME AUTHOR

Sex, Diet and Tanning by Drs. Terence Winters and Robert Dorr. The curious story of the development of the drug to induce a natural tan without sunlight

PROLOGUE

Every so often in the venture capital (VC) business you come across an opportunity that is truly exceptional. Such was the case in 1989 with Hepatix, a startup company out of Baylor College of Medicine in Houston, Texas. It had been put together by a friend of ours formerly with the Hillman Company in Pittsburgh and we were lucky enough to be asked to join in getting the company funded and started. This is known as the seed investment round in the VC business.

This book is the story of this company which we helped to create. During the span of almost 30 years, the company was known by three different names as it chaotically lived the life cycle of a VC startup, raising and spending about $350 million. It went through two bankruptcies and was sequentially known as Hepatix, Vitagen, and finally, Vital Therapies.

It is not a pretty story and does not have a happy ending, at least not yet. But there were some incredible things that happened. Most of these kinds of books have heroes and happy endings but no one comes out of this one bathed in glory. However, it is a story worth telling as you will learn a lot about drug development and the way China does business, amongst other things. You will also meet some incredibly dedicated and hard-working people whose major motivation was to help alleviate suffering in liver failure patients. None of us were in this primarily for the money and several of us, including me, lost a significant amount of money.

The founders of Hepatix were a physician and a scientist from Baylor College of Medicine. They were difficult to work with and caused us much heartache. However, I salute their brilliant idea, their hard work, and their dedication to trying to make it happen. Their concept was to use a special line of live human liver cells outside the body (extracorporeal) to provide liver function to serious liver failure patients. Thereby, either saving their lives while their liver regenerated or keeping them alive while they awaited a liver transplant, known as "bridge-to-transplant." At the time, in 1990, we had not heard of using live human cells to do such a thing. We were fascinated and impressed with the technology and the market opportunity, as were many of our VC friends. As a result, the first financing was a frantic competition to get a piece of the action and possibly sit on the board of directors. Ultimately, the financing came together fast and the company had a flying start but soon got into problems.

Today, this kind of biologic product is referred to as a cellular therapy. Specifically an allogeneic cellular therapy since the same product can be used on all patients in contrast to an autologous cellular therapy which uses the patient's cells and therefore can only be used on that patient.

Unfortunately, after more than 30 years, the product, ELAD (Extracorporeal_Liver Assist Device), is still not approved to treat patients anywhere in the world. Back in 1989, I had no idea that this company would start us on a worldwide development project that eventually moved to China in 2004. Then, after eight years of fruitless attempts to get approval in China, back to the US where we failed to get it approved for a different indication than the one which showed so much promise in China.

I accidentally fell into being CEO of the company from 2003 to 2017. Even though we did not succeed, this has been the highlight of my life and I would not have missed it for the world. I'm sure that the product will eventually get approved and will save lives, but there is still work to do.

Since 1964, I have always operated at the leading edge of science to develop new products. Originally trained as a chemist, I commenced working on the synthesis of tetracycline antibiotics for my PhD thesis at the University of Wales. I then went on to study the medicinal components of desert plants at the University of California, Los Angeles (UCLA). After realizing I was not suited to academia, I became a polymer chemist at Goodyear in Akron, Ohio. While there, I worked on polyester product development during its explosive growth in the 1970s where we developed fibers for tire cord and textiles and stumbled upon the polyester soft drink bottle—it was the only plastic polymer that kept CO_2 in the bottle— among other things. Then I got into the business side and sold Goodyear's technology and know-how around the world, all the while gaining great business experience.

After the oil shock of 1975, I decided that it made more sense to be in the oil business and joined Diamond Shamrock Corporation, an oil and chemicals company, where I was part of a team looking to buy technology as the basis for new businesses. A stroke of good fortune afforded me the opportunity to be the junior of two managers of our corporate VC fund, launched when the VC world was just starting to take off. These were the Reagan Revolution years and in 1983 I accepted an offer as the life sciences partner of a private VC group in Denver, Colorado. This got me involved in the genesis of the biotechnology revolution and I stayed in and around this business until the present day. I am supposed to be retired but VCs never retire because the business is too much fun. I have seen and participated in every boom-and-bust cycle of the biotech business since inception but that is the subject of another book, still to be written.

I have tried to focus on the story in this book and not on the sometimes mind-numbing details of clinical trials. Rest assured that the gathering and analysis of data were going on all the time. However, it is not necessary to get into this detail to tell the story, especially to readers who are not skilled in scientific research. I hope that I have met my goal of making the story comprehensible to the non-scientific reader. If you see a word or term you do not understand, there is a glossary after the final chapter where it is probably defined.

The story starts slowly in Texas but most of the action happens in China. If you are mostly interested in the China part, then start reading at Chapter 5. But be forewarned, you will miss the essence of the VC seed and startup processes described in the first four chapters.

I hope you enjoy the story.

Terry Winters

CHAPTER 1
Hepatix Stumbles and Is Reborn

"Sold!" exclaimed the auctioneer, sounding his gavel on a desk in an empty room in La Jolla, California, in 2003.

My good friend John Lewis, a partner with Paragon Venture Fund, had bid his investment note, amounting to about $500,000, for the assets of Vitagen, the successor company to Hepatix, after its bankruptcy in 1995. Since no one else could match this bid, John's fund was now the new owner of the assets. The technology and know-how included the human liver cell lines which were stored in several places in the US and Europe and which were essential to manufacturing and using the product known as ELAD or Extracorporeal Liver Assist Device.

About three months before the auction, John had called me to discuss our evaluation of the Vitagen business and whether our fund should invest in keeping the company alive. We had sent a team to La Jolla to review the situation and to see if the company could be saved. But our reluctant conclusion was that it would simply be throwing good money after bad. Not only was the company burdened with a large amount of debt by the investment loans that had been made by the existing investors, but It was also not getting what it wanted at the US Food and Drug Administration (FDA), the regulator of this biologic drug product, because it had not achieved proof of principle in its early clinical trials in liver disease patients. These trials had been poorly designed and the choice of indication, a small market known as fulminant liver failure, largely caused by the drug Tylenol, was not attractive to VC's due to the small market size and the very slow enrollment in the trials caused by the patient rarity. On top of all this, it was spending money like it was a successful pharmaceutical company with plush, expensive offices in La Jolla.

I told John that we were still excited by the business but that the company needed to be put through a Chapter 7 bankruptcy so all of its debts could be eliminated and we could restart it from scratch. John was not surprised and understood our conclusion. After he thanked me for spending the time, he skillfully extracted a soft promise from me to join him in an investment to restart the company if an appropriate Chapter 7 bankruptcy could be accomplished. However, before we describe how we restarted the company, we need to explain the technology and business opportunity and explore why the company got itself into this trouble.

CHAPTER 2
Technology and Start-Up of Hepatix

The liver is arguably the most complex organ in the human body. It is the waste treatment facility and the chemical manufacturing plant for most key biochemicals needed for life. Most other organs such as the kidneys, lungs, and heart have a single function and we now have mechanical devices that can duplicate these functions to keep patients alive. The kidneys are filters, the lungs are gas-transfer organs, and the heart is a pump. But no one has been able to successfully duplicate the complex functions of the liver necessary to keep a liver failure patient alive for a meaningful period.

What we do have is the surgical miracle of liver transplant. However, it is very expensive, limited by a shortage of donor livers and requires the recipients to be on expensive drugs to prevent organ rejection for the rest of their lives. Liver transplantation exists because the simple solution of drugs just does not work for the liver.

It is worth spending a moment to explain why there is a shortage of donor livers since many people give permission for their organs to be taken after their death and used for transplant. The problem is that the liver begins to deteriorate minutes after death. For a liver to be viable for transplant, in most cases, it has to be taken from a patient with a beating heart. This is why the transplant unit team gathers around a brain-dead patient's bed before they pull the plug and then immediately harvest the liver. The liver is usually transplanted within 12 hours to have the optimal outcome for the recipient. Unlike the liver, other organs have devices to support them. For example, the kidney has dialysis; the heart has ventricular assist devices; and the lung has ECMO (Extra Corporeal Membrane Oxygenator). As a result, patients can tolerate a period of time in which the transplanted organ does not function well. But there is no such support for livers, and the transplanted liver needs to function close to perfectly as soon as it is transplanted. The need to assure quality liver function decreases the number of organs available for transplant. That's why there are only about 7,000 liver transplants done each year in the US compared with about 10 times as many kidney transplants.

There continue to be advances made in preserving livers for transplant and exciting developments like growing human livers in pigs but it is probably going to be a long time before the donor liver shortage is over. Meanwhile, the search for the liver equivalent of kidney dialysis continues.

The two founders of Hepatix had the brilliant idea of using live human liver cells to treat liver failure patients in a device that passes the patient's blood through these live cells outside the body, known as extracorporeal therapy. The blood then returns to the patient cleansed of waste and with the major biochemical syntheses performed. In other words, liver function outside the body. This was not a new idea but the problem with it was that no one had ever been able to successfully isolate and grow liver cells outside the body, let alone keep them alive in a device that would need to be effective for many days.

So, the founders of Hepatix set out to develop a line of human liver cells that would be stable, could be grown in a manufacturing plant in quantities that were clinically useful, would survive many days in a device treating a liver failure patient, and were allogeneic, meaning the cells grown from this cell line could treat any patient. They worked with the leading human cell storage and development organization, The Wistar Institute in Philadelphia, and found exactly what they were looking for in a rare liver tumor taken from a teenage boy. They confirmed that the cell line produced many of the key biochemicals that a healthy liver produces and processed many of the body's toxins. The cell line, known as C3A, was isolated and stored in several locations and then they looked for financial support to start up their company.

I can feel your shock and skepticism about the words "liver tumor." That means cancer, right? How is it going to be possible to use a cancer cell to help a patient overcome a serious disease? Aren't cancer cells lethal and don't they put out toxic materials? The answers to these two questions are, respectively, yes and no. They are potentially lethal because they have no control over their continued growth and can kill the patient by uncontrolled growth which smothers key organs and systems in the body. They also magnify their lethal effect by splitting off some cells from the main tumor which travel around the body in the bloodstream, take up residence in other parts, and grow new tumors. This process is known as metastasis. Fortunately, the C3A cell line was only weakly metastatic and the cells stopped growing when they were space restricted as in our bioreactor.

Remember also that growing live liver cells outside the body was not possible and that keeping liver cells alive once separated from the human liver was also not possible. The C3A tumor cell line overcame both of these problems since tumor cells are immortal and, under the right conditions, they could be made to divide and multiply in a bioreactor into an almost unlimited supply of cells. Since it was obvious that we were going to need a large number of cells, probably about a pound or more, to do each treatment, these properties were essential to develop a product. The C3A cell line met these criteria.

The issue of the cancer cells escaping from the device and passing into the patient was a bit more difficult to overcome but we got some advice from the FDA that they would not consider this to be unsafe providing the device had a failsafe way of stopping the cells escaping back into the patient. Eventually, we were able to develop this to the FDA's satisfaction and so the cancer cell issue was handled but not without a lot of work. We were also able to demonstrate that even if a C3A cell did pass into a patient, it would not grow into a dangerous tumor which further helped with the FDA.

Hepatix was formed in early 1990. These were still the early days of the biotechnology revolution and capital was not easy to raise. However, the founders were fortunate that Baylor College of Medicine in Houston had recognized the opportunity presented by the Bayh-Dole

Act of Congress, which allowed universities to own the technology they developed under US government grants. Baylor had recently set up a technology transfer office and hired Steve Banks to run it. Steve was a highly competent professional VC player who formerly had been with the Hillman Company in Pittsburgh which had supported many of the early computer and biotechnology companies. The only problem was that Baylor did not have any investment capital so Steve had to come to his friends in the VC industry.

We were lucky that he called my partner Carl Stutts first who recognized the opportunity and brought it to his partners at our fund, Columbine Ventures, in Denver. We were an eclectic bunch, five partners from the computer, semiconductor, biotechnology, and energy industries managing about $78 million of capital targeted for seed and early-stage life science and information technology investments in the American Southwest. That was a lot of money in the 1990s.

In a rare instance of early agreement among the partners, we all really loved this deal. We quickly got our diligence done, committed $450,000 to the Hepatix start-up, and agreed to act as the lead investor. Our friends at Point Ventures in Pittsburgh and Triad in Houston soon joined us with an additional $250,000. This money was meant to set up the company to raise a more significant amount of money to develop the product and plan the initial clinical trials. We closed on this $700,000 investment in December 1990.

The timing was good since the market was in the middle of another boom time in the biotechnology field. After we got the company formation work done and wrote the business plan, we approached many of our friends in the VC business and found ourselves with an excess of commitments to fund the company. We agreed we would accept a maximum of $3 million in the first-round investment with Columbine as the lead investing a total of about $1 million for about 25% ownership in the company. There were several Texas-based investors and also Paragon Ventures out of Silicon Valley, led by John Lewis who was to play such a key role in getting the company restructured in the future. The $3 million investment was closed in January 1992 and we were off and running.

Hepatix was very different from the kinds of biotechnology investments being made at that time. There had been a lot of talk about using live human cells as a therapy for serious diseases but no such products were on the market. We were also not aware of another company trying to develop a product to perform allogeneic cellular therapy on humans. This made Hepatix unique and explained its attraction as an investment.

That was the good news. The bad news was that none of us knew what we were doing and we had no idea of the challenges lying in wait for us as we progressed down the rocky road of trying to develop a cellular therapy for liver failure. All you had to do was grow the cells and use them in the device outside the body, right? Sounds easy. But the reality was very different with the main challenge being to grow the cells in a controlled and reproducible process and satisfy a very skeptical FDA about the safety and efficacy of using cells on real, live patients.

We decided that Carl Stutts, one of our general partners based in Houston, would represent Columbine on the board of directors in the role of chairman of the board and lead director. Carl had been a partner at Tenneco Ventures, an oil company in Houston, before joining us and had experience in the biotechnology field. We felt that his local presence would be a very important factor in developing the company. Carl asked that I attend some of the board meetings with him to provide some more biotechnology experience. This made sense to everybody.

The company took some laboratory and office space in Houston and started to hire some key employees. One of the first was a Chinese physician, Dr. Dar He, a naturalized US citizen, who had experience in cell culture and was given the responsibility to develop the manufacturing process for the cells.

I first met Dar soon after the start-up company moved into its new lab space. I was impressed with Dar's story and his commitment to developing a product to save the lives of liver failure patients. In China, he had lost his best friend to liver failure caused by the hepatitis B virus and he vowed to spend the rest of his life developing an effective therapy. Dar is the kind of person that everybody liked because he was bursting with energy and enthusiasm. He was also a good physician and scientist but readily admitted that he did not have a business mind. However, in our subsequent work together in China, he gained more experience in business than most MBAs. More about that later.

Dar made very good progress with manufacturing the units containing the liver cells. Since kidney dialysis had been around for many years, he could use much of the equipment that was used in that procedure, including the cartridge where the cells are grown. Dar developed the growth procedures and the quantity of cells to be used. He also developed various testing procedures to ensure a consistent product. The final version contained about one pound of the C3A cells in four cartridges and could be kept on the bioreactor for many days before it was needed for use. It could also be shipped under cool conditions and quickly activated for use on a patient.

Word leaked out about what we were doing and we started to get requests for compassionate use of the product on patients dying of liver failure. The FDA did not object and so we tried the product on two such patients with promising results in early 1992. We used the patient's blood taken from the femoral vein, passed the blood through the cells, and then back to the patient. But these early compassionate use treatments showed us that we had a serious problem with blood clotting in the cartridge which, because of the fragility of the liver cells, we could not solve with the common anti-clotting agents. Therefore, we started work to separate the plasma from the blood and to use the plasma to contact the cells. This was a difficult process and continued to give us problems right up to the present version of the product.

Hepatix launched with an interim CEO, George Schapiro, who was known to most of us and was willing to take on the job provided it did not develop into a long-term position. We also began a search for a permanent CEO and focused on getting a market-oriented person since we felt our challenges were going to be in this area and not in the manufacturing, clinical, or regulatory fields. We thought it was going to be a slam dunk getting the product approved. This turned out to be a very serious mistake and proved again that none of us really knew what we were doing in these early times. The manufacturing, clinical, and regulatory challenges turned out to be daunting, and underestimating these probably was the major factor that resulted in Hepatix's first bankruptcy.

Our initial major error was classifying ELAD as a device for regulatory purposes. The FDA initially went along with this classification and we were very happy to have it treated as a device since the pathway to regulatory approval for devices is much simpler and takes much less time than a drug or a biologic. The downside of this is that devices make it much easier for competitors to get a similar product approved. But we felt that our patents were strong enough to stave off competitive challenges for a long time.

In developing the manufacturing process, the two founders and Dar chose two key proteins that are made in significant quantities by the liver to be the markers of the quality of the product and, when they reached a certain pre-specified level in the cartridge output, they were the indicators that the ELAD cartridges were ready for use on a patient. These two markers were albumin, one of the most ubiquitous proteins in the human body, and transferrin, another human protein produced in lower quantities but diagnostic of liver function. These were acceptable to the FDA.

CHAPTER 3
First Clinical Trials and EU Adventures

After the basics of the cartridges' manufacturing were worked out, the company spent most of 1992 running trials of the cartridges on dogs. This generated the data needed to get the investigational device exemption (IDE) allowed by the FDA to enable human clinical trials to begin. The clinical development and regulatory issues were handled by the two founders and we were ready to commence human clinical trials in early 1993. It didn't occur to anyone that the founders were academics and neither of them had any experience in clinical development and working with the FDA, which has the authority to regulate everything we were doing. In hindsight, that was another serious error.

The FDA allowed the IDE in early 1993 and the first trials commenced at Baylor College of Medicine in Houston. Those of you who were around at the time will recall that this was the time of the first heart transplant in South Africa which generated enormous public interest. The press was therefore ultra-sensitized to these kinds of innovative medical developments and so it was no surprise that we had a lot of press and TV coverage of the first treatment at Baylor. This made everybody feel very good since we thought we had a viable product and we were in the lead to develop the first artificial liver.

We decided to focus on fulminant hepatic failure (FHF) as the target indication for this first trial. FHF is aptly described in its name since it is essentially a poisoning of the liver by a toxin that makes it inflamed and causes the liver to fail. There is no drug to treat it and if the body cannot handle it, the patient dies fairly quickly, usually of inflammation of the brain caused by liver failure, where the brain breaks out of its cavity in the head. It is therefore a very serious condition with about

2,000 cases every year in the US. Of these, about half receive a liver transplant, with most surviving. They go to the top of the transplant list and are usually transplanted within one-to-two days due to the urgency of the condition. Of the remaining 1,000, half die within days and half recover spontaneously. It is a very high-profile disease since 80% of the cases are caused by overdoses of acetaminophen, a pain reliever drug known as Tylenol in the US and as Paracetamol in Europe. The reason is that the therapeutic dose and the toxic dose of Tylenol are fairly close together. The typical patient is a young female with a migraine headache who, desperate to relieve her pain, reasons that if two tablets every six hours are good then two every hour should be even better, but this puts her in the toxic range with disastrous results.

The first trial treated eleven FHF patients at Baylor and was supervised by Dr. Sussman in 1993. There was no control group in this phase 1 trial and the main purpose of the trial was to confirm the safety of the product, which was achieved and the FDA allowed us to proceed to the next trial. A control group consists of the same kind of patients, but these are not treated with the product. The results of the treated and control groups are then compared to see if there is any benefit from using the product. In our trials, the standard for the comparison, known as the endpoint, was usually death, euphemistically referred to as survival.

This was the point where Dr. Michael Millis entered the picture. He was serving his liver transplant fellowship at the UCLA Hospital where Dr. Sussman gave a Grand Rounds lecture in 1994 and asked Dr. Millis to lead the protocol drafting for the phase 2 trial at King's College Hospital in London, England. He was to play an increasingly important role in the development of ELAD going forward and in the business part of the third iteration of the company as Vital Therapies, serving on its board of directors for more than ten years.

Mike and I worked very well together. We both had an acute sense of the scientific method and of doing things right the first time. He is an outstanding surgeon and has been in charge of transplantation at the University of Chicago since I first met him in 2003. He specializes in liver transplantation and is well known in international circles, especially in China where he has been working on the ethics of China's liver transplantation program, a difficult job requiring sensitivity to the political climate. This was to be very useful when we moved to do our trials in China in 2005.

The founders had very good relationships with some of the key physicians at hospitals in England who were acknowledged to be the leaders in liver therapy innovations. The first clinical trial was therefore planned at King's College Hospital in London and began in May 1993. This was to be a phase 1 trial for FDA purposes which could then be used to run the definitive trial, known as a pre-market approval, or PMA, trial for a device and could be used to file for marketing approval. Contrast this to the three sequential clinical trials, phases 1, 2 and 3, required for a drug or biologic which would probably take about five years longer and cost much more to complete than the requirements for a device.

The King's College trial was run on FHF patients and we felt that we could use ELAD to either save the patient's life to full recovery or to bridge him/her to a liver transplant. The problem was that not a great deal of thought was put into the availability of these patients and it turned out that there were less than 300 cases per year in the UK. It was difficult to get them to enroll in the trial. Nonetheless, thanks to the high profile of the trial, it was fully enrolled with twenty-five patients, twelve active and thirteen controls, in about a year. This was a randomized controlled clinical trial or RCT, the gold standard in the pharmaceutical industry.

In an RCT, candidate patients are evaluated and, when they are confirmed to qualify, they are randomly assigned either to the treated or control groups. The treated patients are put on the therapy while the controls are given the current standard of care but not the therapy under evaluation. Then, the results in each group are compared to see if there is a statistically significant difference between them based on the endpoint. In our case, it was survival at 90 days after enrollment.

As a phase 1 trial, this one, by design, did not have enough patients to show a statistically significant difference in the survival endpoint between the treated and control groups. It was not designed to give statistically significant results. The results were good but not spectacular, mainly because FHF is such a horrendous condition that many patients die anyway and with just twelve active patients, it was difficult to show a definitive survival result. There was a good control group in this trial and the best part of the result was that you could clearly see that treatment with ELAD slowed down the time to death. On the whole, this was a successful trial and merited going to the next step.

We are going to be using Kaplan-Meier curves to summarize trial results many times as we go forward with the story so we need to explain what they are and how to read them. Any clinical trial needs to have an endpoint which is a way of judging how the patient responds to the therapy. Of course, you have the placebo or control group as well which does not receive the therapy, and so you can see the difference between the two—that is what the Kaplan-Meier curve does. The statistical mathematics behind these Kaplan-Meier curves tells us whether the results meet the FDA's mandated 95% confidence level for significance. It is usually expressed as the percentage chance that the results are the same, as a p-value where $p = 0.05$ or less expresses the 5% chance or less that FDA requires. Therefore, a good result is a p-value of 0.05, or lower.

The endpoint for our trials was always survival. We tried to use other endpoints, such as blood markers of liver function, but the FDA would have none of it. Their argument was that our trial patient population has a high death rate and it happens in a relatively short period of time, usually less than 120 days. Therefore, they would not accept any other endpoint except survival. We had no choice but to comply.

The Kaplan-Meier graph shows each death in the trial by the curve stepping down one place equivalent to the percentage that the death represents of the number of those patients remaining alive in the trial. There are two curves, one curve for the active and one for the placebo/control patients and you can see very clearly if there is a difference. Statisticians have worked out the math to analyze it to see whether it is statistically significant.

After this trial was completed, the problems began for the company. It was time to raise more money if we wanted to proceed to the next trial. But out of the blue, we got a letter from the FDA advising us that the classification of ELAD had been changed from a device to a biologic drug. This moved us out of the regulatory control of the FDA's Device Division, known as the Center for Devices and Radiological Health, or CDRH, and into the Biologics Division, known as the Center for Biologics Evaluation and Research, or CBER. Being regulated by the CBER, rather than the CDRH, was known to be a big increase in regulatory scrutiny and in time and money to comply.

This was a bombshell since it would require a great deal more investment capital to complete the trials. When we tried to raise this money, we received a lot of resistance from new investors. So, the existing investors started to bridge the company with additional funds. This led to some serious disagreements between the founders and the investors.

The existing investors were not willing to put in a significant amount of additional money without the validation of several new investors, which is a standard operating practice in the VC community. But the founders felt that the existing investors were trying to steal the company from them. This poisoned the atmosphere and was the beginning of serious arguments between the founders and the investors which led to a lawsuit that played a significant role in the first bankruptcy.

At the end of 1994, a cease-fire was called in the lawsuit and an agreement was reached with the founders to give them the rights to use the C3A cells for diagnostic testing purposes with Hepatix retaining the full rights for therapeutic use. The founders formed a new company called Amphioxus and started to transition out of Hepatix to raise money for Amphioxus. But it only postponed the inevitable continuation of the lawsuit.

I had been attending every other board meeting and watched this start to play out. I was mostly silent in the board meetings, only asking a few questions and letting my partner, Carl Stutts, carry the ball. We hired a new CEO in early 1993, Dr. Phil Radlick, who was primarily a marketing guy and not comfortable with the manufacturing and clinical issues. However, he knew a lot of people in the medical industry and was particularly well plugged into the community in Europe. Coupled with Dr. Sussman's very high profile in the US and UK liver physician communities, this helped with our credibility in implementing the trials in the US and Europe.

However, I knew we were in trouble when towards the end of 1993, the CEO presented to the board a plan to build a manufacturing plant and to carry out clinical trials in Switzerland. While Switzerland is a very sophisticated medical country, it is not part of the EU and has the highest cost structure of any country in Europe. But we went ahead with the plan anyway and, of course, ended up spending uncomfortable amounts of money even after offsetting the grants that Switzerland gave us for setting up shop there. The first serious manufacturing problems showed up in Switzerland and, despite much work, we could not grow the cells in the cartridges reproducibly, resulting in not being able to enroll and treat numerous patients and slowing down the completion of the trial.

We did manage to raise an additional $5 million in early 1994 with several new investors. At $2.6 million, Columbine was now close to our maximum investment and we ceded the role of lead investor to Chemical Ventures who put in half the money of the new round of $5 million.

In March 1995, the problems in the company had become so serious that Carl asked me to take over and try to figure out how we could get it back on track. I reluctantly agreed to do so and joined the board of directors. However, the rift between the founders and the investors was serious, the clinical trials were not going well since patients were rare and progress slow, and there were significant manufacturing problems that needed to be addressed.

It has been said by people a lot smarter than I am that you should not see laws or sausages being made. I would add board meetings to that list when there are significant problems in the company. Therefore, I will not dwell on the details of the several very difficult board meetings where we tried to work out a solution, but I will summarize the situation.

Prior to the board meetings, I took Dr. Hank Agersborg with me to Houston to try to figure out what we had and how we could proceed. Hank had recently retired from being the head of research at American Home Products, a well-respected large pharmaceutical company, and he was running a pharmaceutical company incubator in Philadelphia for us. I learned a tremendous amount about drug development from Hank because he had already shepherded many drugs through the FDA process to market. He was the ideal person to figure out what we had and where we went from here.

Hank had a dour personality and looked a lot like W.C. Fields, with a wonderful sense of humor to match. But he was all business and bored in on the key issues. At the end of our session on the first day, we were astonished to learn that none of the manufacturing or the trials to date had been run according to FDA requirements and so none of the data could be used in the approval process. We would have to restart the game at square one!

Hank and I worked out a plan to restart and make sure that everything was done to FDA requirements. But we wanted to do this with a minimum amount of capital and use the capability at Hank's company incubator. This meant that we would eliminate most of the Hepatix staff and use a lot of outside services. The rest of the board did not like this plan and so I ended up resigning from the board and Columbine exited the investment. We wrote off our $2.6 million, licked our wounds, and went home, leaving the rest of the board with a new CEO installed to figure out what to do next.

What they did next surprised us. They declared a Chapter 11 bankruptcy, which allowed them to reorganize to discharge debt and other impediments to progress. Then they moved the whole company to San

Diego, changed the name to Vitagen, raised a large amount of money, and started to do everything necessary to be allowed to proceed to a phase 1 clinical trial for a biologic product. This meant they had to do all the work necessary to file an investigational new drug, or IND, application and then start the clinical trials, still focusing on FHF patients. We were glad to be out of it because it required a significant amount of additional capital and we were already close to our limit of $3 million for any one investment.

It is never pleasant to lose $2.6 million but VC is a very high-risk business and losses are part of the game. Fortunately, in the VC business, you can only lose one times your money but you can make ten or more times your money on a good investment. Therefore, we took our loss and focused on new investments that had significant upside. Tough to do but this is creative destruction, the very essence of capitalism.

However, the lawsuit was still active, and resigning from the board did not exempt us from being a target. My wife became apoplectic when, three years later, she was served with the lawsuit at our private residence which claimed multi-million dollars for breach of fiduciary duty by the board members. It didn't seem to matter that the time of the alleged breach of duty was after I had resigned from the board. However, we had good legal counsel, and eventually, it was resolved for a token payment on our part. I have no idea how the rest of the lawsuit was resolved with the then-current board members.

I had plenty of other things to focus on and forgot about the company until it resurfaced again, eight years later, in 2003.

CHAPTER 4
Second Bankruptcy: What Have We Bought?

During the years after the first bankruptcy in 1995, I had no contact with Vitagen. But I did get the occasional update from John Lewis who I met from time to time because of our other investments and at social gatherings in the VC community. John had stayed invested in the company and kept putting in his pro-rata amount of the various financings. Frankly, I didn't pay much attention to it since I had many other investments to manage.

During this period, 1995-2003, the liver research community was still seeking a way to provide liver support and there was a high level of activity. Several other ways to design and operate a liver assist device or biologic support had reached the stage of clinical trials and two devices, which removed the toxic products, were actually approved and marketed. The academic societies had taken note of all of the activity and a "shoot-out" was staged in 2000 at the meeting of the American Association for the Study of Liver Disease (AASLD) in Boston between four competing ways of providing liver assist function. I was not there, of course, but our future chief medical officer, Dr. Jan Stange, provided me with an account of this "shoot-out." The four competitors were:

1. Vitagen, presented by Dr. Mike Millis with the results of their initial clinical trials with ELAD in FHF.
2. Circe, a new company developing a cellular therapy using pig liver cells and, at that time, in the middle of their pivotal phase 3 clinical trial, presented by Dr. Achilles Dimitriou, the founder, from Cedars Sinai Hospital in Los Angeles.
3. Teraklin, a German company marketing the MARS system for liver dialysis against an albumin solution that removed most of

the toxic products of liver failure and provided simultaneous kidney dialysis, presented by Dr. Jan Stange, CEO.

4. Hemotherapies, marketing a liver dialysis device that used powdered activated charcoal in the dialysis fluid, presented by Dr. David van Thiel, CEO.

This debate was really about whether liver support could be of value by only removing the toxic by-products that build up as a consequence of liver failure, such as bilirubin, ammonia, cytokines, bile acids, and many others, which the devices remove physically, or, whether a more complete approach was needed to metabolize these by-products for elimination and to replace the products that the liver produces such as peptides, proteins, and other key biochemicals necessary for life, which the cellular therapy approach using pig liver cells or C3A cells was thought to at least partially achieve.

This debate is still ongoing today but we have got much more information and the state of play is that there are some liver failure conditions that the devices help and some where a more complete cellular approach is needed. The Teraklin albumin dialysis approach in particular had a dramatic effect on some of the symptoms of liver failure. This included waking the patient up from their coma. But this impact on the symptoms has so far had no obvious effect on survival apart from a modest short-term improvement at twenty-eight days which reverts to no difference at ninety days and beyond. The cellular therapy approach still remains to be proven before an approved product can be marketed.

At the end of the debate, the audience was invited to vote and Teraklin was declared the winner.

For the record, the Circe pig cell trial failed, Hemotherapies went out of business. Teraklin was sold to Baxter which still markets MARS for several specialty uses in liver failure and Vitagen filed for bankruptcy in 2003. So, of these four approaches, only MARS is still commercially available around the world, which may speak for the wisdom of the audience at AASLD 2000?

Now back to the story.

When I got John's call in April 2003 and his invitation to take a look to see if we could save the company, now located in San Diego, I jumped at the opportunity. By this time, our original venture fund that had invested in Hepatix had been liquidated. This is quite normal for these funds because they have ten-year lives and are structured as partnerships. I joined my good friend Jock Holliman as a partner in his fund, Valley Ventures, located in Phoenix, Arizona. Phoenix is about 350 miles east of San Diego and so the company's location fitted perfectly into our investment area. Valley had raised a new fund and we were actively looking for investments.

A quick review of Vitagen's fundraising information made it clear that our decision would be based on the progress of the clinical trials and the resulting data, assuming that the financial side was in order. For the on-site evaluation in San Diego, Dr. Randy Steer accompanied me. Randy is a good friend of many years and was well experienced in biotechnology and in clinical trials. He is an MD and PhD and practiced medicine as a pathologist before moving to be the chief medical officer of a large pharmaceutical company and then a consultant based in Palm Springs, California. We had a long-standing relationship with Randy and found him to be extraordinarily knowledgeable in medicine, especially in the design and analysis of clinical trials. Randy was fluent in French and German as a result of an excellent education in Europe. He also had an outstanding sense of humor that fitted in well with my British roots. We got along very well and are still very good friends.

It took Randy and me less than a day to conclude that the company was not salvageable in its current form and that it was best to let a Chapter 7 bankruptcy occur. This is different from the first Hepatix bankruptcy which was Chapter 11 and allowed a re-organization to occur. Chapter 7 is a total liquidation of all debts and assets.

We were astounded at how little progress the company had made in eight years and how poorly it was being managed. They had an office facility overlooking Torrey Pines Golf Course which housed some expensive research equipment and people and then a second facility about twelve miles away for manufacturing and related activities. It didn't seem that these two facilities communicated well with each other and the company did not know its potential markets. It had simply stuck with FHF as the clinical trial indication despite agonizingly slow progress with patient enrollment. The small size of the market for FHF acted as a huge damper on fundraising. Combined with the very slow progress in the trial, it was terminal for the company.

The manufacturing operation was still operating with off-the-shelf bioreactors which produced only a single set of four cartridges with each run of about forty-five days. The cost of producing the cartridges was very high and the manufacturing process could never have been commercial. Since the FDA requires that clinical trials for biologic products are conducted with a product that is representative of commercial manufacturing, this was a crucial problem. This is a very expensive FDA requirement but it is necessary due to potential variations in the production quality of biologic products that are not a factor with single chemical drugs. However, it makes developing a biologic product time-consuming and very capital intensive. One more downside of being regulated as a biologic.

The reason for the problems was probably that the CEO had no experience in the clinical development of biotechnology products and the management team was not well-suited to the tasks. The two key positions, in clinical trial management and regulatory affairs, were being handled by part-time consultants with predictable results.

Although the clinical results that we saw were promising, we could not move forward with the current team or the clinical strategy and trial design. Coupled with a crippling debt load from shareholder note financing, the company's position was impossible and we recommended a Chapter 7 bankruptcy filing to John Lewis. I have already described John's very constructive reaction. We retired to await Vitagen's possible emergence from bankruptcy which would enable a fresh start.

Vitagen and Hepatix had now raised and spent over $65 million, which was impressive considering that the market for biotechnology invest-ment was not exactly booming. However, as we dug into the money-raising materials and the contacts, we became very concerned that they had reached out to just about every potential source of venture-capital money and may have induced investment fatigue among the whole VC community. This did in fact turn out to be the case and made it difficult to raise money, one of the many reasons why we decided to pivot to China in 2005.

In going through this process, we decided that there were only five people on the current team that we would retain in any restarted company. They were highly motivated mid-level people and we used the time to continue to build our relationships with them, anticipating a positive opportunity for restarting the company from scratch.

When I got the call from John Lewis in June, three months later, to say that the bankruptcy process was complete and that his fund now owned the assets, we were ready to move. We rapidly reached an agreement with John that we would recognize the full value of the note that he had used to buy the assets and that Valley Ventures would contribute a like amount in cash, giving us equal ownership. The only problem was that none of us really knew what we had bought and so we agreed that, to start, we would each put up $50,000 as a loan to the company to cover the expenses of the five team members and the various consultants that we would hire to sort out what we had and to help to create a strategy and a plan for moving forward. If we decided not to proceed, this loan would be lost unless we could sell the assets to cover it which we deemed to be unlikely. If we decided to proceed, then this loan would be part of the investment in the first-round financing of the new company.

We agreed that I would act as interim CEO, John would be president and both of us would sit on the board with me as Chairman. We would start searching for a permanent CEO and then John and I could step down from these management roles in about six months. This was wishful thinking and I didn't realize that I had taken on a permanent position that would last for fourteen years!

We also added John's partner Robert Kibble to the board along with my partner Jock Holliman. This gave us four venture capitalists on the board, which was frowned upon. But we saw it as an interim board where we could add some more horsepower if we decided to proceed after we had developed a strategy and a plan. This worked very well. Everyone was excited and highly motivated by the possibility of getting the product to a very large market in a relatively short time. The board worked well together; none of us took any compensation for this evaluation period.

We got to work quickly. John deferred to me for most of the operating decisions and was always there for consultation and to challenge some of the things that I wanted to do. It was a stimulating experience. There was a great deal to do so here's a summary of the major things that we looked at:

1. The top priority was to preserve and safely store the C3A liver cell bank because without this we had no starter cells to grow the cells in the cartridges and, therefore, had no basis to proceed. Aron and Dar were well aware of this and had taken steps during the bankruptcy proceedings to make sure the cell bank was safe. It had been divided into four parts and was stored in the US and a friendly foreign country in four separate locations. The cells were stored frozen at a very low temperature and when we needed a small amount to seed the growth of the cells in the cartridges, we simply called it up from one of the storage locations. We had enough cells in the combined banks to make over 1 million sets of cartridges and so there was no danger of us running out of our key raw material.

2. The expensive office space in the Torrey Pines area of La Jolla was closed and we negotiated our way out of the lease. The useful equipment was transferred to the manufacturing facility in Rancho Bernardo and we all crowded into this facility which was probably only about 2,000 ft.², including the manufacturing space. This dramatically decreased the expense for office space since the rate was about a quarter of the Torrey

Pines facility. We also acquired a bonus since being crowded into a small space really improved communications.

3. We analyzed the clinical trial results from every possible angle and recruited Randy as our main consultant while leaning heavily on the company's Clinical Advisory Board (CAB) which we were delighted to learn contained some of the leading figures from the best hospitals in the liver disease world in the US and the UK. They were anxious to help and it was obvious that they wanted to see an effective therapy developed for liver failure.

4. We needed to learn much more about the potential markets for liver failure and we engaged a very experienced market research team, led by Bob Easton, to do a market study. We had used Bob many times before and he was well respected in the medical industry so his market research report, if favorable, would be of great help in our future fundraising. I also knew Bob was unbiased and he would not hesitate to tell us that this was a lousy investment if the investigation led that way. After all, he had kept me out of a significant number of poor investments over the years. To supplement this, we made calls to about a dozen of the leading physicians in the liver disease area who had experience with running the ELAD trials. Jock, John, and I divvied up these calls. We had all done this kind of exercise many times in our VC careers but, with ELAD, we all agreed that we had never got such detailed and enthusiastic reports on an experimental product and the need for such a therapy. This was very encouraging.

One question that we asked all of the physicians who we talked to was what results would they want to see before they would use the product in standard clinical practice. Their responses were surprisingly similar. All of them said they would want to see at least a 20% difference in survival between the treated and control groups in the clinical trials. But that was not a 20-percentage point difference which, for example, would have been 40% to 60%. It was a 20% numerical difference which, again for example, would have been 40% to 48%. In all cases, we questioned this and most of them said that this simply reflects the fact that nothing works in acute liver failure and that many of these patients were dying. Anything that offered increased survival would get prescribed and used even if the label was only for FHF. They would use it "off-label" which was quite legal but could not be promoted by a sales force.

We learned as much as possible about the regulatory situation and we soon identified this as being the key thing to worry about. It was obvious that we needed to hire a good full-time regulatory person. But for the moment, we did not have the funds nor the stability to attract the right person and so we continued with Randy Steer and a very good regulatory consulting firm that he recommended based in Washington DC, in the backyard of the FDA. Randy gave us a lot of time and his in-depth experience was better than any full-time regulatory person we could have hired!

The five team members that we decided to try to keep were:

Aron Stern had been the Chief Financial Officer of Vitagen and we credit Aron with being the glue that kept the team together to enable the restart of the company. This was the beginning of a very long relationship between me and Aron and he did a wonderful job of keeping me out of trouble on the finance and governance side of the company. He was an absolute whiz with spreadsheets and with managing the company's money so that we got the best deals on everything.

Dr. Dar He is the Chinese American who was introduced in Chapter 1 as being in charge of manufacturing at Hepatix. His enthusiasm was infectious and we put him to work to document all the steps of the manufacturing process. Dar had become a huge advocate of switching our clinical development to China and he was not reticent to frequently lobby me on the matter. At that time, I did not have a good view of China. I felt it was just another Third World country and I could not conceive of doing clinical trials or selling products in China. I would politely brush off Dar every time he raised it.

Dr. John Brotherton is a PhD chemical engineer who was the brains of the operation. He was quiet and unassuming and the perfect foil to

Dar and his sometimes excessive enthusiasm. When we looked at making any changes in manufacturing, John would be there with the necessary calculations and he was always correct. I never recorded an instance where any of his calculations were wrong and I grew to be very dependent on John's abilities.

Shapour Aslani is an Iranian-American analytical chemist who was in charge of the development of all the quality control tests and the routine implementation of these tests to make sure the product was being produced to specifications. Shapour was very good at what he did and we relied heavily on him for the analytical work. He ran a very clean and efficient lab which was located in a small room adjacent to the manufacturing room. Shapour and I also shared a love of football, that is real football, known as soccer in the US, and we shared many stories about the game. I learned that Iran is football-crazy!

Carol Conlin is a registered nurse who was one of the nurses who traveled to the treatment hospitals to monitor the ELAD therapy on the patient. She was quiet and efficient and always willing to do anything to help the company. We called these nurses our "ELAD specialists." When we had a competition to come up with a new name for the company, it was Carol who came up with the name "Vital Therapies" and won a nice bottle of wine donated by John Lewis.

These five people had a really tough time going through the Chapter 7 bankruptcy and, amazingly, they stayed committed throughout the process. However, they had all seen and witnessed ELAD treatments and were convinced that we had a product that worked very well and would be able to save lives. They were committed to ELAD and did not regard their Vitagen employment as just a job that made them peripherally involved with the therapy. This was impressive to me and the rest of the board of directors.

The state of the life science financial markets in 2003-4 was not good for companies such as ours and we knew that we did not have enough money around the board table to get us through to approval and market launch. We would have to raise a substantial amount of additional money that would probably come from venture capitalists like ourselves. However, biotechnology was not very popular at the time and we knew that it would be an uphill battle to raise the money. There had been too many companies formed and taken public and there were not many success stories to give investors comfort to continue to invest in the field. Most of the newly public companies were trading below their initial public offering (IPO) prices. Taking a potential drug through the tortuous regulatory pathway to gain marketing approval was not easy and required a lot of money and a lot of time. This made us determined to get a stellar plan and strategy before we went outside of our investors to raise money. This meant that we had to have the regulatory situation under control and, preferably, be enrolling patients in the pivotal trial needed for approval.

CHAPTER 5
The Pivot to China

After we took over the assets in June 2003 and started to analyze what we had and what to do, it was obvious that we needed a senior operating person out of the drug industry who had deep experience in clinical trials. Within about six weeks, we lucked out with Dr. Kameron Maxwell who came recommended by one of my friends. He lived in Rancho Santa Fe, an upscale suburb of San Diego, close to where the company was located in Rancho Bernardo, and he had just finished running another drug development company, including clinical trials with significant interactions with the FDA. He was interested in joining us and his resumé was perfect. After I completed the reference checks, I knew that this was our person. The board agreed and we offered him the job of chief operating officer, which he accepted.

Kameron immediately got to work. He looked at all the clinical data and engaged several knowledgeable consultants who he had worked with before, including an excellent group in Washington, DC, that consisted of two very hard-nosed former FDA reviewers. They knew how the FDA worked and insisted that we get everything in perfect shape before we met with the FDA to ask for approval of our clinical plan.

We soon found a big problem: no clinical reports had been written on the two clinical trials that Vitagen had run. These were the phase 1 trial in 1999 with twenty-five subjects and the partially completed phase 2 trial in 2001-2003 that enrolled nineteen of thirty subjects before it was halted by the bankruptcy. These trials were all on FHF subjects with twenty-nine   treated and fifteen   controls for a total of forty-four subjects enrolled. We had to take the time to write the clinical trial reports which were done by another of Kameron's consultants, but it took until the end of the year to complete them. This was a very time-consuming process since our consultant had to go back and review every single clinical trial subject in detail and make sure we had the data scrubbed and ready for FDA review.

Writing these clinical reports took a lot of time and money but it was an extremely productive exercise. We got to know a lot about the FHF indication that had been chosen for the trials which was already profiled in Chapter 3. It was not ideal since it was small with less than 2,000 patients per year in the US. It was also difficult to find an endpoint for the trial since the patients automatically went to the top of the liver transplant list where they were usually transplanted or died within five days. As a result, a survival endpoint was not feasible since transplantation had a significant effect on survival and confounded that endpoint.

We then decided that the only feasible endpoint was success in bridging the patients to transplant. When we analyzed the pooled data from the combined phase 1 and phase 2 trials, we were very pleased to see that the p-value for bridge to transplant was 0.02, well within the FDA's target of 0.05 or below. The p-value is the number calculated by statisticians to determine whether two sets of numbers are variations around the same thing or whether they are truly different. It is where the rubber meets the road in clinical trials, the time in the process when you compare the results from the treated and the control (untreated or placebo) groups, which is the way that efficacy is measured in clinical trials. The FDA sets an upper limit of a 5% chance that the two sets of numbers are not different and this is expressed as a decimal of 0.05 for the 5% statistical chance. So, anything below 0.05 is accepted to be a statistically significant difference whereas a number above 0.05 is rejected as a failure to prove that the treatment has performed better than the untreated or control group. The p-values are affected by various components of the clinical trial with a large number of subjects making it easier to see the difference and get a result below 0.05 and a strong difference between treated and control also making it much easier to hit this number. Therefore, getting a statistically significant result with only forty-four subjects was quite an achievement since it normally takes several hundred subjects to achieve this statistical significance. The Kaplan-Meier plot of the combined p1/p2 bridge-to-transplant results is shown in Figure 1.

After we were sure of the 0.02 p-value, we spent a lot of time debating whether we should immediately apply for marketing approval by filing a biologic license application (BLA) submission with the FDA. We felt we could get designation as an orphan drug and we knew that many orphan drugs have been approved with smaller clinical trials and much less robust numbers than what we had. But the consensus was that we should not do this. On reflection, I think we made a mistake and we should have made the BLA filing. Here is the relevant language from the FDA guidance document:

"The purpose of this section is to establish procedures designed to expedite the development, evaluation, and marketing of new therapies intended to treat persons with life-threatening and severely-debilitating illnesses, especially where no satisfactory alternative therapy exists. As stated in 314.105(c) of this chapter, while the statutory standards of safety and effectiveness apply to all drugs, the many kinds of drugs that are subject to them, and the wide range of uses for those drugs, demand flexibility in applying the standards. The Food and Drug Administration (FDA) has determined that it is appropriate to exercise the broadest flexibility in applying the statutory standards while preserving appropriate guarantees for safety and effectiveness. These procedures reflect the recognition that physicians and patients are generally willing to accept greater risks or side effects from products that treat life-threatening and severely-debilitating illnesses than they would accept from products that treat less serious illnesses. These procedures also reflect the recognition that the benefits of the drug need to be evaluated in light of the severity of the disease being treated. The procedure outlined in this section should be interpreted consistent with that purpose."

I think you can see that ELAD fitted these criteria very well.

We also embarked on the first of several CEO searches to replace me since I had only taken on the job under the condition that it was for about six months while we searched for a new CEO. The problem was that we could never find anybody who the board could unanimously agree to hire. With every candidate, there was always at least one of us who dissented and found something wrong. That was fine since we had an agreement that we had to be unanimous on the new CEO and we didn't want anybody saying "I told you so" if things went south. As time went on and I got more comfortable with the company, I offered to move to San Diego several times but was always told that this was not necessary and that investors don't like venture capitalists as CEOs. This was fine with me. As we all know, subsequent events have made California an impossible place to live and to do business and so I was fortunate not to move.

So, I kept running the company and commuting from my Scottsdale, Arizona, residence. It actually worked very well for the fourteen years I was CEO since my typical pattern was to spend about one-third of my time at each of the company, working at home, and traveling. Plus, I did not become a California resident and, therefore, dodged that tax bullet, pro-rating my time and only having to pay California taxes for the days I spent there. I kept my Arizona residency for tax purposes and the commute was either a one-hour flight or a five-hour drive. As time went on, I mostly drove back and forth because the flights became unreliable. It was a scenic drive and I could use the time to make many phone calls.

As the various consultant reports started to come in, we became more and more excited about the opportunity as their analysis of the clinical data revealed that we had a product that seemed to save the lives of FHF patients. It is worth reviewing the criteria that we used to assess the attractiveness of investing in the company. We looked at three main criteria:

1. *Did the product serve a very large market, defined as over $1 billion per year in the US and double that worldwide?* After we received the market research report, it was obvious that this was an unserved market of at least this size.
2. *Did the company have a dominant competitive position in this market, preferably with no other competitors?* Many companies had tried but all had failed and there were no life-saving liver

failure products on the market, except for liver transplantation which was a surgical procedure and not a product. We felt it was complementary to ELAD and not competitive. ELAD scored high on this competitive criterion.

3. *Was there a moat around the business to keep margins high and deter competitors?* At the time we were evaluating it, there was good patent protection but we were aware that the patents would expire by about 2010. Even after that, as a biologic with orphan drug designation, we could get an additional twelve years of exclusivity after marketing approval was granted by the FDA. As time went on, we also realized that there was a tremendous amount of technical know-how in the process of consistently manufacturing the cartridges to specifications. The business was therefore well protected competitively.

We concluded that the main features of the business were very attractive but we had to spend time on fixing the problems that Vitagen had not paid attention to. This required capital and we increased our loan to the company from $100,000 to $500,000 in August, with Valley and Paragon participating equally. We continued to finance the company with these shareholder loans through the end of the year and then did a first closing on a preferred stock equity financing in February 2004, with a final closing in May 2004, converting all the loans to the preferred stock for a total of about $3.4 million investment. Valley and Paragon owned about 35% each with the balance being smaller investors, founders' stock to the five ex-Vitagen employees, and a significant stock option pool set aside as an incentive for hiring new people.

The Clinical Advisory Board (CAB) proved to be extraordinarily useful as we went forward. We asked Dr. Michael Millis, who was introduced in Chapter 3, to chair the CAB. We retained on the CAB all of the members from the Vitagen days. Their knowledge, experience, and wisdom were pivotal in the decision to move forward and in the design and implementation of the clinical trials. This was a working CAB and not just there for window dressing for money-raising purposes. However, the names of their institutions (Mayo Clinic, Massachusetts General Hospital, University of Chicago, NYU Medical, etc.) did not hurt us.

As we dug further into the regulatory situation with the FDA, we became increasingly concerned that there was a lot of work to be done. We were surprised to find that Vitagen had never had a face-to-face meeting with the FDA and that they had not worked out the details of the specifications and controls for the manufacturing and use of the product. The FDA regulates all aspects of biologic products but the best way to look at it is that there are two main parts of the final package to be submitted for approval.

The first part is everything surrounding the manufacture and use of the product itself, known as CMC (chemicals, manufacturing, and controls). This aspect is not trivial and is the main reason why products do not get approved for marketing.

The second part is everything associated with the clinical trials where you have to prove safety and efficacy in the selected clinical indication with trials at multiple clinical sites and enough patients to get to statistical significance for a meaningful clinical endpoint. In our case, this was patient survival over three or six months compared with an untreated control group of patients with the same disease level.

We had a lot of work to do in the CMC area which was managed by Kameron with Dar, John, and Shapour doing much of the work. They had to work out and document all the procedures for growing the cells in the cartridges and using them on the patient. In addition, they had to work out the quality control methods that would be satisfactory to the FDA to show that we could produce the cells in the cartridges consistently every time.

There was also the question of animal studies which are required before you initiate a human clinical trial. Vitagen had done animal work with dogs but the value of this was questionable since liver failure had to be created in the dogs with noxious chemicals and they did not live very long after this was done. We felt we had enough experience with the Vitagen clinical data on human patients in their two clinical trials and we banked on this to be sufficient for the FDA.

But an unexpected complication arose: the company that supplied the cartridges that the cells were grown in had recently withdrawn that cartridge from the market and substituted a new one. They had done this with meticulous care and had documented that the new one, made with safer and more stable materials, was fully equivalent to the old cartridge. This should have been an acceptable change for the FDA to allow but it proved to be a real problem.

By March 2004, our team and our ex-FDA consultants at the DC regulatory firm felt we were ready to go to the FDA to request approval to move forward with a phase 3 trial and we requested an "end of phase 2" meeting with the FDA. This had a ninety-day waiting period and the meeting occurred in June. We carefully prepared for the meeting and asked Dr. Michael Millis, the CAB chairman, and Dr. Win Williams, a CAB Member from Massachusetts General Hospital, to accompany the team to the FDA meeting in Washington, DC. Kameron led our team which included John, Dar, and Dr. Randy Steer, our regulatory consultant. By this time, Randy had joined our board of directors and was a key team member. I went with them to DC but did not go to the FDA meeting because the FDA did not like executive management at these meetings.

The meeting did not go well. First, the FDA did not seem to like the fact that we had two physicians with us who had participated in the clinical trials and they found a lot wrong with the analytical work and release criteria. They also requested more animal work and we reluctantly agreed to test the cartridges on three sheep, a better animal model than the dogs. The FDA agreed we could simply connect the cartridges to their vascular systems without creating liver failure in the sheep.

We felt we could fix the analytical work and release criteria but we ran into a buzz-saw on the issue of the new replacement cartridge. The FDA was adamant that this makes it a new product and said we have to start from the beginning and could not use the existing phase 1 and 2 data since it was generated with the old cartridges. This would be a death blow to the company unless we could get it changed but in subsequent phone calls with the FDA, they would not budge.

We spent a lot of time looking at our options and presenting more data from the supplier on the comparison of the new and old cartridges but all to no avail. We all agreed that the FDA's position was unreasonable but the question was how to fix it. We had many discussions with our consultants, especially the two former FDA people in DC. They pointed out that there is a mechanism to resolve things like this, which can be requested and results in a meeting within thirty days. It is known as a Type A meeting and we felt that there was no alternative but to request it even though it is an unusual and high-risk strategy. The question was then who would lead the meeting and the consensus was that it had to be the CEO. My science was rusty, but I could logically make the arguments, so we agreed to apply for the Type A meeting. Most of us felt that this was a long shot and would not succeed but all pitched in to prepare the documents for the meeting.

Then fate intervened and pointed us towards China.

Dar had continued to be in contact with his old friends in Beijing and he had shared some of the Vitagen data with them. They were impressed and two of the leading Chinese liver physicians worked with Dar and arranged to visit us in San Diego. It was a fait accompli and Dar pleaded with me to meet with them. Being fresh off the very troubling FDA meeting, I was softened up for some way out of our problem. We met with them at the company on July 19, 2004.

These two Chinese physicians looked a lot like Laurel and Hardy but they turned out to be incredibly well-informed and much more knowledgeable about liver disease than anyone we had met to date. The Laurel of the pair was Dr. Duan Zhong Ping from the Beijing You'an Hospital. He was a diminutive middle-aged hepatologist who spoke broken English but had a command of the liver failure world that was impressive. The hospital had been one of the two that treated the SARS outbreak patients in Beijing the previous year. He had also tried every device and product that had ever been developed for liver failure, a fact that we confirmed when we visited him later that year. He calmly told us that it was his opinion that ELAD was the answer to what they were looking for—a product that could save the lives of hepatitis B patients with serious liver failure. He invited us to move our operation to China where he would introduce us to the Chinese FDA, known as SFDA, and assist us in running the phase 3 trial and commercializing the product in China.

The Hardy of the pair was Dr. Zhu, a rotund cheerful liver transplant surgeon who had been trained at the University of Pittsburgh, then the leading US liver transplant center. He divided his time between Beijing and Chongqing in Sichuan, southwest China. He echoed Dr. Duan's comments and told us about the transplant activities in China which, at the time, was the leading country in the world for the number of liver transplants. Together, they quoted some numbers about liver disease in China that truly shocked us: 120 million people are infected with hepatitis B, leading to over 400,000 deaths per year, over 1,000 per day, making liver failure the 4th leading cause of death in China compared to the eleventh in the US. These were truly shocking numbers but they pointed to an enormous market in China even though the pricing would be nowhere near as attractive as in the US. They talked about large 1,000+ bed hospitals devoted entirely to liver disease in China and painted a picture of it being an unsolved problem that we possibly had the answer to. Remember, I was a venture capitalist and was used to people trying to impress me with numbers and so I was skeptical but a few days later I agreed to send an exploratory team to China to meet with some key people to determine whether this made sense for us.

We started planning for the China trip but meanwhile, we still had the Type A meeting with the FDA to get through and we still regarded the US as the main opportunity. We submitted the documents in September and we were granted the meeting well within the thirty-day statutory time. It occurred on Friday, October 8, 2004, at the FDA's offices in Bethesda, Maryland, just outside of DC. The timing turned out to be unfortunate, as you shall see. We took the same team to this FDA meeting: Drs. Mike Millis, Win Williams, Randy Steer, Kameron Maxwell, and John Brotherton. I was the addition and was to lead the meeting. We were scheduled to leave for China on October 17 which turned out to be very good scheduling.

Ahead of the meeting, we sent carefully worded briefing documents to the FDA detailing what we had done to fix the analytical and release testing, the sheep treatments, and further information on the cartridge. However, we decided that we would give a brief presentation that focused on asking the FDA whether they would allow us to solve the cartridge problem by treating six FHF subjects in sequence at two clinical sites and sending them the data in real-time so that they could see that the cartridge was safe and no different from the old cartridge. Providing everything went well, we would then move directly, with no delays, into a phase 3 trial of forty FHF subjects plus forty controls which would be targeted for approval of the product for marketing, if the results supported it.

I need to explain why we decided to stay with the FHF indication. Although it was a small market, not more than 2,000 patients per year in the US, we already had the results of two clinical trials in FHF which, when combined, gave us statistically significant results on a bridge-to-transplant endpoint. If we stuck with this medical indication for the final phase 3 pivotal trial, we stood a chance of getting to market in about two years. If we started over with a new indication, such as another form of acute liver failure, we faced about five years of clinical trials and another year for approval in the best possible case. In these times of capital scarcity for biotech companies, we felt that we could raise the capital needed for a two-year path to market but not for a six-year or more path.

We, therefore, decided to keep with the bird-in-the-hand rather than the one-in-the-bush. We confirmed this decision by talking with our CAB members and several other liver physicians who said that there was a good chance they would use the product off-label for other indications if we had the approval for FHF. This would have been legal provided we did not promote the product for these other indications. This was therefore a no-brainer providing the FDA would allow us to pursue this route to approval. Bearing in mind the guidance the FDA had issued for life-saving products, quoted earlier in this chapter, we felt there was a good chance that we would be allowed to proceed.

There were 12 FDA representatives at the meeting including the acting director of the Office of Cellular Therapy, our regulator, and part of the Biologics Division of FDA (known as CBER), making eighteen people in the room. Having so many FDA attendees was a good sign and indicated that they were taking us seriously. But it did not start well. I introduced Drs. Millis and Williams and they each described ELAD treatments that they had done at their hospitals, University of Chicago and Massachusetts General Hospital, respectively. It was obvious that our FDA audience was bored with hearing about experimental treatments and did not assign any value to the presentations by two very eminent physicians. This was not encouraging. I decided to move directly into asking the question as to whether we could proceed with the trial to first validate the new cartridge and then move seamlessly into the phase 3 trial.

Several of the FDA people asked questions and made comments that indicated it was not going well. I decided to force the issue and emphasize that our company was going out of business if we could not get their agreement to do what we felt was a reasonable evaluation of the new cartridge and a pivotal trial to bring a life-saving product to market for a condition with no current therapy. The FDA was dithering and so I had to force the issue by asking the question directly to our lead reviewer. He paused and then said that they could not allow this. I saw no point in prolonging the meeting once we got this answer so I got up, gathered my papers, and said that the meeting is over. We had our answer and we were going out of business. I thanked them for listening to our presentation and we all turned to leave. But as we were doing so, our reviewer said that we should sit down and discuss this some more.

Miraculously, we worked out a way to get this done and even worked out a schedule to do it with a call three days later, on the following Monday morning, with the key FDA people. We were surprised to get this decision but very happy with it and managed to catch our flights back to the West Coast late that Friday afternoon.

But then fortune dealt us a cruel blow.

Over the weekend, the news broke that a Merck drug, Vioxx, was being voluntarily withdrawn from the market by Merck because of safety issues with cardiac side effects that had not shown up in the clinical trials. The FDA came in for a lot of criticism for approving a drug that had subsequent safety issues and it was a major news item that Monday morning. We called at the appointed time on Monday to try to work out the details of implementing our agreement but could not get anyone at the FDA. We continued to try over the next few days but no one would speak to us. We were obviously very concerned. I continued to call several times a day and finally, in the following week, the acting director, who had led the FDA in our Type A meeting, picked up the phone. We had a short conversation where I said that we were surprised that we had not been able to reach anyone to implement our agreement. She said that there was no agreement. I was dumbstruck but said that I had six people in the meeting and they all heard the agreement. She responded that she had twelve people there and that there was no agreement.

It was checkmate by the FDA.

I said that I understood the situation they were in with the Merck drug withdrawal but that I would have appreciated it if she could explain the reason why they were not implementing the agreement rather than simply saying there was no agreement. She did not respond and we ended the conversation.

Although the FDA did not explain the situation, it was obvious that the safety issues with Vioxx leading to its withdrawal had created an earthquake in the FDA and had pushed them into a much lower-risk mentality. So much so that they could not agree to our request. But we had to figure this out for ourselves.

China beckoned!

CHAPTER 6
CHINA!

For eleven years, from 1972 to 1983, I traveled the world buying and selling the technology of two multinational companies. I have done business in many developing countries including Indonesia, India, Egypt, Turkey, Mexico, Taiwan, etc. But nothing prepared me for what we found in the People's Republic of China (PRC), a.k.a. China. I had never visited mainland China before and I expected to find a typical Third World country but instead found an incredibly high-growth teeming metropolis in Beijing with beautiful buildings and wide streets. Gone were the hordes of bicycles that I had seen in the photos. In their place were modern cars in traffic jams on wide, spacious streets, high-end shops, great restaurants, international hotels, billboards, and all the modern city features. There were, of course, areas of obvious poverty but, in 2004, it was a very impressive place!

We took a team of five to China, including myself, Kameron Maxwell, Dar He, Aron Stern, and Hal Gerber of Wells Fargo Bank, who we had retained to help us raise funds. We were met at the airport by Drs. Duan and Zhu with bouquets of flowers and whisked in limos to our five-star hotel, The China World on Chang 'An Boulevard, about two miles east of Tiananmen Square. This hotel was indeed five-star and would not have been out of place in the capital cities of the developed world. The whole place was bursting with people. At lunch, I fell in love with Dan Dan noodles and continue to love Chinese food.

We were made to feel like royalty and well taken care of throughout the five-day trip. The days were full of meetings with influential people in the liver disease world and dinners at excellent restaurants around huge circular tables. I was always directed to the seat furthest away, facing the door, and learned that this seat was always given to the highest-status guest. Thus began my experience in China as CEO of an American company. In China, the head of the company makes all the decisions and is treated like the king of his or her world. I was not used to this but I could not fight it.

We visited Dr. Duan at his facilities at Beijing Youan Hospital. He had a separate building called "Beijing Artificial Liver Treatment and Training Center" as well as "Cell Biology Research Unit of Artificial Liver." The facilities were spacious and well-equipped, including one room that was the graveyard for all of the artificial liver devices and products that he had tested over the years. He told us the only one that seemed to do any good was the plasma exchange unit where fresh donor blood plasma is infused as the patient's own blood plasma is removed. He was very excited about including ELAD in his evaluations.

We also visited the second hospital that he wanted to collaborate with in our phase 3 trial of ELAD in China, 302 Military Hospital, about ten miles away. This hospital had also been one of the hospitals treating the SARS patients and it was a very big hospital, with well over 1,000 beds, run by the PRC army. We were well received at 302 Military Hospital and shown the facilities where our treatments would be carried out. Most of the physicians here were in military uniforms and the hospital was part of the large military medical establishment in China. It was generally regarded as the number two hospital in China behind 301 Military Hospital, also in Beijing, where all the China Communist Party dignitaries were treated when needed. The statue of Florence Nightingale in the foyer of 302 surprised and comforted us.

In addition to the scale of everything and the obvious competence of the medical community in treating liver disease, the thing that most impressed me was the size of the liver disease problem in China. Most of the leading physicians that we met with stressed the importance of the problem and the fact that there was no therapy except liver transplant which was available only to a lucky few and then only to the rich since it was not covered by any insurance. Over 1,000 people per day were dying from liver failure due to hepatitis B infection in China with about 120 million people testing positive for antibodies to the virus in their blood. This meant that they either had been infected and recovered or they were harboring the virus and it would reach serious infection levels in future years. The gestation period for break-out serious infection and symptoms could be more than twenty years. The disease caused an acute liver failure crisis that most people recovered from the first time. But the infected person then moved through a series of ever more serious crises about every two years. Eventually, a crisis would kill the victim.

The insidious nature of the disease meant that the victims did not know they were suffering from it and their first indication was the first crisis. Several of the Chinese physicians explained to us that the reason why this was such a widespread disease in China and much of the Far East was that South East Asian people had a genetic susceptibility to these viral infections of the liver and little natural resistance so they did not do a good job of fighting off the virus. Hepatitis C was also a problem. It is another viral disease of the liver but progresses slower and it proceeds to cirrhosis of the liver rather than acute liver failure. The numbers were much lower than for B with "only" about 40 million testing positive for the C antibodies in China. Interestingly, hepatitis C is a relatively common disease in the US, with about 4 million people infected, with very few hepatitis B cases.

The fact that hepatitis B progressed, albeit slowly, to acute liver failure and hepatitis C to cirrhosis was a significant difference between the two diseases and it is worth explaining why this distinction was important to us.

Cirrhosis is a chronic deterioration of the liver where the hepatocytes and other cells are replaced with fibrous material. The liver shrinks and goes from a healthy red color to black, slowly deteriorating in performance until it cannot support life.

Acute liver failure in hepatitis B is an inflammatory disease where the liver actually becomes swollen and cannot perform its usual functions. We felt we had enough factual information to conclude that ELAD would be successful on the inflamed, swollen liver of acute liver failure but not on the shrunken liver of cirrhosis. We were not totally sure of that and, when we came back to the US to continue the clinical trials later, in 2013, we felt we had to prove it, which we did.

I made a mental note to get a professional market research firm to confirm these large numbers of viral liver disease infections in China as soon as possible because, if they were true, this was a major unserved medical market and an opportunity to make a real impact on a dreadful disease.

After one of our meetings, a famous Chinese liver surgeon pulled me aside and, almost with tears in his eyes said, in perfect English, "Dr. Winters, we need you to come to China to develop and market your liver failure product because we have so many people dying of liver disease. I see many of them and there are over 1,000 deaths per day so please hurry up and get your product tested and available. We will give you all the help you need." This was strong stuff that tugged at my heartstrings and influenced me emotionally in favor of going to China. It also confirmed that we were getting a full-court press to put all our attention on China. This should also have warned me that we had something that the Chinese really wanted and that they will get it at all costs but I was naïve to how China operated along with all the other "barbarians."

During our leisure time, we went shopping and explored Beijing a little. A visit to the Forbidden City was incredibly impressive and walking around Tiananmen Square was a real experience. The sheer number of people in that area had to be seen to be believed on the day we were there. Shopping was a delight and we found the prices to be very attractive. All of us brought some great presents back for our families. But we did not discover Silk Street on this trip. I will describe it in a subsequent chapter.

We had several detailed discussions with Dr. Duan and the 302 Military Hospital physicians about the conduct and design of the clinical trials, especially with respect to the cost and the pace of subject enrollment we could expect. The cost was a small fraction of the US number and the pace of enrollment was expected to be about three-to-four patients per week at the two centers which was much faster than we could expect in the US or Europe at just two clinical sites. They recommended that we accept all types of acute liver failure subjects into the trial and said that about 80 percent of the patients would be acute liver failure from hepatitis B. This was starting to look good but we still had to get an idea of the regulatory situation and how the Chinese FDA, known as the SFDA, would treat us. We got an indication of that at the final dinner.

The dinner was at the Diaoyutai (pronounced Dayo-oo-tie) Guesthouse, west of Tiananmen Square. It is one of the ten great buildings in China, built as one of Mao's palaces in 1959 to celebrate the tenth anniversary of the Communist Revolution. If we were in doubt as to whether we were important guests, this dinner settled the issue. The building and dining rooms were impeccable and it was truly one of the finest dinners that I have ever experienced with perfect ambiance, service, and food. There are some photos of the dinner on our China-trials.com website.

We were pleasantly surprised that two senior people from the SFDA joined us and took an active part in the dinner conversations. In between the multiple courses, there were many speeches and toasts, which are typical of Chinese dinners. All of the speeches had to be translated and Dar worked overtime as our trusted translator. The speeches were obviously meant for us to be in no doubt that we were being invited to come to China to run our clinical trials and to make China the first place to commercialize our acute liver failure product. This was repeated by many of the Chinese participants including the two SFDA representatives.

Toward the end of the dinner, I said in my speech that we were honored by the invitation but that we needed to go home to the US to consider our options. We would probably accept their invitation but we would then need to come back and do a lot of planning to implement the trial. They in return said that they stood ready to give us any help necessary and the SFDA representatives said that, if the trial gave good results, they would give us a decision on approval within 120 days of filing our application. This turned out to be the only promise that they did not keep.

Before we left China, we met with some lawyers in the Chinese office of one of the large Washington regulatory law firms to investigate the logistics of running the trial and the corporate and legal structures necessary to do the job. They recommended that we do it by setting up a 100%-owned subsidiary of our company in China and funding it to do the job. There were other structures but this was best and we could then use the subsidiary as our marketing company in China. We were also assured that there would be no problem in getting any profits out of China and back to the US in dollars, which surprised me. However, if we ever wanted to close down the subsidiary, it would be difficult to repatriate any funds left over. The only problem seemed to be that it would take at least a year to get approval for the subsidiary in China. This was a great concern because we did not want it to delay starting the trial. We decided to see if we could call on our new Chinese friends for help.

We then had a quick tour of a new business park south of Beijing where we could establish our offices. It was impressive, a huge development with multiple manufacturing and office buildings on a very large scale and it seemed ideal for our purposes.

We returned to the US thinking that going to China was a real possibility and very attractive but well aware that there were a lot of things that we had to consider before we made such a game-changing decision. The fact that we were being invited figured very highly in our deliberations and the deadlocked situation with the US FDA eventually pushed us over the brink.

CHAPTER 7
The China Decision

We arrived back in the US on October 21, 2004, and had numerous meetings to discuss whether we should recommend to the board to accept the China offer and to move our trial and our commercialization plans from the US to China. We all realized that this was a big step but I sensed that not all of the management team was on board. We still had not got the situation sorted out with the FDA and had not received their minutes of our October 8 meeting. We were anxious to get these minutes to see what the FDA was willing to put on paper and to judge the magnitude of the mountain that we needed to climb to keep going in the US.

We had a board meeting by phone on October 27 where the main discussion was the China trip. The board members were very interested in moving operations to China but we all agreed that we needed to wait until we had worked out more details and a better reading on the US FDA situation, and the overall cost and logistics of a China operation. Then most of us headed to Boston for the annual meeting of the American Association for the Study of Liver Disease (AASLD), the leading US liver disease society. We saw most of our CAB members at this four-day meeting and sounded them out on a China trial and initial market launch. Most of them were not enthusiastic and had not had good experiences with medical work in China. This made us pause and think very hard.

I need to explain America's view of China in 2004 since it was very different from the way we now see China in the 2020s. China had exploded on the scene in the early 1990s with the "free market" policies ushered in by Deng Xiaoping. None of us really knew much about

China except that it was regarded as a fast-growing country and that it was expected to take its place in world commerce as a large economic powerhouse, to the benefit of China and the world. It was the place to be and, in 2004, it seemed like all the large multinationals were jumping into China and doing very well. There were minimal to no concerns about things that are known to be issues today, such as theft of intellectual property, manipulation of currency, repatriation of profits, and arbitrary actions of the communist government. Everyone wanted a piece of China in 2004!

We had a company planning meeting in San Diego on November 9 and in the middle of it, the minutes of the FDA meeting arrived. Taking over a month to get the minutes out was a long time even for the FDA and we speculated that they had taken extra special care. After reading them, it was obvious to all of us that we had a steep hill to climb. The FDA introduced some additional issues and there was no mention of the agreement that was reached at the meeting. We all agreed that this was now not a viable route for our first marketing approval and that we could not raise enough money to take care of all these FDA issues. Those of us who had not been on board for China suddenly became China advocates. The only alternative was going out of business. However, it was still a daunting and scary prospect to put all our eggs in the China basket.

After numerous management team meetings, I was satisfied that everyone was now fully on board and we started to work out the logistics of doing the trial in China. Importantly, we would manufacture the cartridges in our plant in San Diego and ship them to China. This would keep the manufacturing process under our control and it minimized the danger of technology leakage in China. Growing the cells was the single most important proprietary technology that we had and the less risk we took exposing it, the better. We had taken the conscious decision not to patent the various proprietary features but to keep them as trade secrets. We needed to protect them as closely as possible.

The cells would tolerate transportation in our special shipping box and there was a perfect daily non-stop Air China flight that left Los

Angeles International Airport (LAX) at 2 a.m. and arrived in Beijing the next day at about 5 a.m. Youan Hospital would then collect the cartridges from the airport with an ambulance which would subsequently speed through Beijing to the hospital with alarms ringing and then be ready for initiating the therapy at about 10 a.m.. We could get all of the international regulatory and customs approvals handled and this solved the main logistical question. The rest of the clinical trial issues could be addressed on our next visit to Beijing which concerned the cost, design, and implementation of the trial and, most importantly, the regulatory pathway, which we could work out with the SFDA.

We also had to work out the governance issues to see if we could get a subsidiary formed in China in a reasonable amount of time. We insisted that this trial be in the name of our US mother company, not the China subsidiary, and that VTI US own all of the intellectual property results and all of the various permits required. This would keep our commercialization options open.

From the information that had been given to us on the first trip, we were able to estimate that the trial would cost less than 50% of a comparable trial in the US or Europe. This proved to be a fairly accurate estimate and, plugging in all the costs, including the additional travel and living costs of getting back and forth to China, we estimated that we were going to need to raise about $10 million to complete the trial and make an official filing for approval in China. Again, that turned out to be a pretty good estimate.

Over the next few months, we had continuous deliberations about whether to shift our clinical operations to China. We also continued to try to work with the FDA to keep our US option open but it became increasingly clear that this was going to be a very long haul. The decision to go to China wasn't made suddenly in one meeting, it just sort of happened and everybody slowly came to the conclusion that it was our only viable way to keep the company going. I reached this verdict fairly early but I decided not to do a hard sell to the board and management. I preferred to let them all reach their own conclusions. This was a particularly difficult decision for most of the employees since they would have to do a lot of travel and be away from their families for long periods of time. But they slowly became reconciled to that course of action and it was obvious to me that they were all very committed to getting ELAD commercialized. It didn't matter whether it happened first in China, the US, or elsewhere. Dar was a huge help in getting people over the line since he was a believer not only in ELAD but he felt that China was the best place for our product since that's where the largest market is situated.

When I was comfortable that the board and employees were committed to accepting the invitation to take our operations to China, the key thing I wanted to do was to get a professional market study done to be sure that we really were addressing a very large market. This was not easy to do and I worked with a good friend, Bob Easton, who ran his own market research company and had done a couple of studies for us on the US market for a liver assist product in 2003 when we were evaluating what to do with the new company.

Bob was candid that he was not qualified to do work on the China market and introduced me to several other entities that had a presence in China and were capable of doing the study. The standout candidate was the US company IMS (now IQVIA). Their main business was collecting data on drug prescriptions worldwide and selling the data to pharmaceutical companies. But they had developed the market research capability as a related business and had a large office in Shanghai. We engaged them to talk with thirty physicians, mainly infectious disease, gastroenterology, and liver transplant specialists, in Beijing, Shanghai, and Guangzhou to dig into the actual market in China for ELAD. We wanted to confirm that some of the numbers we had heard during our initial visit to China were realistic.

IMS did an outstanding job for us and delivered the market study in January 2005. The study confirmed that these numbers were sensible although not quite as large as we had been quoted. The big market was hepatitis B with 120 million people infected and 20 million symptomatic at any one time. The hepatitis C market was about one-third the size of this but the numbers were pretty much in line with what we had been led to believe. Overall, more than 10% of the Chinese population was infected with hepatitis B/C. These were incredible numbers.

For comparison, in the US, there were essentially no hepatitis B infections and about 4 million, or just over 1%, hepatitis C. They also estimated that at any one time, there were 1.6 million liver failure patients in Chinese hospitals. These were astoundingly large numbers. In addition, IMS confirmed that there were no effective therapies. Now we knew why there were so many large hospitals in China that specialized in only liver disease. While we felt great sympathy for these patients, we recognized that this was a major opportunity where we could really make an impact and build a large company. This market study was expensive but it was worth every penny since we now had an independent, unbiased expert view of the market opportunity which was very helpful in our fundraising.

This is a good point in the story to make some comments about the FDA and the way they treat life-saving product development. Despite their own guidance document, which was quoted in Chapter 4, they seem to be overly fixated on unimportant details related to safety and quality. This was the first time I had seen the FDA bureaucracy in action and up close since I continued to have to deal with them. After the Vioxx debacle, they obviously became fixated on safety and were no longer going to allow a product on the market if there was the slightest question about safety. This is fine but the FDA never counted the cost of lives lost by delay in approving a life-saving product. This would move the needle in favor of earlier approval which would have saved thousands of lives.

The truth is that there have not been many lives lost from allowing products on the market and then finding safety issues. But think of the number of lives that have been lost by the delays in getting life-saving products on the market. There are too many of them to count but the whole process is so time-consuming that the number of lives must be in the thousands rather than just a few from drugs that develop safety issues after marketing approval, and most of these are not life-saving drugs.

The FDA clearly says in the guidance document that patients suffering from a life-threatening disease are willing to take more risk than those with non-life-threatening conditions. But the FDA does not behave as if they believe this. The patients are not the ones holding up progress. If a patient has a life-threatening disease such as acute liver failure, they're not going to bother too much about the niceties of a potentially arcane safety issue since they will be dead in a short time. This is unfortunate and very demotivating to those of us trying to develop drugs that save lives. The FDA treats us like we are trying to sell them a bill of goods and that we are trying to hide something. I can assure you that rarely goes on, certainly in my experience with developing these kinds of products. Anytime you try to attain perfection the old adage, "The perfect is the enemy of the good" comes into operation. And I am reminded of Winston Churchill's observation that "Perfection is spelled P-A-R-A-L-Y-S-I-S". He knew a thing or two about this as he prodded his military and government bureaucrats to take risks to win World War II.

The other side of the argument is that safety is paramount and although few people have been killed by unsafe drugs that have been approved, it is always likely to happen. There's also the argument that any patient can get access to a life-saving product in development through the FDA's compassionate use program, known as Expanded Access, which has now been further legitimized with the "Right to Try" legislation which was championed through Congress by President Trump in 2017 after the leadership of The Goldwater Institute in my home city of Phoenix, Arizona. This, of course, helps but the reality is that companies do not have to provide their product for compassionate use, insurance companies will not pay for it, and patients can usually not afford to pay. Further, companies are terrified of the FDA taking action, or tarnishing their FDA standing, as a consequence of any adverse reactions which occur during the compassionate treatment. The FDA allows payment for compassionate use but limits the price to actual out-of-pocket costs so there is little incentive for companies to make their unapproved products available for compassionate use. If it is a breakeven proposition, then why would any company take the risk of making the product available for compassionate use, especially considering the FDA risks involved? As you will read later in the book, we ran a compassionate use program for several years and we were only paid for one treatment even though we politely sent a bill, but, by policy, never followed up to collect.

There is also the argument that the accelerated approval process addresses this issue for life-saving drugs. I could go into detail on why it only helps a bit, but let's get back to the story…

CHAPTER 8
Fundraising for the China Trials

The initial funding that we had raised was now running low and we had already engaged the investment banking side of Wells Fargo to help us to raise more capital. Our original guideline was $20 million but we reduced that to $10 million because it was going to be a much lower cost to operate in China. In addition, it became obvious that it was going to be very difficult to raise funds. In 2004, biotechnology was not particularly popular and venture capital funds were not prioritizing it as an investment area. We had talked to some of the West Coast VC funds that we knew and had not received a good reception.

Our situation was not helped by the fact that Vitagen had blanketed the VC world with its business plan, fundraising documents, and meetings and had worn out its welcome. We had to overcome that stigma and show how we could get a product on the market quickly to have a chance of raising the money. We felt that China offered that prospect. For now, Valley and Paragon continued to fund VTI, supplemented by some angel investors.

Later in November 2004, while we were still in the planning stage, Dar informed me that the word was spreading in China that we were getting ready to do a clinical trial and that some business friends of Drs. Duan and Zhu, the Chinese liver physicians who had visited us in July, were requesting the opportunity to invest in our company. This was surprising but we felt that we should investigate it while the interest was hot.

We ran into a problem immediately when we probed how to take Chinese money to fund our US company. The Chinese currency, the yuan, was not a convertible currency and Chinese investors could not convert their yuan into dollars to invest outside the country without the approval of the aptly-named SAFE, the State Agency for Foreign Exchange. Such approvals were difficult to acquire and generally only covered $50,000 per year for each Chinese citizen. Since we were thinking in millions, we were well short of this. By the way, this non-convertibility of the yuan is the reason why it will never become a world reserve currency, despite what you hear and read in the media. If it did become convertible, the money would drain out of China as water out of a bath when the plug is pulled.

We then retained legal counsel and auditors in Beijing and they were not very sanguine about being able to make this happen. We even looked at accepting the Chinese currency, the yuan, into our subsidiary in China and then using the yuan to pay all our bills in China, which would be substantial. But this was not allowed. It was hinted that there were other ways to get money out of the country but we assumed these were illegal and did not investigate. We decided to meet with the potential Chinese investors and see what else we could learn. Our main caveat was that we kept everything legal under both China and US law.

These potential Chinese investors were in Taiyuan, which is in Shanxi Province, about 200 miles west of Beijing (even though it sounds like it, it is not Taiwan which is the island off the coast of China where the Nationalist Chinese retreated after the 1949 revolution). We had never heard of Taiyuan but we were assured that these investors were legitimate, had significant funds available, and were well aware of the liver disease problem in China. So, we decided to meet with them ASAP. I suggested that my partner in Valley Ventures come with us. He was a member of the VTI board and it was essential that at least one of the board members got to experience China. Jock Holliman had been my partner for about ten years and we had a close relationship based on open and honest dialogue. As a result, I knew that Jock would point out any problems that I was not seeing. We were like brothers. He was also more of a financial man than me and was excellent in fund raising.

We arrived in China for our second visit on December 4, 2004. In addition to Jock, Dar came as a translator, and Aron was our CFO and financial person. We were amazed to find that Taiyuan was a very big city, the capital of Shanxi province, with a population of over 4 million people. We were even more amazed to find out there were about fifty other cities in China with populations over 4 million, most of which we had never heard of. The Chinese population of over 1.4 billion was becoming real to us.

We were welcomed and treated with typical Chinese hospitality with good food and camaraderie. We were even introduced to the governor of Shanxi Province. However, the negotiations did not go well. They were interested in investing about $3 million but they wanted to control the company and have significant ownership. This was not acceptable to us and we politely terminated the discussions and headed to Beijing, less than a one-hour flight away.

During the next three months, Wells Fargo introduced us to several potential US investors but most found the story to be too complicated and did not like the China connection. In April 2005, we had another contact from a potential investor in China that was credible. It came through Dr. Zhu and a prominent liver transplant surgeon who had transplanted a new liver into a government executive in Chongqing (pronounced "Tong-ching") in southwestern China's Sichuan province, about 1,000 miles from Beijing. The investor was a real estate developer in Chongqing who had operations in Canada and had dollars to invest from his foreign bank accounts. After a couple of phone calls, he invited us to Chongqing for further discussions. I was scheduled to fly to Australia for a board meeting of another of our companies and went a few days early to stop in Chongqing on the way.

Dar and Dr. Zhu came with me and we arrived in Chongqing in March 2005 to be greeted by the investor at the plane door. We were treated extraordinarily well and stayed in an outstanding hotel in the city. These discussions went well and we were talking about an investment of up to $10 million with no complications.

We learned during our meetings that Chongqing is the biggest city in the world with a population of about 30 million. Yet another big city that we had never heard of but this time on a grand scale. It is on the Yangtze River where the Jialing River flows into it. It looks like a cross between New York and Pittsburgh and has a very large downtown area with many high-rise buildings. It is one of the four areas that the central government directly administers. Beijing, Shanghai, and Tianjin are the other three. At night, it is impressive.

In the very interesting conversations that we had over our lunches and dinners, we learned that most families in China have been touched by serious liver disease. At one of the dinners, the government executive who recently had the liver transplant mentioned earlier joined us and we heard first-hand the moving story of his problems with the acute crises of hepatitis B. We were to have these kinds of conversations many times in the future in China because liver disease is so pervasive.

One evening they entertained us at an impressive nightclub which was the full equivalent of anything that you would get in Las Vegas. Also, in the realm of entertainment, it turned out that the sons of our potential investor were golf nuts and I had a game with them on a lovely course set on the banks of the Jialing River. This was the first of many rounds of golf I was to play in China and all the courses were first-class. Golf is a game for the rich in China and the clubhouses and other facilities are fully equivalent to what we have in the US.

Our investor eventually wanted to meet some members of our board so we agreed to return to Chongqing in a few weeks with a couple of our board members for more discussions.

It was now becoming clear to us that there were a lot of rich people in China and it certainly appeared to be a free market economy. As we learned more about it, that proved to be the case for the economic side, but there was a different situation politically. There seemed to be a devil's bargain that a Chinese citizen could be free to succeed economically so long as he or she toed the line politically. We wondered how long that could last.

We returned to Chongqing in mid-April with Jock Holliman and John Lewis, who, with me, made a majority of three VTI board members, along with Dar, John Brotherton, and Dr. Zhu. The discussions were excellent and we ended up with an agreement for our investor to invest $10 million into VTI US, in dollars, so there were no problems with SAFE and currency exchange. We came away with a memorandum of understanding, the investment being contingent on the investor completing his diligence. He was to invest $8 million with US investors adding $2 million for the $10 million total. But it did not go smoothly.

The diligence was done and we were satisfied that the investor was serious but his conclusion was that the risk was too high since ELAD was not approved in the US yet, a fact that had been clearly stated at the start of discussions. However, we were presented with an alternative where he would invest $10 million in Yuan in our subsidiary for 70% ownership. Aside from the fact we could not accept investment in the subsidiary, we did not want it under Chinese control and we did not want to sell off 70% of the huge Chinese market. I made several visits to China to try to find common ground but after a month of doing this, it became obvious that this was not going to happen and discussions petered out. We then worked with Wells Fargo to look at other investors and possible partners for the Chinese trial.

There was no shortage of potential partners who were interested in talking with us. To mention a few: we talked with a Shanghai company in the blood products business, a US company that was already selling a product in China with a full sales and marketing organization, and a large Chinese generic drug company. We even got down the road with a large, very well-known US pharmaceutical company that was very interested in the cellular therapy business. We had one of the few interesting products in the field (fast forward to 2021 and there are still only about four cellular therapy products on the market, mostly in the cancer area in the US). We also talked to several Chinese VCs (there were not many at that time) and to several US-based VCs who focused on China investments.

China was starting to boom and a lot of people wanted in on the game. However, we began to see a pattern in the excuses that potential

Chinese investors and partners used to say no. There were three main reasons: First, Chinese investors were not used to investing in companies with no revenues that were still in the development phase. For example, there was no tradition of investing in R&D. Second, they were afraid of the highly regulated medical field and wanted a product that was already approved. Lastly, it was all about control for the Chinese. They did not like being minority investors.

By the end of May 2005, we were staring at being out of money in about six weeks. We then began to focus on US investors and particularly those who had been excited by the prospect of a US company going to China to get its drug approved and commercialized. There were two standout VC funds that shared our vision of going it alone in the China market and wanted to be directly involved in such a company. Both were run by successful women and one of them, MedVenture Associates, got really involved in the diligence and sent one of their people with me to China to kick the tires. They continued to like what they saw and stepped up to give us a commitment to lead the investment with the majority of the money.

MedVenture Associates was led and managed by Annette Campbell-White who was known to John, Jock, and me. She was a remarkably successful medical device investor and had an outstanding strategic mind. She could clearly see what was happening in China and wanted to be a part of it. Once she made that commitment to us, she stuck with it even though numerous other funds that she introduced to us did not join in.

By the middle of July, we were totally out of money and had to forgo salaries to make it to the end of the month. If you have never been in the position where you don't know how to make the next payroll, you can never understand the pressure you are under when this happens. Annette agreed to a first closing to get some funding to the company at the end of July and then we had a final closing of the investment on November 1 with Valley Ventures, Paragon Ventures, and Toucan Capital as co-investors in a total combined investment of $9 million. I will always be thankful for the confidence that Annette showed in VTI and regret that we were not able to be successful to reward her commitment. The delay in funding slowed us down and our plans to start the China trial by July had to be postponed to early 2006.

We can't close this fundraising chapter without mention of several social things. First, the food in Chongqing. Sichuan province is famous worldwide for its hot food dishes and it did not disappoint. To a lover of spicy food like me, the food was wonderful. I even had some dishes that were too spicy and seemed to burn my mouth away. But I loved it. I got on particularly well with Dr. Dong, one of the physicians at the huge government hospital that we went to see in the city of Chongqing and he guided me through a wonderful lunch with many traditional, very spicy, dishes. When he ate the head of the big fish that was served to us, after initially offering it to me, I was somewhat surprised but gratified when he explained that it is the best part. The hospital was impressive and had its own liver intensive care unit (ICU), taking up a whole floor, which is the first time I had ever seen that.

I must also share the story of our flight out of Chongqing to Shanghai. John Lewis and I were flying to Shanghai to meet with some potential investors and some people who could assist us with money raising in China. The Boeing 737 flight was packed with not one empty seat and we were sitting about halfway back with John in the window seat and me in the middle. We were the only Westerners on the flight.

The takeoff was normal but while we were climbing there was a scary impact and the plane noticeably slowed and then flattened out and went around in circles for about an hour. Something was obviously wrong but there was no announcement. Then when the pilot finally made an announcement, it was in Mandarin. We could not understand it but the reaction of the passengers was not good and we started to worry.

I poked the Chinese gentleman sitting next to me in the aisle seat and said very slowly: "Do - you - speak – English?"

He looked at me and replied: "Yes, - a – little." So, I asked what the pilot had said.

He responded slowly, "He - say, - we - in - big – trouble."

I looked at John, we both were very scared. However, the plane was soon coming into land. It made a flawless landing and stopped next to another plane on the tarmac. Then the announcement came in Mandarin and English. We had hit a flock of pigeons and lost an engine while we were climbing after takeoff. This plane could not continue and we were to transfer to the other plane next to us. The passengers all wanted to look at the engine which was a very sorry sight. The fan blades were mangled and we thanked our lucky stars that the pigeons didn't hit the other engine as well. I mentally added this to my personal stock of narrow aviation survivals from traveling the world. We then boarded the replacement plane and arrived safely in Shanghai. This incident made the international news and we only realized how lucky we had been after a few days. The pigeons that we hit were specially bred for racing and I don't know what happened to the poor fellow that was breeding them. I suspect we don't want to know but there will be no more pigeons raised around Chinese airports.

This was the first time that we had been to Shanghai and it was much more impressive than Beijing. The Bund area on the east side of the river had beautiful old buildings, whereas Pudong on the other side of the river had huge new buildings that rivaled New York. Our meetings in Shanghai were not productive but the shopping was great!

And, finally, I must mention my wife's first visit to China. I had been trying to get her to accompany me on one of the trips for many months but she had resisted, insisting that she had no interest in visiting yet another Third World country. She finally agreed to join me for a first visit in May 2005. From touchdown in Beijing, she was in shock at what she saw and was obviously hooked and very impressed by China. She was even more impressed with Shanghai. We brought back an incredible amount of stuff, all of which was high-quality and a fraction of the price we would have paid in the US. From that visit on, she was always clamoring to join me and she ended up making fourteen visits to China, really enjoying every one of them.

Meanwhile, there had been a lot going on with Kameron and the team getting us ready to run the clinical trial, an ocean, and a different culture away.

CHAPTER 9
Preparing for the China Trial

One of the key items for Kameron was whether ELAD would be regulated in China as a device or a drug since it made a significant difference to the size of the trial that we had to do. Device trials in China had to enroll 120 subjects and drug trials, 360 subjects. Both had to be randomized to equal numbers of control and treated patients so that together the control plus treated patients totaled the requisite number. So, for devices, it was sixty control and sixty treated subjects.

Kameron was advised that SFDA would decide on the device or drug issue and a meeting was set up to work that out with SFDA. Recall from Chapter 2 that Hepatix had started out with ELAD regulated as a device by the FDA which was changed without warning to being a biologic drug, a change that increased the time and cost of efforts to gain approval. The SFDA meeting was scheduled for February 28, 2005, at the SFDA building in Beijing. Kameron and John were our attendees. It was a short meeting and SFDA said that ELAD will be regulated as a device, requiring only 120 subjects in its pivotal trial, split equally between control and treated.

SFDA also approved the protocol for the trial, enrolling all acute liver failure subjects who met the criteria regardless of the cause; in practice, these were 90% hepatitis B patients. During the trial, both treated and control patients were allowed to be on any other drugs or devices to treat liver failure although this was mainly done for control patients as part of the standard of care. Dr. Duan insisted that we start all patients in the trial, control, and treated, with a session of plasma exchange, before the ELAD therapy was initiated. He was concerned about enrolling subjects in the trial and he felt that this would put all patients on an equal basis, plus it would give a reason for the controls, especially, to participate. Plasma exchange was called "artificial liver" therapy in China and it had been shown to have a small positive effect. We felt that it would improve the outcome for both treated and controls and that it would make it more difficult for ELAD to get a positive result but we did not object.

It remained for SFDA to complete the testing and approve the trial devices and components. This was time-consuming. In addition, we needed to make sure everything was in order at the two hospitals, set up the China subsidiary, acquire the final approval of SFDA to run the trial and raise the money. These were not trivial issues. The money raising has already been described so we will now address the other issues.

Dar was a major player in resolving these issues and setting up the China subsidiary was a case in point and a lesson in how to get things done in China. One of Dar's old friends in China, Fu Chang Luo, was working for an international medical device company that was selling its products in China and we took him on as a paid consultant. He came with us to our second meeting with the lawyers from the DC regulatory law firm and Mr. Luo heard the discussion that it would take about a year to set up the subsidiary.

We had glum faces coming away from that meeting but over lunch at the China World Hotel, Mr. Luo quietly said that he could get it done in seven days. I was in the middle of enjoying a bowl of Dan Dan noodles and dropped my chopsticks! I asked him how he would do it. He explained that it was not a problem since the new business park south of Beijing wanted tenants and he could persuade them to do it for us. He had done it before. The rest of us exchanged skeptical glances but I challenged Mr. Luo to show us how to do it and he accepted the challenge.

The five of us piled into a large taxi and headed down to the business park with Mr. Luo on his cell phone, all the while in animated conversations. We went straight to the administrative building, where we were well received and were welcomed into several meetings, all in Mandarin. As we were leaving, Mr. Luo announced that we will have the subsidiary, called a WOFE (Wholly Owned Foreign Entity) set up in a few days and they will let us know when we can collect the certificate.

Four days later, we had the very impressive certificate in hand and we were giving instructions to our San Diego office to wire some funds to capitalize the WOFE which was called Vital Therapies Beijing Limited. There is a photo of the certificate on our China-trials.com website. They even gave us office space in the business park with a nice sign on the door. We were all stunned that we were able to get this done so quickly when we thought it was going to be the slowest item on our list. We had a new respect for Mr. Luo and this changed the way we viewed China! It taught us an important lesson: most things could be done in China if only you can find the correct people. Regrettably, there was another lesson we were still to learn: questionable payments were sometimes required, something that we never did.

These payments were a sensitive subject and, at the outset of our China adventure, we learned all we could about the law on facilitation payments or bribes. Both the US and China had very stringent laws outlawing these kinds of payments. We had to comply with both countries' laws but the US was the key since it was strictly enforcing its law with many successful prosecutions and massive fines, even for offenses committed outside the US.

The US law to combat such illicit activities is the Foreign Corrupt Practices Act, or FCPA. We hired a lawyer who specialized in the FCPA and had a session on the subject that included our key management people. I think I speak for all of them when I say that we were chastened by what we learned and we resolved to strictly abide by the law. This was particularly important in my case since the CEO was held totally responsible for compliance. We had a written policy in place and I made sure that everyone was aware that we did not make these kinds of payments either in cash or gifts. We could make small gifts to the key people that we did business with but they could only be of token value. The fact that we did not make these kinds of payments probably did not help us and could have been one of the main reasons why we never got approval to market

ELAD in China. But the subsequent events with the commissioner of the SFDA laid this subject wide open for all to see; these kinds of payments were part of doing business. More about this shocking story later.

Now that we knew we were regulated as a medical device, we needed to get everything approved for a device trial. Kameron, Dar, and John worked this out directly with SFDA who determined that they needed to test the cartridges that the cells were grown in and the bedside unit that housed the cartridges by the patient's bedside. But strangely, they did not need to test the cells which were the active part of ELAD. This surprised us but maybe it should not have since we had very detailed testing results on the cells which had been specified by the US FDA and which we provided to SFDA. It was apparently satisfactory for these purposes.

The SFDA testing of the cartridges and the bedside unit took a long time but gave us a chance to try out the shipping and operation of the units in China. We also used the time to make sure that our production process in our San Diego plant was operating correctly and we made several dummy runs of empty cartridges from our San Diego plant to the Beijing hospital. The cartridges were in a special insulated container cooled with solid carbon dioxide, known as dry ice. We included a temperature monitor in the container to be sure that the cells were not exposed to any harmful temperature changes. We found that we could use a courier to get the cartridges to LAX in the evening. To make matters even more beneficial, the timing of the Air China flight at 2 am was fortunate in that the courier was traveling and avoiding traffic delays on the busy LA freeways in the late evenings.

The flight and the customs clearance at either end surprisingly did not present any problems, thanks to Mr. Luo again! We were worried about customs clearance at Beijing Capital International Airport; the cells could not have tolerated more than a few hours delay in customs and the Beijing customs could have taken a week or more for clearance. Once again, Mr. Luo came to the rescue and introduced us to a trading and customs company called, in English, the Angel International Transport Co. Ltd. Mr. Luo and Angel solved the problem and we never once incurred a serious delay through customs in Beijing.

However, because of the shipment time, the cartridges only had a 48-hour window when they reached the Beijing Hospital before they expired. We were assured that would not be a problem since we would only ship cartridges when a patient had been enrolled and was waiting. As a result, we did not have to take any special measures to preserve the cells at Youan or 302 Military Hospitals. We always got the cartridges to the hospital within twenty-four hours of leaving our San Diego plant which was a great performance since it was a fourteen-hour flight.

The logistics of growing the cells in the cartridges were always a challenge for the clinical trials. It was an expensive process to grow the cells since they had to be continuously fed with a very expensive growth media. The first stage was to grow the cells in flasks until we had enough to seed the four cartridges of a set, usually taking about forty-five days. Then they needed to be grown on a bioreactor until they met the specifications for the output of the two proteins already described, which took another twenty days. The result was that a fraction of an ounce of cells grew into about a pound of cells in about sixty days. They could then be kept on the bioreactor, waiting to be sent to treat a patient, for another sixty days after which they had to be discarded. We also had to hold a spare set of cartridges ready to go in case there was a problem with the first set.

It was expensive to manufacture the cartridges and we ran the whole process in our San Diego manufacturing facility. If we got the timing wrong, it was very costly, so we needed to plan. The problem was that most of the physicians were overly optimistic about the number of patients that they could recruit. We learned to apply discount factors to the physicians' estimates but these could be wrong for reasons out of the control of anyone. In our San Diego plant, we were hampered by only being able to use an old model bioreactor that could only accommodate four cartridges, which amounted to one patient set at a time. So this limited our capacity even though we had four of the bioreactors in operation.

At the top of Kameron's wish list was the need to develop a new manufacturing process that could handle about thirty-six cartridges at a time. This was the only way we were going to be able to supply commercially in a cost-effective way. Kameron got started with planning this project even though we all knew that implementing it was going to have to wait until we had a successful trial and could raise a significant amount of capital. Nonetheless, the team moved this forward to the point where it was ready to go as soon as we had the funds available to build it.

Working with Dr. Duan on plans for the trial, we came up with a forecast which, if implemented, would have led to full enrollment of the 120 patients by the end of the year 2006, peaking at sixteen patients per month in the summer. When SFDA reduced the number of patients we needed to ninety we were then able to scale this back to a forecast trial completion by the end of September. This turned out to be wildly optimistic, as you will learn.

We needed to get many documents translated into Mandarin for the SFDA to review, in particular, the phase 1 and phase 2 US clinical trial reports that were described in Chapter 4. Dar insisted on doing this because he wanted it done right and he spent an incredible amount of time on these translations. This was a good decision since a professional translation would have been very expensive and we probably could not have found someone used to all the medical terms which were used in these documents. Each hospital dedicated a special room to ELAD therapy. We would have preferred to have an intensive care unit (ICU) room but the assigned rooms looked good and were adequately equipped.

We started out on this adventure thinking that we could run the trial in China according to FDA procedures and then use it for approval in the US as well as China. However, it became clear very quickly that this was not going to work. The way the hospitals were set up and the fact that we had to use a clinical research organization (CRO) to help us run the trial made it impossible for us to adhere to US standards and procedures. There were only three hospitals in Asia and the Middle East that the FDA had certified as clinical trial sites and none was in

China with the closest one being in Singapore. So, we recommended to the VTI board that this trial be run solely to file for marketing approval in China. The board reluctantly agreed but as things proceeded it was obvious that this key decision helped things to run smoothly and made us a lot of friends in the hospitals and the CRO.

Both You'an and 302 Military Hospitals were very cooperative and clearly excited about being selected as trial sites. We ran a constant procession of potential investors and VTI people through the hospitals and they were very patient and willing to help us. Dr. Duan at You'an and Dr. Xin at 302 Military were seasoned clinical investigators and used to being the principal investigators in clinical trials. The military uniforms that the doctors wore at 302 Military Hospital were impressive and always surprised our visitors.

We became very comfortable delegating most of the decisions to Drs. Duan and Xin; the most important being the selection of patients to fit the inclusion criteria in the protocol. The language issue would have made it very difficult for us to make these decisions and so it was fortunate that we had two competent physicians; Dr. Duan was the principal investigator and Dr. Xin was the co-investigator. They worked well together and were only about ten miles apart, so that was not a problem. Both of them were motivated by wanting to see a new therapy come to market for them to use. As the trial progressed, it became obvious that the main problem was that they sometimes let their emotions interfere with their decisions because right from the start it was obvious that this therapy worked very well. They desperately needed a therapy so they included a few patients who were out of the protocol criteria and were beyond saving. This hurt our results but the therapy was robust enough to rise above this issue.

We were very concerned about the role of liver transplantation in China and the threat it posed to running a straight survival trial. In the US, an egalitarian way of prioritizing patients on the transplant list according to the severity of their condition had evolved and it was not possible for anyone to buy their way to the front of the line. Not so in China. All liver transplants were private pay and only the rich got transplanted. In practice, liver transplants only occurred when death was almost certain so you can see why it would have ruined a survival trial because most transplanted patients survived whereas they would have died without the transplant; this would have wrecked the survival trial results. This is a good example that sometimes what is good for the patient can be terrible for the clinical trial results which are needed to make the therapy widely available.

The only way we could run a trial in China that would show if ELAD was safe and effective was to use a different endpoint than overall survival. We chose transplant-free survival as the endpoint which eliminated the possibility of a transplanted patient compromising the trial results. In transplant-free survival, a transplanted patient is counted as not surviving and so this kind of trial is limited to where transplant is only used on terminal patients. We came in for some criticism on this change in endpoint but if you think about it, it is the only way to proceed in a place like China.

We had to decide how many specialists we needed and who would fill those roles in China. The specialists were VTI employees, usually registered nurses, who traveled to the hospital treatment site to be in the treatment room with the patient all the time to be sure that ELAD was operating correctly and to fix any problems that arose. Importantly, our specialists were not allowed to treat the patients in any way but only to observe and make changes in the equipment as needed. Patient care could only be provided by the hospital staff.

From prior US clinical trials, we had learned that the minimum qualification needed for a specialist was to be an experienced registered nurse. We thought about hiring local Chinese nurses but felt that this was premature as we needed to gain experience with operating in China before we tried to train China personnel. ELAD was a 24/7 treatment for at least five days, so we needed to have enough specialists to work twelve-hour shifts and provide continuous coverage. As the trial proceeded and was obviously going to be successful, we started to hire and train our own Chinese nurses so that we could hit the ground running when we got approval to sell.

It was also obvious that we needed to provide our best people to be specialists and that the minimum number to cover the treatments and the rest periods was three. We hoped to be able to train some of the hospital nurses to become specialists and to take over to give our three a break from time to time since we did not have the funds to hire our own China employees yet. Dar and John Brotherton agreed to do the job and we reached out to one of the former Vitagen specialists, John Carlins, to fill the third spot. John was living in Pittsburgh but readily agreed to join us. He was a cheerful person with a very good sense of humor. His only drawback was that he was a supporter of the Pittsburgh ice hockey and football teams but we forgave him for that.

We found a really good Marriott hotel close to Youan Hospital and negotiated good room rates so that it became the home for our specialists. The Marriott staff were terrific and helped make life interesting and enjoyable for our Beijing staff. It also helped that there was a really good chili crab restaurant nearby and we were very frequent and addicted customers.

On a lighter note, by now we had all discovered Silk Street. It was a former open-air market that was now housed in a six-story building on Chang'an Boulevard between the China World Hotel and Tiananmen Square. It was the best shopping market that any of us had ever found anywhere in the world. You bargained for everything and could get some high-quality deals in clothing, shoes, golf clubs, food, tourist mementos, carpets, jewelry, watches, in fact just about everything. All of us developed our own way of negotiating but we quickly learned that the Chinese vendors began with a price at least five times the amount that they were willing to accept. So, you haggled until a bargain was struck. The best negotiator among us was Kameron and he implemented a very simple strategy. After the first price was on the table, he would offer a low first counter and then, when the vendor came back with a slightly reduced price, instead of coming up a little bit he would cut his price in half. The look on the vendor's face when this happened was priceless and it always led to a very favorable bargain for Kameron.

There were still two important issues to resolve. First was that we had to get FDA permission to export the cartridges with the cells grown in our San Diego facility. As time went on, we became increasingly nervous about getting this approval in time. However, we then had a stroke of luck in that the law changed and after February 2006, we no longer had to get FDA approval for exporting these cartridges to China. It was a closely run thing.

The other issue was to get the bedside unit and the cartridge approved by the Chinese SFDA. This was done by having the units examined and validated at the SFDA's Guangzhou facility. We then had to get enough of the bedside units so that we could handle two patients at a time at each hospital if needed. We would need two bedside units operating together if the randomization of the patients yielded two successive treatments since, obviously, a control patient did not require a bedside unit or cartridges. But we had all experienced the some-times-capricious nature of the randomization process and we knew that this would happen several times (and it did!). Each treatment could last for 14 days or more and then there was substantial cleaning and maintenance required, so we decided that we needed six bedside units in China. This was a substantial commitment of funds since the bedside units cost about $100,000 each but we decided we had to do the job to the highest standards and that delays because of unavailability of a unit would cost us even more. SFDA approval of the cartridges and the bedside unit took more time than we had planned for but it was all done and ready in place by February 2006.

We used this time to get to know the personnel in the hospitals and we held an investigators' meeting in Beijing in January 2006 with our CRO and our newly hired VTI-Beijing VP of clinical development which was very useful and helped us to plan the treatments and the recording of the data from the trial.

With all the issues resolved, we were ready to proceed with the trial. Understandably, Dr. Duan wanted to proceed slowly and carefully so we set February 14, 2006 as the start date of the trial.

Travel to and from China was becoming very hard on our people and potentially very expensive if we put them in business class. So, Aron took the initiative to negotiate a $3,000 round-trip business-class agreement with Air China for the LAX to Beijing flights, 14 hours non-stop each way. Air China was not a great airline and the service was not up to US standards but the seats were fully reclinable and the timing with the flight leaving at 2 a.m. every day was perfect for us to sleep well. Everybody was happy with this deal and with these flight arrangements.

We were now up to about 12 people in the company. I was happy to leave most of the operating details to Kameron who proved to be an outstanding COO. I was spending much of my time worrying about the financing of the company and the care and feeding of our investors. I also had several other companies to worry about since I was still a partner in our VC fund in Phoenix. I had originally taken this job as CEO for six months on an interim basis - but the work was growing exponentially. I was also CEO of another start-up out of Arizona State University that took quite a bit of time and I was on the board of an Australian company developing a drug for tanning that was also very demanding. I took many trips to Australia via China and vice versa. Looking back, I don't know how I handled it but it got done primarily because we had very good committed people in the company.

CHAPTER 10
The Surprising First Trial Patient

We had two sets of cartridges ready to go by early February 2006 and Dr. Duan did not disappoint us since he had a patient ready to be treated. We packed up the set of 4 cartridges, sent them out with the courier, and then waited. Everything went very smoothly for this first set of live cartridges. They arrived in Beijing at 5 a.m. on the morning of February 16, quickly cleared customs (which was a big relief), were driven through the streets of early morning Beijing in their special ambulance with sirens wailing and were received by our specialists who prepared them for the ELAD bedside unit. They were treating the patient by 10 a.m. We had a full complement of our operating people at the You'an hospital and the initial reports were encouraging.

However, I got a phone call from Kameron after about two days of treatment to tell me that this was not a patient that would count in the trial. This was a test patient to see how we did and to test the efficacy of the therapy. Dr. Duan had surprised us by using a patient who had no liver. He wanted to see if ELAD could keep this patient alive. We were pleased that it did.

During the first day of zero liver function, when a patient has no liver, there is little effect on the patient. But then, the body's waste builds up and is not metabolized and all synthetic functions of the liver are absent. Life functions slowly deteriorate and it generally takes about seven days for the patient to die. Therefore, if we could keep this patient alive for more than seven days, that would be definitive evidence that ELAD was providing liver function - we did a lot better than that.

After the patient had been on ELAD for about two weeks, I decided that I had to be there to participate in these events and, at short notice, traveled to China. I found a triumphal scene at the hospital with Dr. Duan celebrating the long history of cooperation with the United States and obviously delighted with the fact that ELAD was operating like a liver and keeping his patient alive. He explained to us that he needed to observe ELAD on a patient without a liver to gain confidence in putting very sick liver failure patients into the trial and to use it to recruit patients into the trial. He said that there was no problem with SFDA since he cleared it with them first. I wasn't very pleased about this but it worked out very well and we didn't violate any SFDA regulations.

There is a photo on our China-trials.com website of the group at Yuan Hospital during this first treatment. We are all looking very serious and it was indeed a very serious time. There were tears from many people, including me. It is a wondrous thing to be able to save someone's life. We sang Chinese songs and "America the Beautiful" and we were very optimistic about the outcome of the rest of the trial.

Later that week, I left to go on to Australia. I was at Beijing airport waiting for the flight when I got a call from Kameron to ask me whether we would pay for a liver transplant for this patient, a cost of about $40,000. Kameron explained that there was no endgame for this patient since he did not have a liver, he could not afford a transplant and we could not keep him on ELAD any longer. This put us on the spot because funds were very tight pending the closing of our main venture capital financing. However, after talking with Kameron we both agreed that we had to do this - it was the right thing to do and we would find the money somehow. In addition, we did not want to be tagged with the reputation of being a hard-nosed American company operating in China and callously letting this patient die. I was in a melancholy mood throughout the flight, thinking of this unfortunate patient and the serious situation that he was in. But the prospect of prolonging his life with a liver transplant made me feel a lot better.

The first thing I did on landing was to call Kameron to find out what happened. He sounded very sad and said that the patient would be taken off ELAD in a few days and was expected to deteriorate quickly. The patient's family had declined our offer of a transplant since they did not know how to take care of such a transplanted patient and were nervous about the ongoing costs of the anti-rejection drugs. I screamed into the phone, "Tell them we will pay for them!" but Kameron said that he had already made that offer and they still declined. I was very upset to hear this but there was nothing I could do about it. The patient was taken off ELAD a few days later and died in about a week. It certainly brought the message home to all of us about the seriousness of the disease that we were trying to treat.

This first patient had made a very important contribution to the development of our liver assist product by showing that we could provide liver function and this helped to give confidence to the Chinese physicians and the staff who were treating the patients in the trial. It was a prime example of "the operation was a success but unfortunately the patient died!"

With this test case successfully completed, we started to enroll patients that would count in the trial in early March 2006.

CHAPTER 11
The Trial Starts

We started to enroll patients in the trial at a rate of about one per week. Dr. Duan wanted to enroll the first few patients himself before 302 Military Hospital started enrollment. This was quite understandable since his reputation was on the line.

A serious problem showed up with these first few patients when two of them died from infections apparently as a result of the treatment. But when Kameron and the team looked closer, they found that the real problem was that the treatment room was not clean. It was hot in the hospital and the windows were open, but they faced a construction site, and a lot of dust and debris were taken into the treatment room. We quickly surmised that this was the cause of the infections. We kept the windows closed and cleaned the room and we had no further problems with infections. But these two deaths in treated patients counted against us in the trial and set up a higher bar for us to meet for success.

We had let the two principal investigators, Drs. Duan and Xin, take the lead in writing the protocol and it worked out well. The main thing was the entry criteria. We wanted to restrict it to hepatitis B patients but they persuaded us this would be unduly restrictive, for the trial and for the scope of the approval that we would get for marketing purposes. So, we agreed that we would accept all comers with a diagnosis of the kind of liver failure seen in hepatitis B patients.

The entry criteria that the patients had to meet to get into the trial were defined by the components of the MELD score which had been developed at the Mayo Clinic after observation of a large number of liver failure patients (the acronym was formed from Mayo End-stage Liver Disease score). It is a complex algorithm comprised of three components measured in the blood which could not be altered by the hospital staff. This was done to create an unbiased score that could be used to prioritize patients for liver transplant and avoid emotional and judgmental factors that could give a patient preference on the transplant list; remember that donor livers available for transplant are always less than the number of potential recipients and some way of prioritizing the candidates is always necessary.

The three MELD score components are bilirubin, a yellow substance from the degradation of red blood cells which is responsible for jaundice; INR, a measure of blood clotting capability; and creatinine, a measure of kidney function. The patient entry criteria were defined for the trial to give a MELD score where 50% of the patients would likely die in 30-90 days. These were very sick patients.

The thing that we wanted to avoid was enrolling cirrhotic patients since we were pretty sure that ELAD would not be effective for these patients since cirrhotic livers cannot regenerate. In practice, about 80% of the patients enrolled in the trial were hepatitis B victims.

Kameron and the team spent a great deal of time in China in the early phases of this trial. They were really committed. They also saw the Chinese healthcare system up close and were amazed at the huge differences from the US system. There were also some amusing incidents - most of them resulting from the perception amongst potential patients that this therapy was successful and therefore nobody wanted to be a control patient. The SFDA was very sympathetic to this problem since it was impossible to blind the trial and the ELAD system at the treated patients' bedside could not be hidden. Each patient knew whether they were assigned to treated or control treatments. When we started to have problems enrolling controls, SFDA made it easier for us by halving the number of control patients that we had to enroll so it became 60 treated and 30 controls for a total of 90 patients. We very much appreciated this change.

We had several incidents where, when told they were assigned to be a control, with no treatment, the patient refused to participate. Some of them went into fits of depression upon hearing this news since they regarded it as a death sentence. One enterprising patient, assigned to a control slot at 302 Military, refused to participate and traveled the 10 miles to You'an Hospital and tried again. This time, he hit the jackpot and drew a treated slot. We did not find out about this until after the treatment was over and there was nothing we could do about it nor should have done about it.

Then there were several patients who were enrolled for reasons that the staff were sympathetic to their condition but who should never have been in the trial because they were outside the enrollment criteria. One of them I remember very well. He was a 15-year-old boy, three years under the age of participation, and he also did not fit the liver failure criteria. We are not sure exactly what disease he had but he fought valiantly and eventually died. We were all really saddened by this but none of us objected to his enrollment. Although he counted against us, we simply decided that we needed to keep working to enroll enough patients to overcome these problems. We felt we had a robust therapy that could handle a few deviant patients, even though they counted as deaths against us.

We were able to keep a running tally of the treatments and the outcomes, with no objections from SFDA. This would never have been allowed in the US for a pivotal trial but the SFDA was very practical and did not worry about this. The US FDA always argues that you cannot do this in a pivotal trial because as the results unfold, it can cause you to change the therapy or how you run the trial and, therefore, result in bias. That is always possible but when you are using the gold standard of survival as the endpoint, it is pretty difficult to influence the survival of any of the patients. The disease is the key issue and we had chosen to enroll only those patients who had a 50% chance of death within 30-90 days of enrollment. In this very sick patient population, if we could extend that survival outcome, we would have proved that we have an effective therapy that is unlikely to be influenced by bias. However, this was yet another issue that made this trial unsuitable for FDA's consideration for approval. We were not worried about this since we were doing this trial only to satisfy the SFDA's criteria for approval.

There were two serious issues that we had to contend with. About halfway through the trial enrollment, I received a call to say that my presence was required in China ASAP. A patient had died while being treated with ELAD and we were being accused of causing this death. It was a complicated situation that resulted from the attending Chinese physician's decision to give plasma to the patient in spite of a plasma allergy and to do it again after it could clearly be seen that the patient's red blood cells were rupturing and causing a red discoloration of the treatment fluid. Before I left for China, I was able to talk to several members of our Clinical Advisory Board, and I learned that these hepatitis B patients frequently had very fragile red blood cells that could be susceptible to rupture due to the shearing energy from the plasma separation process. The Chinese physician should have known this and terminated the treatment, but he did not.

I was met at the airport by the team and they spent the ride into Beijing bringing me up-to-date on everything that had gone on and emphasized that the hospital management wanted to question the CEO who they regarded as the sole person responsible for the safe conduct of the trial. I got the uncomfortable feeling that I may be the sacrificial lamb and had visions of a long stay in a Chinese jail! The team made it very clear to me that this was an irresponsible decision by the attending Chinese physician and that the hospital seemed to be trying to cover this up and put the blame on us. The consensus of our group was that we should play for time and get everyone to agree that we needed an independent study of the event.

When I got to the hospital I was conducted to a large room where there were about eight people waiting to question me. All the members of our team joined me in the room. It was a hostile environment and the meeting was conducted in Mandarin Chinese with translations. This was one of the times when I was grateful for the language difficulties since the translation time gave me additional time to think before I spoke. Having just got off a 14-hour flight, I was not exactly in prime condition for such a hostile meeting. It was important that I kept a cool head and did not overreact. I asked a lot of questions and made it clear that I had only just arrived and that I was trying to establish the facts.

At the appropriate time, I suggested that we put the whole thing in the hands of an independent inquiry team. There was some discussion and all agreed that would be done as soon as possible.

The independent team started work quickly and had a report ready in about two weeks. Thankfully, it exonerated us from responsibility but it was vague on who was actually responsible. I think this was exactly what the hospital wanted and they were able to prevent any guilt from landing on the Chinese physician.

We immediately started work on an automatic alarm system which would be triggered by the red coloration of the blood plasma. In all the subsequent trials, we only saw this situation once more and we were able to head it off quickly.

The second serious situation happened as a result of a shortage of blood plasma in China. Plasma was always in short supply in China and the hospital staff were constantly having to go to great lengths to get sufficient plasma for use in the trial. It was an essential part of the trial and was used to keep each patient's blood volume in the normal range because of losses during the therapy. In one of the treatments, plasma was not available and the patient died. This was a tragic event and seemed to be because a promised batch of plasma did not materialize.

There was a formal investigation into the patient's death but no blame was assigned since the plasma shortage was well known to everyone in China. We were very concerned about this and we offered to make a significant payment to the patient's family. However, the hospital did not want us to do this since it would set a precedent and would be misunderstood by the public in China. We did not agree with the hospital but we felt we had to go along with their request.

We thought this was the end of it but the patient's family continued to work with lawyers in China and filed the equivalent of a civil lawsuit against the hospital. This went on for four years and we were not aware of it until we were suddenly asked to make a payment for the judgment against the hospital of about $50,000. This was in spite of the independent report that exonerated the hospital and us from blame.

We were obviously not very pleased with this but we had taken out very good clinical trial insurance and we discussed it candidly with our insurance carrier. They had experienced events like this before and agreed to pay the $50,000 to the hospital for settling the judgment. But this was not before I had received some threatening letters that promised to put me in jail if I ever set foot in China again without paying the judgment. The payment was made but I was very concerned the next time I visited China. However, everything had calmed down and nothing happened to me.

Memo to fledgling biotech CEOs: always make sure you have the best clinical trial insurance you can buy before commencing a clinical trial. We had an excellent insurance broker who chose a gold-plated carrier and we were delighted with the way they treated us. This could have been very much worse.

By the end of the clinical trial, we had hired several Chinese nurses and had trained them to become specialists. They had been taking over for our US specialists in some trial treatments and did a very good job. We did this not so much to help in the trial but to make sure that we had some well-trained people available to assist in marketing the product after it was approved for sale in China.

By the end of the trial we had a small but nice office about three blocks east of Tiananmen Square on Chang'an Boulevard in a high-rise building with about 12 employees in China including an experienced CEO of Vital Therapies China. We remembered the promise that had been made to us by the SFDA executives at the famous dinner at Mao's Palace in Beijing in 2004 that we would have a decision on marketing approval within 120 days of filing the application to market ELAD in China. We wanted to be ready to go as soon as we had that approval. There were a lot of lives that needed saving!

CHAPTER 12
Slow Progress

We made a good start enrolling patients in the China trial in March 2006 but then quickly fell behind. By June we had only enrolled 19 patients vs. a forecast of 48. This led to some cartridge losses but more importantly time was money since our corporate burn rate was about $500,000 per month (burn rate is a VC term to describe how much money a company uses each month; divided into the company's cash in the bank gives the number of months to dry well, or running out of money).

We tried everything we knew to increase the enrollment rate but we had to be very careful that we didn't push so hard that we enrolled patients that did not fit or, worse, put undue pressure on the hospitals that could lead to sloppy patient treatments. The plan was to raise a significant amount of money after the trial was finished with, hopefully, good results. This was targeted for September 2006 but it became obvious that we were not going to finish until mid-2007.

This necessitated going back to our investors to ask for more money and we were gratified that all of them participated plus a couple of new ones in raising an additional $3.5 million in September 2006. The problem was that our burn rate was accelerating and by the end of 2006 we had 19 people in San Diego and 11 in China (this was still very lean for a company in a phase 3 trial). We also had to invest about $500,000 into VTI China to cover equipment and operating expenses. The money raising climate was still not very good for biotechnology in the US or Europe but we did get some very forward-thinking and helpful investors in addition to MedVentures who were outstanding in their support.

By this time, the board of directors had changed with Jan Barker from Med Ventures joining the board along with Dr. Michael Millis, head of transplant at the University of Chicago and an early supporter of ELAD.

Jan is a registered nurse and helped us in the practical aspects of the trial and with money raising. She was an extremely hard worker and very committed to making this company work. She also had an excellent sense of humor and deep experience in medical device company investing.

Dr. Mike Millis brought the knowledge and experience of a liver transplant physician to the boardroom which was essential. It was difficult to get him to join the board and we had to drop the University of Chicago as a clinical trial site because that would have been seen as a conflict. He was devoted to being a transplant surgeon and excited about having, finally, a way to provide temporary liver function for his very sick patients. He also brought good scientific balance to the board in that he could see the pros and the cons of every situation and did not let us go off on tangents due to our enthusiasm and commitment to making this work.

Dr. Millis also brought to the board his practical experience of working in China. He was well known in the liver physician community in China and was an advisor to the Chinese government on their liver transplantation policy with an emphasis on the ethics of sourcing livers and selection of patients to be transplanted. This was a very difficult political situation since China was the target of much criticism about their sourcing of donor livers for transplant with much of the world suspecting that they were using the organs from executed prisoners without consent. There was no proof to confirm or deny these accusations. However, China was at that time the leading country for number of liver transplants and attracted many medical tourists from around the world who were seeking and getting a liver transplant in China that was not available in their own country.

The obvious thing to increase our enrollment rate was to sign up some more hospitals as clinical trial sites. We got introductions to several hospitals in and around Beijing and I particularly remember the visit that we made to the First Central Hospital (FCH) in Tianjin, a port city about 70 miles south of Beijing on the South China Sea. FCH was a large high-rise hospital and, at the time, the largest liver transplant facility in the world doing about 3 liver transplants every day – this was about 5 times the number that the largest US center, Pittsburg at the time, was doing.

The scene at FCH was all hyperactivity. The lobby was as busy as Grand Central Station and the physicians had little time for us, but they did show us around their facilities, which included a large liver intensive care unit (ICU) on three floors which appeared to have over 40 beds complete with all needed space and services. They were interested in our therapy and saw it as a way to bridge patients to transplant and thereby increase their business. They said that they would be happy to be a center and only required SFDA approval. We got the same story from a couple of other hospitals and then approached SFDA but, for some reason that we did not understand, they were reluctant to give us approval to expand the trial to other hospitals and we never were able to add more centers. There also appeared to be a cooling off on the part of our clinical investigators at You'an and 302 Military. In hindsight, this time in the fall of 2006 was probably the beginning of the corruption scandal at SFDA (more about this later) and it probably explained the treatment that we got. However, we were blissfully unaware of this at the time.

The visit to Tianjin was also remarkable for the road we had to drive from Beijing to get there. It was a 4-lane highway and it was littered with wrecks of cars and big trucks from accidents. Many of them were in grotesque positions and were a sobering site as we drove past. My observation about driving in China is that I would never ever do it. There was no discipline and no enforcement of traffic laws and so we always saw outrageous driving errors and horrendous accidents. The only place I ever saw worse drivers was Iran.

We also learned that Tianjin was the favored city for the current 5-year plan and so it was having development dollars heaped upon it. We never saw so much construction going on in any other place that any of us have visited. The Chinese development miracle was awesome to see and you had to admire it.

There was a complete hiatus in the trial for 2 weeks in August 2006 when the key staff from You'an and 302 Military Hospitals decided to come and visit us in San Diego. This was not so much a request to visit as a statement that "we are coming to San Diego." We were delighted to receive them in San Diego but not so pleased that it further slowed down the trial enrollment progress. On balance, we decided that the visit was a positive and indicated increasing interest and commitment on the part of the Chinese. Both of the lead physicians and their medical support people were in the party of eight and we had our three US-based "specialists," Dar and the two Johns, along with two of our VTI China staff in the group which visited us for 5 days.

We split the time between seminars on various aspects of the trial and sightseeing in the area, which our China visitors loved. The seminars included the manufacture of the cartridges, operation of the system, and reviews of the trial and the data. There were several minor issues with the operation of the system that got a thorough review in these seminars. Nothing that could have been a showstopper but all of it served to improve our operation.

After we got through with all the sightseeing in San Diego, the party of eight elected to visit Las Vegas and, of course, we had to send our people with them. The feedback I got was that they were enthralled with Las Vegas and had never seen anything like it before. We were naïve to the ways of the Chinese world and it didn't occur to us at the time that this visit may have been part of the plan to get as much information as they could on the technology but, with the benefit of hindsight, this may have been the case. There is a photo of the group on our China-trials.com website. Two of the Chinese were not known to us and were probably the Chinese Communist Party (CCP) "minders."

In July and August, we only enrolled a total of five patients which put us further behind schedule. However, when the delegation arrived back in China and got organized, we enrolled nine patients in September. But this rate was not sustained for the balance of the year.

In the year 2006, I visited China six times and was beginning to get familiar with the way of life. At You'an Hospital, I got to see a lot of patients both pre- and post-treatment. A patient with liver failure from hepatitis B is not a pretty sight. They were usually strongly jaundiced with the yellow color particularly noticeable in the eyes, had severe ascites, which is a distended belly caused by fluid accumulation, and frequently had minor wounds which were weeping blood due to their coagulation disorders. They were also very lethargic and not amenable to conversation. However, the post treatment patients were the opposite and looked very good. Typically, when I entered the room of a recovered patient, our physician guide would explain who I was, and the patient would break out in tears and motion me to come towards them. At first, I was hesitant but then I got used to it and would hug the patients who had learned to say "thank you" in English. Both of us would cry. Fortunately, hepatitis B is only transmitted through blood mixing and so I made quite sure I had no minor open wounds. It was very emotional to participate in the trial in such a close way and it had a lasting effect on me. That is why we are in this life science business!

As the trial progressed, it was obvious that ELAD therapy was working well and getting the patients over their liver failure crisis to survival. We, of course, measured all of the usual medical parameters but we learned a lot from the Chinese physicians since they measured a lot of soft responses such as the patient's appetite, what they eat, and numerous other hard to quantify parameters. They put as much emphasis on these criteria as on the ones that they could measure numerically and they were excited about the trial since their softer parameters were consistently moving towards recovery in treated patients but not in the controls, especially appetite. Most treated patients asked for food at about the 24-hour treatment mark in contrast to the controls who were unchanged. This impressed the Chinese physicians.

We started to notice that many of the requests for cartridges to treat patients were coming to us on a Saturday afternoon. This was Sunday morning in China and we questioned why this was happening. What we found was intriguing and should have been obvious to us as we got to know the lethargic Chinese hospital system.

Most Chinese physicians and staff worked a five-day week and by requesting the cartridges on our Saturday for shipment on their Sunday and treatment on Monday morning, the trial could run the required 72-hour course and then the staff could clean up on Friday and everybody was free to enjoy their weekend. The cartridges would be sent to LAX on a Saturday evening to be put on the 2 am Sunday morning Air China flight arriving in Beijing at 5 am on Monday morning. Customs clearance and transport to the hospital could be done to start the therapy at 10 am on Monday and it would be complete by 10 am on Thursday. As you can see, the communist system did not exactly encourage hard work! As you will see later, this attitude also influenced the last part of the trial as the Chinese searched for a possible much shorter treatment regime which we already knew did not work as well as the minimum 72-hour treatment. These later patients in the trial did not do as well and negatively influenced the overall results of the trial. But, fortunately, the first 49 patients gave us a statistically significant result for the survival endpoint.

As the trial proceeded, there were three strategic priorities that we were trying to advance:

1. *Make sure that the trial progressed as close to plan as possible and that we kept up high standards so that the data would be accepted by the SFDA.*

Kameron did an outstanding job of running the trial and I soon became very comfortable with his management so that he did not need any supervision from me. It was just a matter of keeping each other up-to-date with what was going on.

2. *Raise the funds necessary to keep things operating and be ready to raise a large amount of capital when the trial was completed and we had filed for marketing approval with SFDA.*

I learned a lot about fundraising and investor relations in my 25-year venture capital career and this experience helped a lot in working with our investors. They were an incredibly supportive investor group and all of them recognized that we were breaking new ground here since no one really knew how China operated and where this could all lead. I tried to get as many of our investors and potential investors as possible to visit China to see the hospitals and meet the staff working on the trial patients. I think this worked very well.

We also started to think about the possibilities of financing the company in China from China investors, met with some very interesting people, and explored taking on a Chinese partner. However, after we did a few months of this, it became very obvious that, unlike the US and EU, there was in China no tradition of financing companies that did not have products on the market generating revenues and profits. After spending time with people, companies, and institutions in China, we concluded that Chinese investors were not going to fund us until we had SFDA approval, had launched the product and were generating revenues – we had multiple verbal offers of tens of millions of dollars to finance us at the launch stage because everybody realized the severity of the liver problem in China and the huge market that was awaiting us. Otherwise, we were seen as far too risky for Chinese tastes.

Two things that really made it difficult to raise money were that, in China, most financing was done with debt and not equity; over 90% of all funding was debt financing. And secondly, there was no network of investment banks and brokerage houses that could raise money for biotechnology as there was in the US and Europe. At this early stage of China's development, most banks and investors were only interested in commodity-type products that would support the commercial development of the Chinese economy.

3. *Prepare for SFDA approval and launch of the product.*

While we did not want to repeat the most serious mistake that US biotechnology companies can make namely, building a commercial structure before having regulatory approval to market, we did want to know all we could about the market and start planning for the product launch. This led us down some very interesting paths.

CHAPTER 13
Filing for SFDA Marketing Approval

Into the fall of 2006, we continued to enroll patients at the two hospitals at an average total rate of about one per week, with encouraging results. Dr. Duan seemed to be getting more comfortable with the treatment as the number of patients climbed and he asked us to come with him to a conference that he was organizing in Dalian, a city about 300 miles east of Beijing, close to North Korea. He wasn't yet ready to make any kind of presentation of the interim results but wanted us to get a taste of how the Chinese did conferences and to introduce us to a number of his influential friends. So, at the end of September, we took a group of about six of us to Dalian for the:

"2nd National Annual Meeting of Artificial Liver and Blood Purification".

The conference title implied that work in this area had only recently got underway and was probably being prodded by the government because of the serious situation with liver disease.

Dalian is a port city in Liaoning province, formerly known as Port Arthur, at the tip of a peninsula jutting south into the Bohai Sea. It has a fascinating history and has seesawed back-and-forth between Chinese, Russian, Japanese and Korean hegemony since it is close to all four countries. There are some older buildings there which show the architecture of these other countries and it also has another of Mao's palaces which looked beautiful. We were amazed to find that it is a large city with a population of over 6 million people. Again, a huge city that we had never heard of. The city square is gigantic and is the beating heart center of the city with much activity. We got to do some sightseeing and I was delighted to encounter the Golden Pebble Beach golf course north of the city in a splendid location on the sea. Regrettably, we did not have time to swing a club!

As 2006 came to an end, we had enrolled a total of 49 patients in the Trial. More importantly, our analysis of the results by the Kaplan-Meier method, with transplant-free survival as the primary endpoint, resulted in a p-value of less than 0.02 which meant that we had a statistically significant result that could be used to file for approval. See Figure 2.

As it became obvious that we were well below the limit of statistical significance, which is 0.05 (below is good since it shows a much lower chance of a random result), we had several discussions with the two principal investigators, Drs. Duan and Xin, to see if we could get SFDA authorization to close the trial early, declare victory, write up the results and apply for approval. The basis would have been that the therapy was proven to be safe and efficacious and it was therefore unethical to continue the trial since the control patients go untreated and had a high likelihood of dying. Continuing the trial would be delaying the availability of a life-saving therapy to all patients in China.

But the two physicians were not anxious to do this and they obviously felt that it would get them into trouble with the SFDA regulators. So, we continued the trial into the new year. However, before we could enroll the 50th patient, Dr. Duan presented Kameron with an amended protocol that would have totally changed the trial. The main change was that the duration of the therapy was reduced from a minimum of 72 hours to a minimum of 24 hours. Dr. Duan argued that this was necessary since Chinese hospitals did not like to run these kinds of therapies for a long period of time. The problem was that we already knew that a 24-hour treatment was not long enough and making these changes could invalidate the whole trial. Kameron quite rightly refused to sign and approve these changes in the trial protocol. We discussed it numerous times and agreed that we had to hold the line on this issue.

However, then it got interesting, since the Chinese went ahead with the new protocol with the changed duration of therapy anyway, without our approval. This only became apparent after they had treated a couple of patients and it presented us with a very difficult dilemma. We could obviously withhold the cartridges and our people which would stop the trial or we could go along with it under protest and continue cooperating. It did not take us long to decide to continue cooperating since the other option would have alienated everyone in China and probably brought everything to a screeching halt. Kameron and I thought that we could eventually persuade our Chinese friends to apply for approval based only on the 49 patients since the result was so strong.

Enrollment continued with mixed results. However, with the strong 49-patient trial result, Dr. Duan was now confident enough to plan to present the trial results in China and we all started planning for the next major conference which was in Luoyang, about 400 miles south-west of Beijing, in April 2007. Luoyang is one of China's oldest cities and was the capital during several of the ancient dynasties. It has many historic features including carvings of Buddhas by the side of the river that date back to the fifth century. We were able to get a very good look at them and there is a photo of some of them in this book.

We all agreed that this should be a major event for the ELAD therapy and Dr. Duan asked us to support it financially and to bring several of our well-known physicians from our Clinical Advisory Board (CAB) to Luoyang to underscore the importance of the trial results. We were happy to comply with all of these requests and we put a lot of work into the conference plans.

Four of our CAB physicians joined us in Luoyang. They were:

1. Dr. Michael Millis, head of transplant at the University of Chicago. Mike has already been profiled earlier in the book and was now on our Board of Directors. He was one of our earliest supporters and ran the first six patients in the Vitagen FHF clinical trial.

2. Dr. Win Williams, hepatologist at Massachusetts General Hospital in Boston. He was also a clinical investigator in the Vitagen FHF trials and saw some remarkable recoveries.
3. Dr. Guy Neff, hepatologist, formerly at the University of Miami who was a participant in the Vitagen trials and treated a number of FHF patients including one bridged to recovery which preserved a donor liver to use to save another patient.
4. Dr. Rajiv Jalan, hepatologist at University College London who had been one of Dr. Roger Williams supporting physicians on the early Vitagen FHF trials at King's College Hospital in London. Dr. Williams was an icon of liver disease physicians and known around the world in liver circles. He recently died at 94 years old.

To anyone active in the liver field, this was a star-studded group of physicians, well known internationally.

We all agreed that the main presentation should be made by Dr. Duan or one of his supporting physicians from You'an Hospital. It had to be someone who had been present at many of the treatments in order to provide credibility. Dr. Duan chose one of his young physicians, Dr. Zhang, who fitted the bill and he insisted that they would prepare the presentation without any help from us. We did not like this idea but we had to play along with it at least up until the day of the presentation.

We welcomed the four US physicians to Beijing and showed them around the hospitals and the main sights in the capital city, also managing to give them a chance for some shopping which they dived into with relish. The next day, we flew to Luoyang and were met with great ceremony on the tarmac at the airport with presentations of flowers and other expressions of the importance of this event.

The conference title was:

"3rd China National Annual Meeting of Severe Liver Diseases, Artificial Liver and Blood Purification"

Obviously, a continuation of the Dalian theme but with some additions. There were a lot of people present and they seemed to be a Who's Who of China liver physicians plus several SFDA people. The conference was held in the large conference center that was modern and well equipped with simultaneous translation capabilities. I estimate there were about 300 people in the audience for the presentations.

We finally got a look at the You'an presentation the night before. It was in Mandarin with English translation on each slide but the presentation was not clear and did not transmit the success of the trial. Even Dr. Duan admitted that major surgery was needed on the presentation. All of us were severely jetlagged but we somehow stayed up until about 3 am in the morning to put a new presentation together. Only when we were happy with it did we finally get some sleep.

This presentation had been informally promoted and purposely put on the agenda towards the end of the conference, to increase the expectation level. The conference room was packed and Dr. Zhang did a good job although the presentation was in Mandarin and we were listening on the simultaneous translation channel. Many of the Chinese physicians in the audience were taking photos of each slide so that was a testament to the interest level. Afterwards, we were the center of attention and were asked to give an informal seminar that evening to which we readily agreed.

Dinner was served in the seminar room which was a large meeting room with about 40 people present around a huge U-shaped table. The Chinese physicians wanted to hear from our US CAB members and we decided to give them about 30 minutes each. All four gave outstanding informal talks about their involvement in the development and in the clinical trials and gave detailed descriptions of some of the patient treatments which brought tears to the eyes of many in the room. They presented in English and Dar performed the translation for the group, in roughly two- or three-sentence pieces. It was an impressive informal seminar, like a fireside chat. The interest level of the audience was extremely high.

After the seminar, Kameron and I had a long discussion and we decided that we had to talk seriously to Dr. Duan again about an early filing for approval. We had now enrolled about 65 patients and the goal of 90 to complete the trial seemed to stretch until the end of the year. We arranged to have dinner with him that evening. We were joined by Dr. Win Williams and 3 VTI people.

We went over all the arguments and explained how this would be handled in the US if we had such good interim data. The trial would be stopped and the documents prepared to file for approval. Dr. Duan was obviously very happy with his reception at Luoyang and was a lot more receptive to stopping the trial early than he had been before but he was still worried about how to handle this with SFDA. We understood his dilemma and learned that he was agreeable to an early filing with just the first 49 patients but he did not want to stop the trial. So, we worked out a pathway to do this that involved working with the SFDA Advisory Committee responsible for review of our application. This committee was chaired by a nephrologist (kidney physician) from Tianjin and included Dr. Duan as a member. If the committee agreed that we could file for early approval with the 49 patients, we would continue the trial, as a separate protocol, to answer the question about the minimum treatment time. If the SFDA committee signed off on this, it would almost certainly be accepted by the SFDA reviewers and decision makers.

The turning point in this discussion came when Dr. Win Williams pointed out that it would be unethical to delay filing when the treatment was so safe and efficacious. After a very interesting discussion, Dr. Duan agreed with our plan.

When we returned to Beijing after the Luoyang meeting, it took Dr. Duan a month or so to get the SFDA Advisory Committee to accept this plan. They had to consult with the rest of the Committee and with the SFDA's in-house statisticians. Then the statisticians took another month to analyze the data and to agree with this plan. By mid-June, we finally had agreement from all parties to file for early approval with the first 49 patients.

We were surprised to learn that it was standard procedure for the lead investigator on the trial to write the application for approval; we saw no reason to change this. Dr. Duan assured us that he had done this several times and he knew how to structure the application correctly. We offered help to Dr. Duan to write the approval application documents and he gratefully accepted it. Knowing how complex this process is in the US, we couldn't conceive of how he could handle it himself but this was a "when in Rome" situation and we let it happen. Dr. Duan did a lot of the work himself but began to work closely with Kameron and our VTI China team as the writing progressed.

We remembered the SFDA promise to give us a decision on approval 120 days from filing and so we stepped up the pace of preparing for the market launch.

But storm clouds were gathering over the SFDA.......

CHAPTER 14
Preparing for ELAD Market Launch

We had been thinking about preparing for the market launch since the decision to go to China in 2005 but we got serious about it in early 2006. There were multiple aspects to consider but we decided to focus on the size of the market, pricing, and how to reach it, plus how we would handle providing product to those who could not pay, usually called indigent patients. Jan Barker stepped up and we took her on as a special consultant since she had a good background in device marketing. We also decided to use the staff of VTI China for all aspects of the market launch since they were intimately familiar with the Chinese situation. Jan did an outstanding job of interfacing with our VTI China People and creating a strategy for product launch and marketing.

We already had a good idea of the Chinese market from the IMS study that we had commissioned at the beginning of 2005. We now needed to find out where these patients were located and what hospitals we could use to provide the therapy. We quickly decided that we could not simply provide the bedside system and cartridges to any hospital and leave them on their own to administer the treatment. This would have been disastrous and an invitation for them to try all kinds of variations such as using only one cartridge and only a few hours treatment or, worse, reusing the cartridges on multiple patients with probable catastrophic results. We had to keep control of the delivery of the therapy.

This meant that we should probably limit the number of hospitals where ELAD would be available and where we could provide training to the staff and our own specialists to make sure that the treatment was delivered to a very high standard. Patients in the outlying areas would have to be referred to these treatment hospitals. We, therefore, commissioned another study to specifically identify the candidate hospitals and physicians. We selected an American consultant who had been in China for many years and knew the hospital situation very well. He did an excellent job and the report he put together was outstanding.

With this report in hand, we set out to meet with each of the candidate hospitals and were gratified that they agreed with our strategy. This would enable them to be differentiated from other competing hospitals in their region. I tried to visit most of these hospitals with the team and we even visited the hospital in Wuhan which is close to the infamous Wuhan Institute of Virology, suspected source of the coronavirus pandemic. It is an enormous hospital and I will never forget the sight of about 100 or more closely packed beds in a large room, with their occupants all receiving kidney dialysis at the same time. It looked like organized chaos! Also, meeting with three impressive hepatologists at the largest hospital in Guangzhou, all of whom were named Dr. Li. Very confusing.

But the highlight of these visits was to the Eastern Hepatobiliary Hospital in Shanghai, known as EHBH, and getting to meet the famous liver surgeon, Dr. Wu Meng Chao. He was over 90 years old at the time and still doing surgery. We were told that patients undergoing liver transplants and resections would pay significant amounts of money just to have him in the operating room while the surgery was underway. He was that famous and in that much demand. He was a gentle person and very interested in what we were doing.

EHBH is a 1,000-bed hospital, only for liver disease, specializing in liver cancer resections. This surgery cuts out a portion of the patient's liver where the tumor is located and discards it. The liver then regenerates and grows back in about two weeks with the cancer hopefully cured. Dr. Wu explained that the problem is when the tumor is large and they have to remove a larger piece of the liver. There is a real possibility that liver regeneration would not be sufficient and the patient would die. What is needed is a way to support the liver while it regenerates - that is his main interest in ELAD. This is a market we were not aware of and we started asking questions about the number of operations that were performed. The number was incredible and indicated another market of at least 1 million patients per year in China.

This exercise of meeting with the target hospitals also led us to suggest an alternative and possibly more acceptable form of market approval of ELAD by SFDA. Rather than requesting a complete approval to use it anywhere in China, we could request a more limited conditional approval at, for example, 20 named hospitals in China. We expected this to be more palatable to the SFDA and it would be all that we needed. We discussed this with Dr. Duan and the chairman of the SFDA advisory panel and they were favorably disposed towards it.

The subject of indigent patients was a little more complicated because it needed a detailed knowledge of the Chinese healthcare system. We gave the problem to Kent Lam who was the CEO of VTI China and he came up with a very innovative suggestion. He was aware of an official charity in China called the China Kind Fund, or CKF. It appeared to be politically plugged in and reported into the government system at a very high level. We were introduced to them in early 2006 and had numerous meetings. They were all over the issue of providing the maximum number of indigent treatments and suggested a very creative game plan:

- CKF would set up a special department to handle the indigent treatment selection and payments.
- It would be financed by us donating 5% of all of our treatment revenues.
- CKF would supplement this fund by going to wealthy Chinese businessmen and soliciting donations which they felt would be very productive since this was addressing one of China's big unserved health problems and could give such a businessman a lot of intangible credits in Chinese society.
- CKF would administer a separate committee to select the patients for treatment and would pay for the treatments at full cost from the donated funds. This way VTI was not involved in the selection process and therefore was insulated from the decisions on who qualified for indigent treatment.

We all liked this proposal and we entered into an agreement with CKF. They were very helpful to us as we progressed to filing the approval application with SFDA and we felt we were ready to handle this part of the market.

We also started to address promotion and public relations (PR) aspects of introducing one of the first innovative cellular therapy products in China. Fortunately, Medventures had an existing relationship with Kevin Knight and introduced us. Kevin was like no other PR entity that I had dealt with in my VC career in that he only got paid for performance. This was unusual in PR circles because everybody simply wanted a monthly retainer for them to do undefined PR work. Kevin's way of working was really appealing to me and the VTI board agreed. We entered into an agreement and set Kevin the task of getting several full-page articles on VTI into the major US business magazines. Business Week was the first one that expressed interest and we hosted one of their reporters in Beijing for a couple of days in April 2007. The reporter did a very thorough job and produced an excellent article in the May 28, 2007 edition of Business Week using the VTI trial as the focus of a larger article on clinical trials in China. Over the next two years, several other articles followed in Forbes, Fortune, etc. Kevin did a great job and really earned his keep.

We had the first of our meetings with 12 ELAD-recovered patients in October 2006 that we put together for some visiting investors. We had met individual recovered patients but never together as a group and we were all very moved by their stories. They were incredibly enthusiastic and all of them said that they would help us in the promotion and marketing of ELAD, spontaneously without us asking. There's a photo of this group meeting on our China-trials.com website. We thanked them and started to think about how we could use this unique promotional source. The CKF people had lots of ideas about this.

We spent some more time in Chongqing in 2006 trying to raise some money and also looking at possibly putting a manufacturing facility in one of their business parks if we got marketing approval and had to manufacture the cartridges in China. We were very impressed with the various developments that we saw and our hosts insisted that we take a short vacation on the riverboat that went from Chongqing to Yichong through the Three Gorges Dam project. They insisted that we be accompanied by two of their people who acted as our guides and did a really fine job. It was a 3-day cruise down the Yangtze River through really impressive country where monkeys could be seen on the banks of the river. The boat stopped at some very interesting places and we learned a lot about the history and culture of China. The boat was very impressive, neat and tidy, and the crew was also the entertainment in the evenings.

The Three Gorges Dam was overwhelming, it was so large. Our boat was an insignificant presence in the huge lock that we needed to negotiate to get downriver. We learned that when it was completely finished, it would provide 10% of the electric power used in China. I find this statistic difficult to believe but apparently, it is true. When we disembarked from the boat in Yichong, we had some time to look around the city and found it to be a fascinating place with incredible fossils in the rock above the river. We brought two of them back and they are still displayed in our house.

I could write a separate chapter on this cruise but let's get back to the story.

CHAPTER 15
The Execution

After we were a month into the writing of the application for SFDA approval to market ELAD in China, the news of a serious corruption scandal in SFDA broke on July 11, 2007. It was announced that the former Chief Commissioner of the SFDA, from 1998 to 2005, had been executed on July 10 for corruption that involved taking bribes for approving several unsafe drugs that had seriously harmed people in China. In addition, his senior assistant was given a suspended death sentence, and several others in the executive management of SFDA were sentenced to long jail terms. We learned that serious economic crimes are capital crimes in China and can carry the death penalty.

The news was a shock and a case of unfortunate timing for us. No one could tell us with any certainty how this would affect the SFDA's decision-making process but the consensus among the people we talked to was that it was a housecleaning and that SFDA would still be in the business of approving drugs but may take a little bit longer. In retrospect, I should have realized that it would upend everything in SFDA and totally change the way that they worked, especially with American companies that were trying to get their drugs approved in China before they had been approved in the US. But we had to find this out over the next 3 years as we tried to work with the new SFDA.

Our team, led by Dr. Duan, continued their hard work and had the application completed by the beginning of September. It was filed with SFDA on September 14, 2007. It was rejected a few days later because of a technicality surrounding the inspection of our manufacturing facilities. But this was worked out and the final application was filed and accepted on September 21. The application was based on the data from

49 patients under the original protocol. The revised protocol data, which had enrolled 20 more patients by then, was filed as a supplement for reinforcement of safety. The trial was then officially terminated with 69 total patients enrolled under two protocols.

CHAPTER 16
Venture Capital Financing

While all this was going on in China, we were anxiously looking at our dwindling cash balance and realized that we needed to raise a significant amount of capital to pursue approval and then market launch in China and to plan and initiate clinical trials in the US and EU to gain US and EU market approval.

Before we could make serious approaches to US VC funds, we had to come up with a viable clinical strategy for US/EU approval. We reasoned that this plus the China trial results and the pending approval would make us an attractive investment. Because of the radically different liver disease situation in China and the US/EU, this was not easy.

In China we had stumbled upon the hepatitis B situation and found that we were very effective in that market, almost by accident. However, there was very little hepatitis B in the US or EU, certainly not enough to run a credible trial. There was a lot of hepatitis C, about 5 million cases in the US, which is a similar viral liver infection but we were fairly certain that we would not be effective in hepatitis C because the disease progresses to cirrhosis of the liver and those kinds of livers could not regenerate.

And so, between the frequent trips to China, we were looking at all of the other liver diseases to see if we could find one that would give us an ideal entry point into the US/EU markets. Our Clinical Advisory Board (CAB) and liver physician friends were invaluable in this process but we did not come up with an ideal liver failure condition that we could focus on.

We could, of course, always fall back on the FHF market but those kinds of patients were so rare that we did not want to go through that waiting game again. We were acutely aware that slow progress in FHF had been the main reason why Vitagen failed. We were also concerned that any market approval might be limited to FHF and may not allow any off-label usage. Finally, it would be difficult to sell such a small market strategy to new venture capital investors.

Among the markets that we looked at were:

1. Liver cancer resections. There are a lot of these done in both the US and EU, about 100,000 per year in each, but the mortality is very low, less than 1%. making this unsuitable for a survival clinical trial. The reason that the mortality is so low is that the surgeons are careful to only cut out that amount of the liver that ensures regeneration and survival.

Therefore, in order to show a difference in survival at a 1% mortality rate we would have had to enroll over 1,000 patients in any trial. This was simply not feasible. To make it feasible, we would need to do a survival trial that required the control patients to die at a rate closer to 50%, and that would mean that the surgeon would have to resect the patient's liver beyond the accepted limit of recovery. That was obviously unethical and so, although this may have worked in China, it was not possible in the US or the EU.

2. Numerous orphan diseases of the liver. There are a lot of these and we looked closely into a genetic defect disease of children where bilirubin is produced in high quantities. We thought there was a good chance that we could alleviate the suffering of these patients but the prospect of enrolling children in a clinical trial was not attractive. None of the other genetic liver diseases were obvious candidates either.

3. Fatty liver disease in all its forms was an attractive market since there were millions of these people but we doubted whether we could make a difference since fatty livers would not regenerate.

4. Acute alcoholic hepatitis (AAH) was the stand-out opportunity. This is alcoholic liver disease caused by binge drinking where the liver is

swollen and in acute failure in contrast to chronic alcoholic liver failure where the liver shrinks, is cirrhotic, and loses function. There were about 100,000 cases of AAH per year in the US, enough to provide a significant market and still be within the annual 200,000 case orphan drug limit.

However, we had to be realistic and recognize that AAH was a self-inflicted disease and it was not one that generated much interest or sympathy. At that time, AAH patients were not eligible for transplant primarily because most of them went back to drinking again and destroyed their liver a second time so it was regarded as a waste of a precious donor liver. We felt that a focus on AAH would make it difficult to finance the company.

5. There was a new market classification known as acute-on-chronic liver failure, or AOCF. It is a hybrid condition where an acute eent such as an infection or a binge drinking session causes liver failure because the liver was already starting to fail for a wide variety of possible reasons.

We chose AOCF as the subject of the US and EU trials and spent quite a bit of time trying to figure out how to keep cirrhotic patients out of the trial. This was not easy and we ended up getting some cirrhotic patients and proving that we were ineffective in cirrhosis, as expected. This is one of the decisions we made that I would like to take back. It was a mistake and we should have gone directly to AAH or even to a mixture of FHF and hepatitis B since we later found we could get some of the latter in immigrant populations.

So, we now had what we thought was a viable US/EU strategy to add to a successful China trial with a decision on the application for China market approval being expected, according to SFDA's promise to give a decision in 120 days, in January 2008. But obviously, the cloud hanging over the China FDA muddied the waters. We thought we had a winning story and started to talk to a number of medically-oriented venture capital funds in the fall of 2006 when the China trial results were available.

We were very disappointed with the reception that we got from most of the VC funds. They were obviously intrigued by the fact that we had run the trial in China but they were skeptical of our China clinical trial results and put most of their focus on new clinical trials in the US/EU which for many of them was like starting the trial process again. However, we kept plugging away and eventually, in July 2007, got a term sheet for a substantial investment from one of the leading medical funds on the West Coast.

We also had some verbal offers from some Chinese investors but all of them wanted to invest and control VTI China, our China subsidiary, which was not acceptable to us. However, two China funds located in Shanghai and affiliated with large EU and US VC funds, wanted to participate in the US financing. This was not very popular with the US participants in the VC term sheet financing but I argued strongly that we should accept these investors since they could help us with the China approval. After I spent some time with the China investors' partners and introduced them to the key US investors, we decided to accept this Chinese investment and to allow them to observe our board meetings. As you will hear, this turned out to be a decision that we regretted - it did not turn out well, and certainly did not help us with the China approval. Yet another example of US logic not being effective in China. I was dead wrong about this and we would have been better off without these China investors.

We raised about $27 million with this VC financing and had several of the leading US medical VC funds participating. They were investing in the US and EU business opportunities and that is where they wanted us to focus. They liked the China results, saw the potential upside of a China approval and product launch and agreed that we should continue to try to gain SFDA China approval. If this happened, our investors would consider it as icing on the cake since they did not expect us to be able to make money in China.

In the two years since we had raised the first venture capital investment round of $10 million, attitudes towards China had significantly changed. There had been several scandals with drugs produced and exported from China, such as the heparin scandal, and the execution of the SFDA commissioner fed the negative attitudes. Further, there had been several successful prosecutions of US companies under the foreign corrupt practices act (FCPA) in the US courts for bribing Chinese government employees to gain business.

The fines in these FCPA cases had been eye-poppingly high and had been levied on the individual executives and not on the corporations. This made everyone doing business in China very nervous. We hired the best lawyer we could find and further strengthened our procedures against anything which could be considered as a bribe. The key was to get the message out to everyone in the company and I spent a considerable amount of time making sure that everyone understood our rules which were to make no payments that could be construed as bribery.

The FCPA law was written so that it only applied to bribing government employees. But one of the problems of doing business in China is that just about everybody can be considered to be a government employee since the government has its hand in every business. This was especially the case in the medical field since virtually all the hospitals were owned by the government and all the physicians and staff were employed by the government. All of the SFDA people were, of course, government employees. We had to be very careful. The FCPA law also had a very long reach and applied to any consultants that a company hired; if they used some of the money that you paid them as bribes then you were guilty of bribery even if you did not know about it – you should have monitored them better. We got the message and so did our employees and anyone that we engaged as consultants or in any other capacity.

This kind of bribery in China was not just a concept, it really happened. The execution of the SFDA Commissioner and the penalties on his minions are an obvious illustration of the problem. We also saw and heard of numerous other such happenings, sometimes close-up, and we had several demands for us to participate. We refused all such "opportunities." I will not go into any specifics since it could put others at risk but our steadfast refusals probably hindered our progress.

We closed on the VC financing on September 7, 2007, and immediately began construction of our improved cartridge manufacturing facilities. We kept the small 4-cartridge bioreactors but we planned to replace them with the 36-cartridge bioreactors that could also be run with as few as 4 cartridges. This gave us much more flexibility and would decrease our costs significantly when we got into commercial operations. As these improvements were made in the facility and with the new bioreactors, my confidence in our team was reinforced. They did a really good job and we were ready for scale-up.

You may ask why we had to do this and the answer is that, for a biologic product, the US FDA insists on the company running its phase 3 trials with the product produced in the same facility and with the same process that is intended for commercial production. This becomes very costly but it is logical since biologic production can be variable and the FDA wants to make sure that you can produce your product to the same standards every time.

An interesting anecdote is that we had a visit from the governor of one of the Australian provinces who wanted to see a US company that was carrying out innovative clinical development. When he saw our manufacturing facility and all the supporting operations, he asked how much is invested in it all. We gave him the approximate figure of about $20 million which obviously surprised him. He thought for a moment and then said "You mean all this is speculative and could be lost if the product is not successful in the clinical trials?" We explained that this is what the FDA requires for a biologic product and he went off shaking his head in disbelief.

We also restructured our board of directors after the financing. Several of the VC investors joined the board and the other key investors attended our board meetings as observers. The board meetings had about 10-15 people in attendance and several more by phone. VTI China was also set up with a functioning board of directors including our China investors and several members of our management. We had regular meetings of the China board that were very useful.

The China trial was halted in May 2007 with 69 total patients enrolled under two separate protocols, as already explained. But then some disagreements started to show up with the staff at the two hospitals over publications and who takes credit for bringing ELAD to China. We stayed out of these but noted that success has many fathers...

In the US/EU, Dr. Mike Millis presented our China trial results at three prestigious meetings: the European and then Japanese Societies for Artificial Organs in September and October, and the American Association for the Study of Liver Disease in November. He was well received with all three presentations and most of the questions were on the design of the trial and the way that the transplanted patients were treated in the data analysis.

We also heard that over 6,000 applications for approval of drugs and devices in China had been withdrawn over the past few months, presumably because the SFDA was tightening its approval procedures. That is not a misprint, it was 6,000. This sounded ominous.

CHAPTER 17
Seeking China Approval

We had no idea what to expect from SFDA now that they had accepted our application for approval and were presumably working on it. We spoke to a lot of people and got every possible opinion from business as usual to total paralysis. So, we decided to wait for about three months before we gently pushed to see what was going on.

Meanwhile, we were approached by Dan Zhang, through a credible, long-time acquaintance, to see if we needed a China clinical development VP to take control of the China clinical trials and data analysis and to help with the approval. He already knew our Chinese investors very well. Dan had an impressive resume which included a senior position at Quintiles, the leading clinical research organization (CRO) in the US. CROs are specialized companies that the pharmaceutical business uses to run most aspects of their clinical trials. At the time CROs were well-established in the US and the EU but were new to China. Dan wanted to return to China (experienced people returning to China were known as "sea turtles") and eventually form his own China-based CRO but in the meantime he wanted a position to fill the gap before he set up his own company. This was a very good fit since we probably would not be running many more trials in China but we needed someone to polish the data and help us with the China approval and so Dan joined the VTI China team in the fall of 2007. We were delighted to hire someone as experienced and well-known as Dan.

Our China investors took a serious interest in VTI and were helping us with the China approval and being very active as board members of VTI China. They were also very pleased that Dan had joined the team and I met with them several times in Shanghai to discuss various aspects of the approval plans. They suggested that we arrange a seminar in Shanghai to discuss liver support in general, introduce ELAD, and invite the key Chinese liver support opinion leaders, SFDA people, and one or two key US liver physicians.

This seminar was held at one of the large Shanghai hotels over two days in January 2008. Dr. Mike Millis, one of our board members, agreed to come to Shanghai for the seminar and to make a presentation. We were pleasantly surprised by the number of key Chinese physician opinion leaders that attended but disappointed that no one from SFDA was there. The seminar seemed to be a success and certainly spread the word to the Chinese physicians, some of whom were on the SFDA advisory panels. We were particularly pleased that Dr. Wu Meng Chao, the grand old physician of Chinese liver disease from the Eastern Hepatobiliary Hospital in Shanghai, who was mentioned earlier, made an appearance – this was a big deal since he was such a famous person. See the photo section.

At the urging of our China investors, we restructured VTI China in March 2008 and brought in a new CEO of their choice. He was an impressive individual who was running one of their companies in the city of Xiamen, in Fujian province, about 500 miles south of Shanghai, opposite the island of Taiwan. Before we signed him up as CEO of VTI China, I traveled to Xiamen to meet with him at his then current company. The company was manufacturing and marketing nerve growth factor (NGF), a natural protein that stimulated the growth of human neurons. The offices and manufacturing plant were new, clean, and impressive with the NGF being isolated from mice since mouse NGF was almost identical to human NGF. The only problem was that the large market that was envisaged for NGF had never materialized and they were not even covering their manufacturing costs with the small revenues. However, the candidate was acceptable and we agreed that he would come on board as VTI China CEO.

The city of Xiamen was delightful. It was a coastal city on the Taiwan Strait and had very nice freeways and buildings. My hotel had to be six stars – it was that good! Driving along the coast road I asked about some enormous Chinese language characters which were behind the road but elevated and faced Taiwan. They told me that the characters spelled out "One country, two systems" and were aimed at ships passing through the Strait. There were also subtle signs of defensive fortifications along the coast. Let's hope they are never needed. We played golf on a very nice course close to the sea which was fitted with lights which enabled play 24 hours per day in order to accommodate the large number of people who wanted to play. In my travels around the world playing many golf courses, this was the first time I had ever seen a fully-illuminated golf course ready for night play. I do not think the Scots would be amused! Other features of Xiamen included its western-style restaurants reminiscent of a university town and a fantastic piano museum on an island offshore which had to be seen to be believed. Back to the story.

Although we were sorry to have to part with the current VTI China CEO, we accepted these changes since they were all in the name of boosting our chances of SFDA approval of the ELAD marketing application. Also at the urging of our Chinese investors, we hired some consultants who were supposed to have close ties to the SFDA reviewers and could help us in finding our way. These were similar to the Washington DC regulatory lawyers that are essential to have when pursuing an application with FDA in the US and so it made sense to us. I never liked hiring Washington regulatory counsel to get approval for US FDA applications and I liked hiring these China consultants even less. However, I am a realist and recognize that this is the way the system works.

The problem was that we kept getting requests for relatively large sums of money where we couldn't figure out what we were paying for. Suspecting that these may be potential bribes, we turned them all down and were not very popular with our consultants. We are not saying that they were potential bribes but we wanted to be safe and not sorry. I was particularly interested in staying out of both Chinese and US jails!

The 120-day time limit we had been promised for a decision on approval passed in January 2008 with no direct contact from SFDA. But our consultants were in informal contact with the key SFDA officials and advised us that, in order to move forward, SFDA specialists needed to inspect our production plant in the US since we intended to supply the China market from the US facility and had no immediate plans to build a China plant. The problem was that SFDA had no funds to pay for such a visit of several of their people to our facility in San Diego. We, of course, offered to pick up the cost but they said that SFDA could not legally accept our payment for the visit. This circular logic made us concerned about SFDA's intentions. But we were in the hands of Chinese "experts" endorsed by our Chinese investors so there was no need to worry!

I became even more uncomfortable when our Chinese investors approached us a few months later and said that they would take over all the contacts with SFDA in return for us paying them a monthly fee. I discussed this with the Board of Directors and we were all uncomfortable with it but recognized that we were not in control of the situation. So, expecting that the investors would have the company's best interest at heart, we agreed to this arrangement. Unfortunately, it did not yield any tangible results in spite of a lot of activity and assurances that our investors were close to the SFDA reviewers. I should have remembered the old saying that hope is not a strategy, but we had no other viable alternatives to move things forward and we had no playbook to learn from since everything had changed after the SFDA commissioner's execution. The situation reminded me of Macbeth's famous "tomorrow" soliloquy in Act V, where he says "It is a tale, told by an idiot, full of sound and fury, signifying nothing."

At the end of March 2008, we got news from SFDA that they were going to start reviewing our marketing application in April, and then in early May we were invited to meet with SFDA at their offices in Beijing. Kameron and I landed in Beijing about 5 p.m. on Monday, May 12.

As we disembarked from the plane at the airport, it was obvious that something was wrong. There were not many people around and those who were there had long faces and bowed heads. We could not figure it out but then we saw images of devastation on the airport TVs and realized that, while we had been flying, there had been a major earthquake in China, in the province of Sichuan, with tens of thousands killed. It was a force 8.0 earthquake, one of the top 20 ever since records had been kept. The streets of Beijing were strangely quiet.

Our meeting with SFDA was delayed for two days. There were about eight people from SFDA in the meeting which was in Mandarin with translations. Our reviewer said that the inspection of our San Diego plant was no longer needed and then the meeting turned to primarily discussing manufacturing. In the application, we had been very careful to put in everything that was required but not to give the full details of how to grow and maintain the cells. So that was what the meeting was mostly about. Kameron danced a lot in responding to direct questions on how to grow the cells. It lasted about an hour and a half and the reviewer was the only one to do any of the talking on the SFDA side. Towards the end, we tried to get some form of commitment from him about timelines but he gave vague responses. He did tell us that they were assembling the SFDA review committee for ELAD and questioned whether ELAD would continue to be regulated as a device. The meeting ended with no conclusions and we felt it was not productive. We produced minutes of the meeting which were sent to SFDA but never got the SFDA version of the meeting as was usual in meetings with the FDA in the US.

It was not until about two years later that we understood what was going on here. It seems that the SFDA reviewer had quit his job a couple of months after our meeting. He took with him a copy of our application and set up a company in Guangzhou, South China, to manufacture and market a Chinese version of our ELAD cellular therapy product. We can only speculate where he got the cells from with the best guess being from the used cartridges after ELAD therapy. These were supposed to be destroyed but it would have been quite easy for them to obtain intact cartridges with cells. However, this company could not grow the cells and had to shut down after a couple of years and spending a lot of money. It is possible that this was a government-sanctioned effort but we have no information to indicate either way. We do know that the former SFDA reviewer was not punished for this gross act of IP theft. It is a cautionary tale for others trying to get approval for innovative products in China.

The rest of 2008 did not advance the SFDA approval and we continued the waiting game. Our VTI China team focused on:

- Discussions with several of the large hospitals about being sites for commercial ELAD treatment. The five hospitals that we chose as the initial sites were:
- Beijing You'An
- Beijing 302 Military
- Shanghai Eastern Hepatobiliary (EHBH)
- Guangzhou #3
- Wuhan Tongji

The first two were the clinical trial sites and the other three were large, well-known liver hospitals. All were enthusiastic to proceed.

- Four of China's leading liver doctors, including Dr. Wu Meng Chao of EHBH, signed a letter to SFDA urging them to approve ELAD in China ASAP. This was done at China's largest liver conference in Shanghai which was held in the very impressive international conference center on the Pudong side of the river. We were disappointed that the letter resulted in no obvious improvements in SFDA's reviewing pace.
- The Olympic games were held in Beijing in August. The games began at 8 p.m. on the eighth day of the eighth month in 2008. The Chinese believed that 8 was a lucky number – they were not religious but were very superstitious! Everything else shut down in China for about 6 weeks.
- Dr. Duan held his annual artificial liver conference in September in Nanchang, an historic city about 100 miles from Wuhan – we participated and presented several papers.

We did not have any further contact with SFDA and the waiting game continued.

The activity for the rest of 2008 was in the US so we will return to the story there.

CHAPTER 18
US Trials and Compassionate Use

Compassionate use is where FDA grants special permission for an unapproved drug to be used on a seriously ill patient. The US FDA had allowed single-patient compassionate use of drugs for life-saving and serious diseases for many years. However, it had never been organized into a well-regulated and streamlined process where the rules were clear. These single-patient treatments required a lot of work by the sponsoring physician who had to request FDA allowance for each compassionate use. It required a lot of paperwork and discouraged the experimental use of promising drugs on terminally ill patients. Many times, the process took longer than it took for the patient to die. As such, the FDA received an increasing amount of criticism and in response issued some draft guidelines at the end of 2006 with requests for constructive criticism.

We read these guidelines with great interest and realized that we could design a compassionate use program for ELAD that could offer help to patients with no hope and also be useful in moving ELAD along the path to commercialization. But one thing troubled us as we studied this program and the changes that FDA wanted to make. Why had so few companies ever participated in compassionate use? It appeared to be a win-win proposition for everybody concerned. We speculated that there were three main reasons:

1. There was no provision for any payment or even reimbursement of a company's expenses.
2. The paperwork discouraged the individual physician from sponsoring it.
3. Finally, and most important in our analysis, companies did not have confidence in the safety and efficacy of their products and

therefore feared that they could be on the wrong end of the
FDA's wrath if something went wrong.

We concluded that the new guidelines were going to take care of the
first two reasons and that the third reason was not a problem for us
since we had abundant safety and efficacy data that had never been
challenged by the FDA and was now confirmed by the China Trial. We
had very high confidence in ELAD's safety and efficacy in several well-
defined liver failure conditions and we could, with the FDA's
allowance, extend these to several related conditions. After discussing
this with our board and our clinical advisory board, we resolved to
initiate a compassionate use program once the US trial was allowed
and underway. All of the physicians associated with our trial sites
supported this.

While we were still planning our phase 2 US trial and our compassionate use program, our hand was forced by a call that we received on
August 6, 2008. Kameron and I were discussing our plans for the US
trial when we were advised that a well-known physician from the
University of Michigan Hospital in Ann Arbor was on the phone and
would urgently like to talk to us. We decided to take the call.

The situation that she described was indeed an emergency and she was
suggesting that this patient be treated with ELAD under compassionate use regulations. The patient had just had a liver resection for a
tumor but the tumor turned out to be much bigger than expected and
the surgeons had to cut away much more liver than planned, leaving
her with only about 25% of her liver which was fatty and not of good
quality. It was clear that the patient would not regenerate her liver,
especially since she was obese and it was well-known that obese
people did not regenerate well. The patient was expected to live only
about 5 to 7 days.

We had to make a quick decision and so we told the physician that we
would respond to her within two hours. We were in a good position to
take on such a compassionate use treatment since we had cartridges
ready to start treatments in our US phase 2 trial. Our new manufacturing expansion was now operating, including the higher capacity

bioreactors. The start of the phase 2 trial had been delayed until late September and so this gave us a 1-month window of treatment inactivity. We also had our people trained and ready to go.

Kameron made a call to our reviewer at the FDA and got a positive response and I called the Lead Director of our Board of Directors who was also agreeable. We called the U Michigan physician and told her that we would proceed and she was obviously delighted at the news. We swung into action.

The VTI team had a bedside system and cartridges at the Hospital in Michigan in a day. The Michigan Institutional Review Board (IRB) approved the treatment within hours and the FDA quickly allowed the treatment under their Emergency Use regulations, requesting that we follow the phase 2 trial protocol. Cooperation from Michigan staff and physicians was exemplary and treatment was commenced at 10:30 p.m. EST on August 8. Dr. Millis, our board member, took a key role in this treatment even though he was traveling internationally at the time. He was essentially leading the team from wherever he was in the world. For this and many other things, we are very grateful to Mike. His commitment is inspiring.

The results of this compassionate use treatment were really encouraging. The patient was kept alive on ELAD for 35 days, during which time she had five surgeries. ELAD was portable and was kept functioning during these surgeries. We used three sets of cartridges and easily broke our record for the longest duration of treatment with one set of cartridges, running 16 days. Probably the most important result was that the physicians attributed her continuing survival to ELAD. We monitored her biomarkers continuously and we were impressed that several of the key markers, including blood coagulation Factor 5, began to increase to normal levels. We weren't sure whether this was from ELAD itself or from her regenerating liver but it really didn't matter since the increase was all that counted and showed that we were having a positive impact on her survival and regeneration of her liver. The end came because she contracted an infection and sepsis.

The patient's family was supportive throughout the treatment. They realized that their daughter was in a terminal condition and they encouraged our treatment saying that they wanted their daughter to contribute to the advance of medical science. It was humbling to experience their enlightened attitude.

We learned a great deal from this compassionate use treatment. Importantly, this was the first liver resection patient that we had ever treated with ELAD and it pointed out a major market that we had not really taken seriously up to this point. However, the problem remained that we could not figure out how to do a clinical trial in this indication despite having several of our very best clinical minds consider the problem. It was a tantalizing market because it could have saved a lot of lives by enabling the liver resection surgeons to remove much more of a liver tumor without fear that the patient could not recover, making more serious liver tumors treatable. But we could not design a clinical trial to prove this within the bounds of ethics.

We were also making progress with restarting the clinical trials in the US. Our main concern had been satisfying the FDA's objection to the change in the cell cartridge, as described in Chapter 5, so that we did not have to start again at the beginning. To increase our chances of getting the FDA's approval, we decided to write up a special report to the FDA on the clinical trials in China, reasoning that the more than 45 treatments (enrolled patients, minus controls) that we did in the China trial would provide additional safety data for the FDA. So having chosen the acute-on-chronic liver failure (AOCF) indication for the US trial we submitted a plan to FDA that involved treating 18 patients in a phase 2 trial and then, if there were no safety issues, seamlessly moving into a phase 3 trial in AOCF. We were pleasantly surprised that the FDA accepted this plan and allowed us to proceed.

We enrolled the first patient in this US phase 2 trial in early October. We had seven sites open for enrollment but the trial proceeded slowly and it became obvious after about six months that this AOCF patient population was not going to be ideal for our US and EU approval purposes. The main problem was the wide variation in the patient's enrollment characteristics and also the very high transplant rate which exceeded 50%. As has been explained earlier, transplant makes it impossible to run a survival trial because patients who would have died now survive and thereby invalidate the trial. So, we had to think again.

The Board also commissioned yet another CEO search. I was very supportive of this search since I had now been doing this job for six years. While I was 100% committed to seeing the company be successful, the constant travel and demands of running the company left me with little personal time and I was fast approaching 70. However, while we interviewed some really impressive candidates, none of them met with the unanimous approval of the board and so I continued as CEO. My wife and I even looked seriously at moving to California but, luckily, could not see anything that would match our Arizona lifestyle at an acceptable price. Subsequent events confirm that we dodged a bullet!

By the end of 2008, the great financial meltdown and recession were in full swing and we were all living in fear of financial ruin or even worse. Fortunately, Aron and I had a very conservative mindset and, with the Board's approval, we kept the company's cash reserves solely in US treasury securities rather than chasing yield in riskier short-term investments. This served us very well and we did not lose any of our cash while numerous money market funds either went belly-up or lost considerable value. On the whole, we came through this very difficult time in good shape and did not have to lay off anybody. Our investors were also very supportive.

One anecdote about this time still irritates me: the Federal Government in its wisdom made a fixed amount of money available to life science small companies to help them through this difficult time and we obviously qualified. However, the guidelines were clear that the money would be distributed on a project basis but that all projects had to be clearly distinguishable. Like good citizens, we followed the rules and also listened to our financial advisors and therefore only submitted for our liver failure product – one project. However, we were aware that many other companies dissected their business into ever smaller projects, which we expected to be disqualified. When the money was distributed, guess what happened? They funded all the projects without any examination for the same amount of grant money each so that, for example, if you had split up your business into five supposedly different projects you got five awards, whereas we were stuck with one. Each project was awarded the same amount: $90,000. We were suckers for following the rules and listening to our financial advisors!

Our expenses were now close to $1 million per month in spite of our trying to hold the line on spending. Keeping a full operation going in China and the US was not cheap and we saw cash levels dwindling to the point where it was necessary to raise more money by the middle of 2009. We had outstanding support from our existing investors and we raised about $4 million on a note that was to convert into stock at the next significant financing. But we had to decrease our burn rate and the only place that could be done with any significance was in China. We had been getting the runaround from the SFDA in the two years since we filed for approval, and so it was an easy decision to reduce our China operations, which we did in September 2009. More about that in the next chapter.

CHAPTER 19
China Stalemate

In the first half of 2009, the worldwide financial crisis was getting really ugly. None of us knew what the endgame would be and virtually no one at the time recognized the bottom of the stock market in March 2009. We were desperate to get the ELAD China approval that we saw as the key to unlocking investment money and generating our own revenue stream to eliminate our dependence on investor financing.

But the situation with the SFDA did not get any better. Every time we satisfied one of their demands, it seemed that two more were generated like Hercules trying to slay the hydra. Sometimes, we felt that they were generating policies and procedures specifically to prevent us from getting approval. We split our approval strategies into top-down and bottoms-up activities, neither of which produced results.

Here are some of the road blocks that we encountered:

- None of the top-down activities arranged by our China investors produced any results. We submitted a letter from the four leading Chinese liver physicians to SFDA, that was not acknowledged. Our China investors, who were now our paid consultants, arranged a meeting with the new SFDA commissioner that went nowhere and they also arranged a special seminar just for SFDA reviewers and prominent Chinese liver physicians in Shanghai in January 2008 that was described in Chapter 17. I am sure that our China investors were doing their best for us but SFDA seemed to be impervious to any actions making it very frustrating for us. We felt that SFDA seemed to spend their time concocting things to do to prevent ELAD approval. There are some photos of this conference on our China-trials.com website. Relations with our China investors went south and we terminated the consultant arrangement later that year.

- It was announced in early 2009 that SFDA would now report to the Chinese Ministry of Health. This was regarded as a good move since SFDA now had some standing in the medical community. China Kind Fund was very pleased with this but it did not seem to make any difference to the status of our filing.

- Then there were the numerous policy changes, some of which seemed to be directed straight at us. There was a new regulation about tissue engineering devices, a new rule that said no device or drug could be approved in China if it was not first approved in its home country, and new regulations about drug/device combination products. In each case we were told that these changes did not apply to us since our application was grandfathered by virtue of being filed before the new policies were issued. But then SFDA behaved like all of these new rules did apply to the ELAD application. We were confused, to put it politely.

- We were asked for copies of our licenses to operate our US manufacturing facility. Of course, we did not have them since we did not need these licenses in the US but that was not good enough. So, we worked with the FDA and with the California Health Authority to create special licenses to operate and these seemed to satisfy SFDA. Both FDA and California were extremely cooperative with this unusual requirement and we are grateful to them. SFDA also asked for special virus testing data on our cells which we complied with at significant expense.

- The most difficult change and probably the straw that broke the camel's back was that SFDA set up a new biological division to work with its device and drug divisions on hybrid filings that had biologic components. In doing this, they were following the lead of the FDA and the EMA. Again, we were supposed to be grandfathered. Prior to this, SFDA had not had a biologics division and each of the drug and device divisions handled the biologic aspects of filings themselves. We had numerous meetings with SFDA to discuss whether our status as a device should be changed and whether we should repeat the clinical trials as a drug, which would have been expensive and time-consuming. But there was no change, which was a small and useless win for us.

- We were working with some physicians at 301 Military Hospital, the elite hospital for the CCP in Beijing, on running a clinical trial in liver support after liver cancer resection surgery – this has already been discussed. We made good progress and got close to designing a protocol but then it was obvious that we would never get SFDA approval to implement this. This could have saved many lives if we could have got it approved and we were really disappointed not to proceed.

In September 2009, we finally decided to throw in the towel since our cash was running low and with the financial crisis still raging on, the prospects of raising a significant amount of money to continue the fight were not promising. So, with heavy hearts, the board agreed that we should cut back our operations in China and we laid off everybody in VTI China except a skeleton staff of four and moved to a very small, low-cost office to continue the quest for ELAD approval in China. None of us were sanguine that we could get the approval we were seeking, but we had to keep trying, in a much-diminished way.

There were some bright spots. Kameron stepped up to take over the position of CEO of VTI China and he had some outstanding ideas for how to move forward. He had much experience in working with the FDA on difficult US approvals and felt that he could apply much of this to our China situation. As an afterthought, we also gave him the responsibility for raising money for the parent company from Chinese investors, never thinking that this would amount to much. As we shall see, it turned out to be a crucial lifeline. Kameron begin to commute to China and worked very closely with Dar and John. We were delighted to see how committed they were to making things happen. They were an excellent team!

In early 2010, with biotechnology about as popular as rattlesnakes in the Arizona desert and the financial crisis draining investors' pockets, I had to concentrate on fundraising in a serious way. I was reminded of a key saying of one of my partners in the VC business that "Money-raising is war and you need to focus all of your attention and your resources to get it done." He quoted liberally from Machiavelli on the use of resources in war. It was a good analogy and I did just that.

It was obvious that the usual sources of capital for biotechnology were, at least temporarily, missing in action and so we adopted a strategy of throwing a lot of unconventional lines in the water to see which ones would catch fish. We hired motivated individuals to help us raise money in Europe, the US and, on a suggestion from our MedVentures friends, a really enterprising individual who lived in Dubai and covered Middle East money sources. We also hired expert consultants to seek corporate partners in China, Europe and the US. I hated to do this but I hated the thought of going out of business even more. This all meant a lot of work for me and I was traveling most of the time as well as keeping the US trial moving forward, keeping our compassionate use strategy alive and supporting Kameron's work in China.

CHAPTER 20
Singapore Compassionate Use

We were confident that we had a very innovative, safe, and potentially successful product on our hands, with no competition in sight except liver transplant which to us seemed to be complementary and not competitive. With the results from the China trial and the University of Michigan's compassionate use, we did some creative thinking to figure out where in the world might we be able to run a potentially profitable compassionate use program based only on the data we had generated to date. We felt that the correct kind of program could give us very good experience with types of liver failure and, while not taking care of all our capital needs, it could contribute something to the cause and help to give potential investors the confidence to open their checkbooks. We would have liked to run this program in the US but with the FDA's stringent regulations on only allowing companies to charge for actual out-of-pocket expenses, it was a non-starter.

We considered most regions of the world but it really came down to Asia because of the enormous size of the market and the enlightened attitude of some of the Asian regulatory authorities. Three countries stood out as being high potential: Singapore, Hong Kong, and Korea. We proceeded to investigate and to make contacts in all three countries.

In 2009, we hired Rob Ashley as our chief operating officer to take over Kameron's role with the US trial and regulatory affairs. Rob is an old acquaintance of mine who had done an outstanding job with one of our portfolio companies and he had become free to move to another position at just the right time when we needed to add a clinical development executive. He hit the ground running and in February 2009, we traveled together to China, Singapore, and Hong Kong to sound out the possibilities for the compassionate use program. We hit pay dirt immediately in Singapore. Rob was able to put together a meeting with the Singapore regulatory authorities and they were a breath of fresh air. They were vitally interested in what we were doing and understood our situation. They encouraged us to come to Singapore for our compassionate use program and said that, providing that analysis of our data confirmed safety, they could then give approval for each treatment quickly. They also directed us to two hospitals in Singapore that were running medical tourist programs in the liver transplant area whichthey thought would be interested.

We were very impressed with all aspects of Singapore and its medical facilities. We were also astounded to learn that they had the second-largest capacity to produce biologic drugs in the world, after the US. It was an area of strategic focus for them and so they had a natural interest in our product, which was a biologic drug.

We also expected a lot of interest in Hong Kong and this was confirmed by physicians at the two hospitals we visited. However, the HK regulatory authorities were still mostly working under UK regulations and it was obvious they would not allow our compassionate use program. We similarly eliminated Korea as a site, also for regulatory issues, leaving us with Singapore as the place to go.

We met with the two hospitals in Singapore, one a government hospital and the other private. Both were very interested but the private hospital moved much faster. We worked out a deal where we provided the first four treatments free of charge for them to become familiar with the ELAD therapy and then they would pay US$22,000 per treatment.

The facilities at the private hospital were excellent and they handled mostly medical tourist patients from the surrounding Asian countries. Medical tourism is the term applied to patients who are seeking advanced medical care that is not available in their home countries. They are usually high-net-worth patients who are capable of paying substantial sums for advanced treatments such as organ transplantation. Singapore was one of the leading countries in the world for medical tourism because of its sophisticated medical facilities and personnel plus relatively low domestic demand for these advanced procedures because of an excellent state medical system that led to a high standard of health in its citizens. Most of the medical tourists who came to Singapore were from India, Malaysia, and Indonesia.

We worked out the logistics of handling the shipment of equipment and cartridges with a distributor in Singapore and then sent a team to train the staff at the hospital. Jan Barker did an excellent job in leading this team and we were ready to treat patients by the first week of April 2009.

Running a compassionate use program is not like a clinical trial. The sponsor, namely VTI, does not have much control over the selection or treatment of the patients and we are not under any obligation to collect patient data before, during or after the treatment. We could reject any given patient but we would only do this if there were a safety issue. The physician in charge of the treatment is in control. This is a two-edged sword, of course, since on the one hand we are free of the administrative burden of the trial but on the other hand we do not know much about what is going on and about the outcome of the treatments. Further, we cannot use what data is collected in support of regulatory approval filings even though we are required to report the treatments to the regulatory authorities.

The first three free treatments were completed in April and May at the Singapore hospital and were all acute liver failure caused by hepatitis B flares with one also having hepatitis C. Two recovered and went home and the third died as a result of infection and intubation issues, unrelated to ELAD. Both recovered patients had living donor transplants scheduled and canceled them when they recovered. Their treatment was aimed at bridging to the transplant and their recovery was unexpected. This may have raised problems at the clinic where the treatments were run since they probably were not happy about the loss of transplant revenues.

After a two-month gap, the fourth free treatment was completed in July followed by the first revenue patient in August. We duly received the agreed $22,000 payment. This was a milestone for the company since it was the first real revenue we had ever received (it remains the only revenue the company ever received!). Both of these patients had acute liver failure caused by hepatitis B flares and both were successfully bridged to a liver transplant. The revenue patient was treated for six days and was stabilized sufficiently to undergo transplantation, which was successful.

This was now a very interesting situation and we were beginning to understand the market dynamics a little bit better. From the limited information that we were getting we pieced together that, as we already knew, ELAD was excellent in bridging hepatitis B liver failure patients to recovery – we had already learned that in the China trial. This was normally a wonderful result that everybody celebrated but in the private hospital world it was not so great because if the patient recovered and went home, the potential large revenue from the planned liver transplant did not happen. This was especially a problem with transplants in Asia since most of them were living donor transplants where the donor had surgery to donate a piece of his liver immediately before the transplant operation where this liver fragment was transplanted into the patient and then it grew into a full liver over a period of about 3 weeks. So, obviously, if the transplant did not occur then a lot of preparation and expense were lost, especially as the donor was probably being paid, which was quite legal in Asia.

I decided to go to Singapore to see if I could confirm these conclusions and find out more about the outcomes and the circumstances around these treatments. I was well received and learned that our conclusions were correct. The lead physician at the private hospital was candid with me and said that they could only use ELAD in a situation where they were sure it would bridge the patient to a planned transplant, not to recovery. We could live with this but I pointed out that we were concerned that this meant that the therapy would only be used on patients in more advanced liver failure where it would not be as effective. In the sixth treatment, that is in fact what happened since the patient was so far into liver failure that ELAD was ineffective. As a result, we decided that we could not continue these treatments at the private hospital.

However, the government hospital in Singapore was driven by different motivations and they wanted their patients to recover without transplantation which led to big savings and so we worked out a deal with them but after unsuccessfully treating one patient there, it was obvious that the program was not a good fit for Singapore. There was still a transplant mentality that seemed to affect everything and we therefore reluctantly ceased our program in Singapore. We had worked with some really good people in Singapore and were always very well treated. There was a spirit of innovation and an eagerness to adopt new therapies but the market dynamics there did not suit our objectives. We had learned a lot, which was the object of the exercise, and which can be summarized:

1. We treated 7 patients and had good outcomes in 4, which were 4 out of the 5 initial treatments.
2. Compassionate use in a transplant environment will only be for bridge to transplant.
3. ELAD cannot be effective as a desperate salvage treatment.
4. We cannot leave the patient selection decision solely to the local physicians, as we did in Singapore. We must get more involved and make sure patients are in our sweet spot for therapy and, specifically, are not too far advanced in liver failure. Use of our own physicians is preferred.
5. Initial free treatments are not wise. If they are not willing to pay then they do not value the therapy.
6. Medical tourism is not a good basis for ELAD use since it is aimed only at transplant.
7. Future compassionate use sites must satisfy three criteria:
8. High levels of local disease, with no or minimal transplantation
9. Enthusiastic physicians
10. The ability to pay

If any one of these is absent, we should not participate.

There is an interesting postscript to our compassionate use adventure in Singapore. About two years later one of our friends sent us a copy of a prospectus for an initial public offering on the ASX, the Australian stock exchange. We were very surprised to see that it was for the hospital in Singapore which they were taking public. Yes, that's right, the whole hospital became an Australian public company. The timing was around the compassionate use program that we had implemented in Singapore and we were shocked to see that ELAD featured prominently in the prospectus with photos and a description of the therapy to illustrate that the hospital was in the forefront of innovations for liver disease. This could explain a lot of what happened in Singapore and we are disappointed that the physicians in the hospital did not share with us what they were planning to do and their plans to feature ELAD. This IPO probably influenced the situation in Singapore.

We looked again at the various places around the world and Jan Barker visited several including Turkey and Egypt but these three conditions did not apply in either of these countries. But then, we found a region that seemed to be perfect: the oil-producing parts of the Middle East - we focused on the United Arab Emirates (UAE) and Saudi Arabia.

CHAPTER 21
The Middle East

At the suggestion of MedVentures, one of our key investors, we had already hired Jihad Fakhreddin as our representative in the Middle East to help us to raise funds and it was easy to extend that representation to include a compassionate use program. I made my first trip to Dubai, one of the seven states of the UAE, in October 2009. I took the Emirates non-stop flight from LAX to Dubai, an 18-hour marathon that goes north from LAX, then left of the North Pole, over Russia, and then over Iran into Dubai - tough to endure in coach! But it was worth it and I was really impressed with Dubai. Even though it was suffering badly from the worldwide financial crisis, the buildings and infrastructure there were first class and the medical system seemed to be very much First World. You could see billboards all over the place promoting various hospitals and medical centers, many of them being subsidiaries of well-known US hospitals such as the Cleveland Clinic. You could tell from the billboards that diabetes and liver disease were two of the most common diseases in the UAE.

We quickly learned that liver failure was the 4th cause of death in the UAE and throughout the Middle East with slightly more hepatitis C than hepatitis B cases. We soon determined that two of our three criteria, the prevalence of liver disease locally and the ability to pay were satisfied. We learned later that the incidence of liver transplant was relatively low and that they would welcome a therapy that saved lives by regenerating the liver and avoiding the need for transplant, making it a trifecta and satisfying our conditions.

Jihad had set up a whirlwind series of meetings for me with potential investors and with key physicians and I returned to San Diego very optimistic about putting together a good compassionate use program and securing some investment money. In addition to Dubai, we also went about 50 miles up the road to Abu Dhabi which was similarly impressive. They are two of the seven emirates, or states, that comprise the UAE, a former British colony known then as the Trucial States.

Abu Dhabi is the fourth largest oil producer in the world and the city reflected the wealth that came from this blessing. The 7-star hotel and the mosque in Abu Dhabi were particularly impressive. While walking around the hotel we accidentally walked into a room where the Manchester City football team was having a meeting, complete with their light blue shirts. This was quite a thrill for me as a lifelong football fan.

Dr. Millis helped us to put on seminars in the two key hospitals in Dubai and Abu Dhabi. We were well received but could not find an appropriate physician and location to implement a compassionate use program. We also had more than a few issues with getting the regulatory authorities to sign off on such a program. We continued to work towards this and also talked to numerous investors in the two emirates.

Then, we visited Saudi Arabia and were very well received in the two largest hospitals; these hospitals were some of the best that I had seen anywhere in the world with the latest sophisticated equipment and very well staffed with international physicians and nurses. We gave several seminars and were surprised when the key physician at one of the hospitals expressed great interest in being one of our clinical trial sites for the trial that was currently underway in the US and Europe. We were initially skeptical that they could qualify under FDA criteria but we were pleasantly surprised to find that they already had met the criteria and that some of their liver physicians were well acquainted with some of the physicians who were participating in our current trial in the US and Europe. So, we signed them up and had a very interesting experience visiting the Saudi FDA office to get approval both for a compassionate use program and for the hospital's participation as one of our clinical trial sites. We were impressed with the lack of time-consuming bureaucracy at the Saudi FDA – the whole process took only a few hours and then we walked out with the necessary signed documents.

The intensive care units at the Saudi hospitals were close to full and we noticed a high representation of liver disease patients along with many car accident victims. It was explained that the latter were mostly young people who were playing deadly games of chicken with their cars in the desert, with predictable results. Liver disease patients were not only hepatitis B and C patients but a significant number of acute alcoholic hepatitis patients. We found this difficult to reconcile with the strict banning of alcohol in the country but guessed that alcoholics would find ways to sustain their addiction.

We knew that the Saudis were serious when they asked if they could send a team to San Diego, at their expense, to train on ELAD therapy in our facilities. We readily agreed to this and very soon we hosted four Saudi nurses and two physicians in San Diego. They were very well-educated and eager to learn and their visit was most enjoyable for all concerned. As soon as they returned to Saudi Arabia, the hospital enrolled its first patient in our clinical trial who was disappointingly randomized to be a control patient. But we were impressed with the speed of the enrollment and optimistic that this would turn out to be a very good clinical trial site.

Then came a cruel twist. I was in Riyadh continuing to meet with several potential investors when I was asked to stop by the hospital where one of the physicians explained that they had a VIP patient with liver failure who was not doing well and who they would like to enroll in the compassionate use program as soon as possible. My first reaction was to ask what the problem was and to see whether the patient was a fit for our therapy but we were unable to get any details of his condition and they continued to press to allow treatment.

I made it clear that ELAD therapy would not work on a patient with an advanced liver failure condition but they were not worried by this and said they must try since they had no other options. The pressure was great and we had to make a decision so I said we would allow treatment providing they acknowledged that it was unlikely that it would be successful and they would not hold any adverse result against us in our developing relationship. They readily agreed to this and thanked us profusely. You can guess the rest of the story. When we began the treatment, our people quickly saw that this patient was terminal. We had to stop treatment after a day or so and he died soon after. A very sad situation and, of course, they blamed ELAD. The relationship deteriorated and we did not enroll any other trial or compassionate use patients nor raise any funds in Saudi Arabia. I readily acknowledge my mistake but I am not sure it would have turned out any differently if we had refused to treat since this would have alienated everybody. I think the moral of the story is to avoid working in environments that are not used to innovation and the risks of new products and clinical trials.

Meanwhile, our fundraising in Dubai was actually seeming to bear fruit. Jihad advised us that one of the sheiks in Dubai that we had presented to had given us a term sheet to invest $10 million in this next fundraising. Since our cash was slowly dwindling to danger levels, this was very encouraging and we started to make arrangements to close on the money along with several other investors who were waiting for more invested money to appear. Then, while we were preparing the investment papers, a sad report came out of the UAE of a serious accident which led to the death of one of the young UAE sheiks in Morocco while on vacation. It turned out that the victim was related to our sheik who had committed to invest and things went south from here to the point where the investment was obviously not going to happen. This was another cruel blow and we decided to cease our efforts to raise money and treat patients in the Middle East and return to our focus on the US, EU, and China. It had been a valiant effort to open up a new source of funding and compassionate use treatments but we no longer had the time to keep this effort going.

To close out this chapter on the Middle East, I have to relate the story of the European Association for the Study of the Liver (EASL) meeting in Vienna in April 2010. This was a huge meeting every year and was much more international than the American AASLD meeting which has already been mentioned. We felt it was important to participate and took about 6 of our people with us to Vienna to display the ELAD product. It was a great opportunity to meet our clinical trial physicians and most of our European and some of our US physicians who stopped by our booth at the meeting. We also met with numerous other people. Even our Chinese clinical site physicians were there.

However, as the meeting was drawing to a close, reports started to come in of a major volcanic eruption in Iceland, named Eyjafjallajökull, which was spewing debris into the air and forming a huge cloud over Europe that presented a major threat to aviation. Air travel was being shut down in northern Europe and the threat was rapidly spreading south and east towards Vienna. The day before we were scheduled to leave, Vienna Airport and all the airports within about 300 miles were closed indefinitely. We had some important meetings scheduled in the US and had to get back ASAP. But the closings happened too quickly for us to react. We rushed to the Vienna Airport to find every airline closed down with the best estimates of re-opening being in two weeks. We panicked. Our colleagues were at the airport with us and we had heated discussions about what to do.

There were three options: stay in Vienna and wait it out, get a train southwest into Spain and return to the US from Madrid or go southeast to Turkey and return to the US from Istanbul. None of these were certain and all depended on getting flights rearranged.

While Vienna was a wonderful city to be stranded in, the thought of two weeks of doing nothing while the company slowly ran out of money was anathema. Going to Spain was interesting but if the Spanish airports were closed, there were no attractive travel options and you would be stuck until everything reopened. It seemed to us that going to Turkey and outrunning the deadly cloud was the least-worst option. The problem was that there were no good train connections and so we found a taxi driven by two Turks who agreed to take us to Istanbul that night for a reasonable sum in the circumstances. We also had some airline tickets from Dubai to LAX that we had not used and on checking with the Emirates office in Vienna we found we could use them providing, of course, we could get from Istanbul to Dubai for which they guaranteed us a ticket.

So, we loaded up with food, and off we went that afternoon in the large Mercedes van. What a journey! Through Hungary, Serbia, Romania, and Bulgaria into Turkey where we finally arrived at about 8 am the next morning after being ripped off at the Turkish border for visas to enter and getting lost in Bulgaria because of closures to the freeways. We will never forget it. We got an afternoon flight to Dubai, overnighted there, and then took the nonstop Dubai to LAX flight which was in daylight for 18 hours. At least we got home in about two days after leaving Vienna.

But then we were shattered to learn that the European airports had reopened after two days and that those who went to Madrid got home even before us. Those who stayed in Vienna actually had made the best decision and easily got flights out when the airport re-opened. Oh well, you can't win them all!

But now we were home in San Diego and expecting to be faced with a huge hill to climb to raise funds to keep going. But, this time, we had a pleasant surprise.

CHAPTER 22
Kameron Delivers

Meanwhile, Kameron had been commuting to China and diligently working on the SFDA approval and the fundraising with Dar and John.

On the stalled SFDA approval application, he had been carefully analyzing the structure of the SFDA bureaucracy and meeting with the key players to determine where we should focus. When he first presented this complex hierarchy to us, I felt that, for the first time, we were getting a handle on what we had to do to work toward approval. I even felt that there was a good possibility we could get it done. Further, our China team was obviously very motivated and enthusiastic. We even had one meeting with the leader of the SFDA Device Division in the SFDA building in Beijing. This is notable since foreigners were not allowed to enter this building but Kameron and I were able to get special permission to enter for the meeting which we took as being a promising omen. But it did not result in any progress and our frustrating wait continued.

Better news was delivered on the fundraising progress. Kameron and the team had actually been working on the longshot possibility of getting high-net-worth Chinese business owners to invest in our company. Kameron had noticed that Dar's contacts in China ran very deep and many of them were successful private business people who also knew a lot of other successful private business people; they were all looking for places to invest their money. In addition, all of them were well familiar with the liver disease problem in China since just about every family had been touched by having someone close to them with liver failure. As Kameron explained it, all we had to do was ask for the money, since they all knew the incredibly large size of the market and thereby the upside of any company with a successful therapy! It was not quite that simple, of course, but Kameron had verbal commitments for $1 million investments from each of three wealthy Chinese private business people, in Beijing, Shanghai and Taiyuan. They all wanted to meet the CEO in order to close on their investments and none of them had a problem with accessing dollars.

I need to explain a few things before we proceed. First, the unique person who was our Chinese American team member, Dar He. In addition to being a physician, he had a gregarious personality and made friends easily. His family was originally from Shanghai and on one of my trips, I actually met his 90-year-old mother who was a fascinating person and related to me stories of the communist revolution in the 1940s, with Dar translating, of course. He had a long list of friends and acquaintances in both Shanghai and Beijing and never ceased to amaze me with these and the deep roots of his family. Kameron harnessed these contacts to discover our potential investors.

Second, if you were Chinese and had made a lot of money, the opportunities for investing it in China were few and not very attractive. Most rich people liked to park their money in real estate and we saw rows and rows of houses and apartments that were empty and were owned by investors. It was said that there were whole towns that were not inhabited. We never saw anything like that but the examples we did see, mostly around golf courses, led us to believe that this was a common occurrence. The other obvious home for wealth, investing in the stock market in China, was not like in the US and it was generally believed that it was manipulated. There were wild swings and most people did not have a great deal of confidence in it. That did not leave many options if you wanted to invest sizable amounts of money which is why most rich Chinese were interested in investing internationally, in spite of the difficulties. They somehow found a legal way around the currency issues.

Third, is an observation. We met many successful business people in China and we began to see a pattern emerging that most of them had become successful after acquiring Government assets and making them very much more productive. This was, of course, quite legal and it is a wonderful example of the superiority of the private economy over Government activities. This was all initiated and encouraged by Deng Xiaoping's opening up of the Chinese economy. It was incredible to see these results and the success of Chinese capitalism. It was also obvious that there was a developing conflict between capitalism and political freedom. There seemed to be a devil's bargain that the Chinese were free to practice capitalism and to get rich but that they needed to accept the hegemony of the CCP, the Chinese Communist Party. The good news is that the Chinese have somehow managed to handle that, so far.

Fourth, and last, is the difference between the CEO of a Chinese company compared to an American company. In the US, the CEO is primarily a cheerleader who focuses on hiring and motivating the executive team and ensuring that the company's strategy is optimized. He/she delegates responsibility while still taking responsibility for the success of the whole enterprise and for the strategies to make that happen. But in China, the CEO is almost a dictator and gets involved in just about everything with not much delegation of responsibility. It is a surprising difference and became very obvious to us as we dealt with more Chinese companies. What this meant was that there was a disconnect between my role and behavior as the American CEO and the way I was expected to conduct myself as a CEO in China. But I got used to it. It is good to be the King!

We had a persistent problem: we were running out of money and it was going to take several months to close on the Chinese investments. We needed to take in some investment to bridge this gap and we are eternally grateful to two of our individual investors for providing a significant amount of investment at this time.

I headed to China to meet our potential investors. They all had unpro-nounceable names and so we christened them according to their areas of activity: Mr. Coal, Mr. Nails and Mr. Road. None of them spoke English but that was not a problem with Dar's wonderful talent for translation and so we had very enjoyable, separate meetings with all three investors in Beijing, Shanghai and Taiyuan. All of them were outstanding hosts and very generous with hosting meals and meetings.

The meeting in Taiyuan, in Shanxi province, was especially notable since one of the venues was a remarkable golf course in the mountains above the city. When we first climbed up to it in a fleet of black Audi SUVs, we were not sure where we were going to end up since we went through endless small villages with difficult-to-navigate roads. But just as we were beginning to despair, the golf course and the related buildings suddenly showed up around a bend in the road. We had a remarkable golf game on a spectacular golf course with the highlight being our host, who had never picked up a golf club before, joining me and showing an impressive natural ability. We stayed in high quality overnight accommodations at the golf club. At dinner that night, they asked me to give an impromptu presentation on the history and traditions of golf to the group of about 15 gathered around a large circular table. Fortunately, this was something that I could talk about for a long time and they seemed to be fascinated with the story that I told.

Our host promptly fell in love with golf and we played in the future whenever we met at a whole variety of courses in China. He rapidly overtook my limited golfing ability and I was even able to host him at our member/guest event in Scottsdale in 2010 where he performed admirably.

Our Shanghai investor was the most erudite of the three investors and he was very curious about the entrepreneurial situation in the US. We had long conversations about the philosophy of entrepreneurship and the history of Vital Therapies. It turned out that many of the issues that we had to deal with were the same as his issues and I think we learned a lot from each other.

Our Beijing investor was the most experienced investor of the three and he entertained us with stories of his successes and failures. We marveled at the diversity of his activities which included a chain of restaurants that served only duck dishes.

As we got to know these investors and many of the other people in Dar's circle of acquaintances, it became obvious that we were seeing

China as few Americans see it and we really liked what we saw. These people were well educated, highly motivated and very hard-working. They had the same goals and ambitions as we did and they held America in very high regard. For them, America was the shining light of freedom and entrepreneurship and they wanted to come to visit us and to have their children educated in the American school system. We never saw any anti-Americanism among the people in China but the situation was different in the ruling CCP classes with discrimination against American companies such as ours. That will become even more apparent as the story progresses.

It was not easy to close on this Chinese investment money and it was well into 2010 before we were able to have a closing that brought in some additional investment from the US as well. In this 2009 to 2011 time period, I was forced to spend a lot of my time on fundraising as well as keeping the US clinical trials going and trying to secure SFDA approval to begin commercialization in China. Fortunately, I had an excellent management team to whom I was able to delegate much of the responsibility while I focused on the key issues that needed my attention.

CHAPTER 23
Funding and Continuing China Stalemate

Funding required a lot of work in this 2009/2010 timeframe. We found ourselves confronting a very difficult US financing climate with biotechnology still not popular. We tried to solve our funding problem by looking for money in many diverse places. We called it casting multiple lines in the water. I hated to do this but had no alternative since our existing investors were having increasing problems continuing to finance our activities and the conventional sources of funds in the US had dried up. Among the various sources that we tried to tap were:

- Institutional financing through investment banks. We were hoping to be able to engage one of the banks to raise a private round for us and then move on to an initial public offering (IPO) when we had achieved milestones such as China approval. I met and presented to any of the banks that would give me the time of day providing they had capability in the biotechnology area. One of the most promising ones that took us seriously was Pacific Growth/Wedbush located in San Francisco. They had bankers and analysts who understood our business. Their analyst, Dr. Duane Nash, had one of the most unique combinations of academic titles that I had ever come across: MD, MBA and JD. He had worked as a patent lawyer for one of the well-known firms and had done an internship at one of the San Francisco hospitals where he had treated many liver failure patients and so was intimately familiar with what we were trying to do. Duane was to play an important role with the company later on and the bank was very creative and generous with their time to help us. Duane actually went to

China with us in 2011 and we engaged the bank to help us raise money. More about that later.

- We continued with specific geographic programs by engaging some qualified individuals to help us raise money in Europe, UAE and Saudi Arabia, in addition to our own program in China.
- We tried very hard to find a life science investment bank in China but did not find any one that qualified and so continued with the program ourselves. The support services in the biotech field in China had not yet developed.
- We looked at numerous potential mergers, corporate partners and other innovative deal structures in the US, China and Europe. Discussions in the US and Europe, although generating a lot of interest, did not lead to any possible deals but there was a lot of interest in China and we got to an advanced stage with two candidates:

1. A Chinese artificial skin company located in Xian about 300 miles southwest of Beijing. This was a very interesting situation in that the company's artificial skin had been approved by the SFDA on a conditional approval basis as a hybrid device and drug product. The conditional basis allowed them to sell to a specified list of hospitals and the approval would become a full approval if the product was proven to be safe and efficacious over the first couple of years of widespread use. The company was run by a very impressive and energetic entrepreneur and he had leveraged this conditional approval into a lot of private and government money which he was using to build a huge manufacturing plant in Xian. The difference between him and us is that his was a 100% Chinese-owned company and had obviously received favorable treatment because of this. We felt that if we worked with this company, we may be able to duplicate the kind of approval he had.

Xian was a great place to visit and we saw and were impressed with the life-sized model soldiers in the pits that had been discovered recently. It was also a very old city and had some beautiful buildings in the downtown area. We actually got a deal agreed with the company that involved investment in VTI and marketing rights for the company but it fell apart because the entrepreneur became nervous that we would have continuing difficulties getting SFDA approval which did not do a great deal for our confidence level.

2. A small pharmaceutical company in Hangzhou, about 100 miles south of Shanghai. We came a lot closer to getting a deal done with this company but ultimately it did not work out. We spent a lot of time in Hangzhou which is one of the most delightful cities in China. It has an artistic and cultural history and is full of intellectuals. We met some really delightful people in Hangzhou and the hotels and restaurants were outstanding. If you ever plan to visit China, be sure to put this city on your list of places to visit.

The history of Hangzhou is fascinating. It is a very old city and was the capital city of the Song dynasty about 1,000 years ago. The Song era lasted until it was defeated by the Mongols led by Kublai Khan who ruled over all of China for about 100 years after 1,279. There is a theme park in Hangzhou that is devoted to everything about the Song dynasty and this is one of the most fascinating such parks that I have ever seen. There is an amphitheater in the park that has an incredible sound and light show complete with horses and waterfalls on stage. This was the best such show I had seen anywhere in the world. Hangzhou was also the center of a big tea growing region and the types of tea on offer were mouthwatering. We had some of our meetings on small boats on the many interconnected lakes in Hangzhou sipping tea in the cold weather of winter. The food was really outstanding and served in an impeccable way in some of the best restaurants in China.

Our discussions got to the point where several of the executives of the company were invited to visit us in San Diego. The only problem was getting visas. We didn't realize that this was such a big problem until we got a call saying that they had been rejected for US visitor's visas at the American Embassy in Beijing. I was not a happy camper and so I immediately went to the Embassy. There was a long line of Chinese waiting outside but I went right to the front of the line and asked if I could see someone from the Commerce Department in the Embassy. In this case my prior experience traveling the world for Goodyear proved to be very useful. I had learned from my experience that the US Commerce Department people in our embassies could be a useful resource when you are in an unfamiliar foreign country trying to do business. The people are very knowledgeable and very helpful (my strangest experience was at our Embassy in Tehran, Iran which I visited in 1976 just a couple of months before the revolution! But that's another story).

Amazingly, I was put right through to one of the Commerce Department officials who was very sympathetic to our case which I explained in terms of getting our product approved in China and seeking a merger for the funding to keep the company alive. He said that he would help as much as he could but that they had no influence on the State Department which granted the visas. Our potential Chinese visitors got their visas in about a week and this started a very productive relationship with the people in the commerce department at our Beijing Embassy. They had never heard of a pharmaceutical company trying to get approval for its product in China before being approved in the US but they proved to be a great help, even though we were ultimately not successful.

The stalemate with the Chinese SFDA continued through these two years. We were in continuous contact with numerous SFDA officials and were treated politely even though we could not see that any progress was being made. We continued to be reviewed by the device division of SFDA but they got the drug division involved in order to review the biological part of our application. At that time the SFDA did not have a separate biologic division, as in the US FDA, and we spent a great deal of time trying to nurture the review of our biologic product, which at times seemed to be a tennis ball that was being batted back-and-forth between the device and drug divisions. We actually had a meeting in December 2009 with the drug division to discuss our biologic product which they said they had no objections to and then posted it back to the device division, but still no progress to approval.

SFDA wanted to come and audit our production plant in San Diego but they were never able to get their act together to actually get it done. Then we found that they were making a big deal out of a recent guideline that they could not approve a product in China unless it was approved in its home country first. This kept being raised despite the fact that we had been told many times that we were grandfathered in since we applied for approval well before this guideline was issued. However, at one of our SFDA meetings, we raised the possibility of a conditional approval similar to the artificial skin that was described earlier in this chapter. They asked us to give them a written summary of what this approval would look like and we gave them a document that included a list of 12 hospitals in China where the therapy would be implemented. But this just seemed to disappear into the abyss that was the SFDA without any comment. SFDA started to get its website in line and our product actually appeared there under the status of "in review and approval." But it stayed there forever and, for all we know, it is still "in review and approval" to this day.

But we were to have one last fling at getting approval in China which presented itself in a surprising way. But first, let's take a look at what was going on in the US.

CHAPTER 24
US/EU Trials

We continued to search for a suitable liver failure patient population in the US and EU and also to find a better endpoint that was acceptable to the FDA to avoid using survival as our endpoint in the trials. I have already mentioned some of the issues of using survival as the endpoint but they are worth repeating and expanding on. While survival, which is a nice way of saying death, is the gold standard endpoint for any life-saving therapy, there are some serious issues with how a trial is designed to incorporate a survival endpoint. Here are a few of them:

1. The FDA is very rigid in its interpretation of how to count survival. Even if a patient dies clearly from something which is totally unrelated to the therapy under investigation, the death is counted in the trial. The most ridiculous example is if someone gets hit by a bus or dies in some other accident. You still have to count it as a death in either the control or treated groups.

2. Since the control group patients do not take hospital time to implement the therapy, then the hospital can spend a lot of time to extend the survival of a control patient. This is an obvious bias that is introduced and makes it more difficult to show efficacy. This is particularly the case with our cellular therapy since you cannot hide the fact that a patient is either in the treated or control group.

3. There is a circumstance called "intent to treat" which results in a strong bias against the treated patients, if it happens. This is when a patient is enrolled in the trial but for one reason or another does not get treated. This can occur for numerous reasons such as when the patient deteriorates before treatment

can be initiated. If the patient dies before treatment, it counts against you in the treated group. Obviously, the same thing applies to the control group but it is much more of a penalty in the treated patients since the patient has not been exposed to the therapy which could have saved them.

4. Patients do not like participating in survival clinical trials. With a treatment such as ELAD where a placebo control is unethical, patients know whether they are in the treated or control group and this can result in control patients withdrawing from the study after they have been enrolled. It can also be a significant disincentive for patients to participate in the study which makes it more expensive and time-consuming to complete the trial.

5. Insisting on a control group in a survival trial is regarded by some people as unethical since it withholds a potentially life-saving treatment from the control group.

6. Following up and finding each patient after 90 or 180 days can be a real challenge, especially if the patient has died after being discharged from the hospital. If the patient cannot be found they are usually censored from the group which hurts the statistics.

These and other issues are the reason that most clinical trials do not use a survival endpoint. This has especially been the case in the cancer field where surrogate and tumor progression endpoints are used instead of survival. When survival is determined as a follow-up to prove the efficacy of an already approved drug, the survival trial frequently does not confirm the surrogate endpoints which can lead to withdrawing the drug from the market.

However, despite a lot of effort on our part we could not budge the FDA from insisting on a survival endpoint in our trials. We felt that this was because we were regulated by the biologic division of the FDA and we further felt that the cancer drug companies had a signifi-cant advantage in gaining approvals with their surrogate endpoints – they were regulated by the drug division which was more flexible and open to surrogate endpoints. They had to show that their surrogate endpoint was clearly related to the final outcome of death/survival and then they could use the surrogate endpoint as the endpoint in the trial and the basis for approval.

We looked at numerous creative surrogate endpoints with the most promising being the use of the MELD score which has been explained earlier as a composite score based on kidney function, blood coagulation, and bilirubin, a liver by-product from the degradation of hemoglobin. MELD score has been used for many years to prioritize liver transplant candidates. I doubt that anyone in the field would argue that it is a predictor of death but the best we could get from the FDA was that we could measure it in the trial for information only.

In looking for an appropriate patient liver disease state, it became obvious to us that the state of knowledge of liver disease was still in its early phases. There was a spirited debate going on amongst the leading liver physicians as to the causes and classification of liver failure patients. It is a complex argument but I will try to explain the situation and the challenges that it represented for us in designing a clinical trial. We came to realize that we had been lucky in China to find a group of patients who suffered from a disease, hepatitis B, that was fairly clear-cut and reasonably well-understood. This was probably the reason why we had such good results in China and, although it was a blessing that there was very little hepatitis B in the US or the EU, it complicated our situation and made us look for alternative patient groups with liver failure caused by other factors.

A consortium of mainly European liver physicians played a key role in advancing the knowledge and the thinking about liver failure. There was unanimous agreement that liver failure fell into two main groups, chronic and acute:

- Chronic liver failure is a slowly progressing disease where the hepatocytes, the main functional cells in the liver, die and are replaced with a fibrous network with nonfunctional cells. The liver shrinks in size and turns black in color, with the end result being a state known as cirrhosis. This condition progresses slowly over decades and is terminal because a cirrhotic liver cannot regenerate. Only a transplant could save such a patient's life. The main cause of cirrhosis is chronic alcoholism, usually over decades. Cirrhotic livers cannot regenerate.

- Acute liver failure progresses much faster and is an inflammatory disease where the liver is bright red and much enlarged. It is mainly caused by ingested toxins such as alcohol or other drugs and can happen fairly quickly. The usual cause is binge drinking rather than the slow deterioration of cirrhosis. Regeneration of the liver is possible in this condition.

The situation is complicated by the fact that both acute and chronic liver failure could be present in the same person and some external event such as ingestion of large amounts of a toxin or trauma could cause acute liver failure in a person with early or later stage cirrhosis. This condition is known as acute-on-chronic liver failure, or AOCF. The situation could be complicated by many other factors such as when the liver becomes infiltrated with fat in a condition known as fatty liver.

The European consortium gathered a large amount of data on the condition and outcome of many cases of both acute and chronic liver failure. From the study of this data, they developed a way of scoring any patient's condition based on not only the condition of the patient's liver but combined with data on the status of the patient's major organs such as the kidney, brain and lungs. The result was a simple score that predicted the patient's chances of death with time. This worked very well largely due to the fact that most cases of liver failure were in fact AOCF caused by an acute event on top of an existing chronic liver problem.

This was painstaking, brilliant work by the physicians in the consortium and we decided to take advantage of it to see if we could find a group of patients that would benefit from the ELAD therapy. So, we designed a trial where to be eligible, the patients had to have either AOCF or pure acute liver failure caused by either alcohol or drugs. We excluded cirrhotic patients from the trial, and, to handle the confounding influence of liver transplant on the results, we censored any transplanted patients. Censoring meant that they stopped being in the trial just before the transplant and the outcome of the transplantation did not affect the trial results.

We designed it as a phase 2 trial but we included enough patients so that we could seamlessly merge it into a pivotal trial suitable for filing for approval if the results were good enough. Then we set out to implement the trial in the US, the EU and the Middle East at the same time, with a total of 24 trial sites with 16 in the US, 7 in Europe and 1 in Saudi Arabia. This was an ambitious trial and we had very good cooperation from the clinical trial sites which were mostly large academic hospitals.

We got particularly good cooperation from the European clinical site hospitals and the Danes, in particular, sent some of their physicians and nurses to San Diego for training. The situation in Europe was frustrating, to say the least, because the enthusiasm of their hospital staff was not matched by the cooperation of the European regulatory authorities which operated in a mess of bureaucracy:

- In the US, we only had two levels of bureaucracy to satisfy before we could begin the trial at any given site: the FDA's allowance of the protocol and the approval of each site's IRB, or Institutional Review Board, a committee which oversaw safety at that hospital. Even though some of the hospitals took quite a long time to give approval, we were enrolling at most US sites within three months of requesting approval.
- Contrast that with Europe, where there were four levels of approval required before we could start the trial at any given site: the EMA's allowance of the trial protocol (for all the EU), approval of the national IRB for each country, approval of the hospital IRB and finally, the approval of the hospital's R&D Committee (we never figured out exactly what this was). The EMA allowance was logical and usually prompt but the process could be held up for months with any one of the remaining three committees and they sometimes had the most

trivial and difficult-to-overcome issues, especially in the UK. We had some prolonged approval processes in the UK and EU, exceeding a year in some cases, and were treated with suspicion by some of the committees.

As a result, the faster clinical site approval in the US meant that it was relatively low cost to set up the trial but the cost per patient afterwards was very high. The EU was reversed with the costs to set up the trial being very high but the per patient cost being less. The cost for both the US and EU averaged out at about $90,000 per patient and that was simply for the cost of operating to get the clinical site and trial protocol approved and to treat the patients at the hospitals. It did not include any other costs including the ELAD product and the cost of all of our people to manage and implement the therapy.

In retrospect, we would have been better to have focused only on the US which would have avoided the high fixed cost of the European setup and all the travel and wasted time. You couldn't just go to London for a day from San Diego!

At the end of 2010, when we had enrolled and completed the follow-up of about 60 patients, our analysis of the trial results showed that ELAD was not effective on patients with a high degree of cirrhosis. We concluded that we could not help anyone whose liver was not capable of regeneration. However, the data were telling us that we were effective on patients with acute liver failure without a significant degree of cirrhosis, especially on acute alcoholic hepatitis (AAH) patients; these patients had inflamed livers but were not cirrhotic. We speculated that this was because ELAD could regenerate the failing livers of AAH patients which were inflamed but not cirrhotic.

These results also explained why ELAD was so effective on the livers of hepatitis B patients in China: these hepatitis B patients generally progressed to an inflamed liver and then to tumors in the liver. This meant that their livers were regenerable and explained why we got such good results with ELAD. In contrast, hepatitis C patients, which were the overwhelming majority of the viral hepatitis patients in the US, usually progressed to cirrhosis where ELAD was ineffective.

This also meant that we could probably support patients who had their liver resected to remove liver cancer tumors, while their liver regenerated, a large and unserved market that would be difficult to prove in a clinical trial. It was a mixed bag of results but it did point the way forward.

There was, however, a festering problem in that we were slowly running out of money. Towards the end of this trial, we had already cut back the number of patients that we could enroll per month to a maximum of four in order to conserve capital and we had reduced our headcount for the same reason. Laying off people was very traumatic but we tried to do it in such a way that we could rehire them if we could secure financing. Hopefully, they all understood.

The market for biotechnology financing in the US was still not encouraging and the results of this trial did not help us since we had hoped to get results good enough to file for approval without needing a further phase 3 trial. So, we began planning for the next US trial which would focus on acute alcoholic hepatitis patients but we knew that we could not start the trial until we had secured financing.

We decided to focus our last-ditch financing efforts on China since our reception was much better there.......

CHAPTER 25
Aodong

Conventional wisdom is that you do not qualify as a seasoned entrepreneur unless you have been through the trial by fire of not knowing where the money to make your next payroll is going to come from. Unfortunately, such an experience was lying in wait for me sooner than I expected. It was indeed a chastening experience.

After we concluded that we could probably not raise new capital in the required time frame from US or EU based investors, we decided as a team to focus on China. While most Chinese investors would only invest in revenue generating companies, we knew from first-hand experience that there were investors in China who had already shown they were willing to invest risk money. Working with Kameron and the management team, we put together a strategy to blanket what we felt were likely Chinese investors and then we set out to go to meet with them. I was working with Dar, and Kameron was separately working with the rest of the team. This dual approach enabled us to cover a lot more ground which was essential since we were running out of time as well as money.

While Kameron focused on the individual investors, Dar and I worked on the Beijing, Shanghai and northern China institutional investor candidates. We met with a lot of very interesting people and got a very good and hospitable reception wherever we went. We shamelessly exploited the personal relationships that Dar had in China and the relationships that we had built with the Commerce Department at the US Embassy who were very supportive.

Dar and I continued our whirlwind of visits to companies, financial institutions and any other potential source of funds that would listen to us. On March 9, 2011, we ended up in Shanghai at one of the largest healthcare corporations in China. While they were very interested in what we were doing and saw the enormous market that we could address, they would not do anything until we had SFDA approval to market ELAD in China. It didn't seem to occur to them that if we had SFDA approval, we would not need them; we drew the same illogical conclusion from all the institutional investors that turned us down. We finished up the last meeting in a very dejected mood and, with both of us uncharacteristically silent, we headed for Shanghai airport for the flight back to Beijing.

At the airport, while we waited for the plane to Beijing, I was feeling depressed, exhausted and kept on thinking about where we would find the money to make the next payroll and how we would handle closing down the company if we could not find an investor. I shared these thoughts with Dar and, if I had been a drinker, I am sure I would have been drowning my sorrows in alcohol. While I was at my nadir of this depressing talk, Dar's cellphone rang and he spent 10 minutes talking in Mandarin to one of his contacts. I could tell that he was getting more excited as the discussion progressed but my dark thoughts stopped me from getting my hopes up.

After he finished the phone conversation, Dar was ebullient and said that the Chairman of a large Chinese drug company based in Jilin province in North China was in Beijing and wanted to meet with us the next morning to learn more about ELAD and VTI with a view to doing a deal with us. I immediately poured cold water on it and said to Dar that I had had enough and that I thought we had come to the end of the road. It had been a very interesting few years but we had to recognize when we were beaten. On the plane, we found ourselves sitting close to one of the ladies we had met in Shanghai who was the CEO of one of the few private hospital systems in China and we had some cordial discussions but Dar quickly brought me back to reality. Dar was not having any of my pessimism and spent the 90-minute plane ride and the rest of the journey back to our hotel working on me to take the meeting and see what happened. So, what could I do but buckle under the pressure from Dar and agree to meet with the Jilin company?

Next morning, Dar and I met with Chairman Li and some of his executive management from the Aodong Company at a very nice hotel in northern Beijing. I was not my usual self and went into the meeting expecting the usual Chinese niceties that I vowed to myself I would not take and then I would terminate the meeting and make my arrangements to go back to the US. But this was no ordinary meeting, Aodong was no ordinary company, and Chairman Li, no ordinary Chinese leader. I took an immediate liking to Chairman Li who was obviously a very polished businessman, logical and simpatico in his approach to business. He began by telling me that he was very interested in learning more about our product and clinical trials and that he was looking for a company like ours that could help him to upgrade his product line of Chinese natural products medicine to state-of-the-art Western prescription drugs. This was something that I had not heard before and it made a great deal of sense after he explained his line of traditional Chinese medicine products with the lead product being an extract of young deer horns that was marketed for impotence.

We started to talk about ELAD, the clinical trials and the status of our filing for approval at SFDA. All of this had to be translated since none of us spoke the others' language except Dar, who worked very hard translating. But after about 30 minutes I decided that I had to try to determine whether Chairman Li was serious or not and so I told him that I needed to be honest with him and tell him about our precarious financial situation and our need to raise capital quickly to keep going. If he could not provide us with some investment very quickly, there was no point in continuing these discussions. He was obviously surprised at my candor but after a few minutes, he asked me how much we needed to keep the company together and to avoid closing down. I was unprepared for this question and had to think quickly so I responded that we needed enough capital for about three months of operation, which was $2 million, and then we needed another $25 million to complete the US trials and to keep trying to get SFDA approval so we could market the product in China. He slowly responded that Aodong could do this but it would take about 4 weeks to get the necessary approvals from SAFE to secure the dollars and send them to the US. After that, if everything checked out and he felt that we could get SFDA approval then the $25 million would not be a problem.

I was stunned at his positive response! He made it clear that he was well familiar with the hepatitis B problem in China and with the enormous potential size of that market. He was looking for a major product for Aodong to expand with and he felt that we may have what he needed. We explained our situation with the SFDA in a brutally candid way and Chairman Li said that he felt he could really help us since he had a lot of experience in dealing with the SFDA. He was comfortable making the investment before we secured SFDA approval but he would insist that we follow his advice on how to get approval. I quickly agreed to this and readily acknowledged that he was the expert and we were the students. After about 2 hours, we agreed to meet for lunch the next day to work out more details.

Lunch the next day was at a high-end Beijing hotel in a private room with Chairman Li, some of his executives and a consultant that I had seen before. I began to piece together the background that led to such a positive meeting the previous day. Apparently, the company we had been dealing with in Hungzhao had suggested that Aodong meet with us. But, before they moved to contact us, they had engaged the consultant, who was one of the most impressive and competent that I had met in China, to get his opinion which must have been favorable. So, the skids had been at least partially greased before we had the first meeting. This second meeting was spent in a lot of get-to-know-you discussion and then finished up in sketching out an agreement.

Chairman Li is a really exceptional Chinese leader. He had started out at the company working at the deer farm and worked his way up to become the CEO after about 25 years. He had set out to grow the company and took it into most of the branches of Chinese traditional medicine. The company was public and as a result of Deng Xiaoping's opening up of Chinese capital markets and his experience gained from running a public company, he acquired a broker in Shanghai that had done very well and was still very profitable. The head of this brokerage company was at our lunch. Aodong now had a market value of about $3 billion and was a significant player in the Chinese traditional medicine and stock markets. On the way, he had made sure that his employees received stock in the company and we learned later that he was responsible for making many employees into Chinese renminbi millionaires. We were to meet some of these as we progressed with our relationship.

After I described the history and background of Vital Therapies, we talked about a possible agreement. Both sides were very reasonable and the discussions quickly progressed to the key points which were the initial $2 million investment for a minimum of 5% of VTI on the same terms as whatever other money we could bring in at the same time. We agreed to follow Aodong's leadership in working with the FDA to get approval; when we had secured this approval, Aodong would invest an additional $25 million for 30% of VTI. We verbally agreed that marketing would be the responsibility of VTI but left open the possibility of Aodong being our marketing partner. We agreed to allow three weeks for each side's diligence and then meet again to finalize the agreement and begin to implement it. Chairman Li agreed to initiate the process of getting SAFE's approval to send us the $2 million investment but stressed that this could take about 4 to 6 weeks. I agreed to return to China about April 1 and said I would bring Kameron with me. Chairman Li asked that we come to Dunhua, Aodong's HQ city in Jilin province, and make presentations on the company and ELAD to his management team at that time and we readily agreed.

After lunch, there still a narrow time window for me to call Kameron who was already back in the US and to tell him that we had an agreement with Aodong and will be bringing in at least $2 million in a few weeks. I could tell that he was shocked and his first reaction was to ask who or what was Aodong. Now we knew where the next payroll was coming from since, with this agreement, we could either front it from our personal resources or get additional bridge money from our investors. I asked Kameron to inform the rest of the management team in San Diego and I called our lead board member and investor in the Bay Area the next day. He was similarly surprised and relieved. The diligence went well on both sides and so Kameron, Dar, and I headed to Dunhua, Jilin province for April 1 meetings.

CHAPTER 26
Negotiating the Agreement

Getting to Dunhua was not easy. We flew into Changchun, the biggest city in Jilin province where Chairman Li met us in his chauffeured black Audi for the 200-mile drive east to Dunhua. We drove on a beautiful 4-lane freeway at fairly high speed since there was little traffic around. This area used to be known as Manchuria and it has been back and forth between Russia, Japan and China over the centuries with the most recent nation change being when the Japanese occupied it in the period before and during the second world war. It is a very fertile plain and every square inch of it seemed to be farmland. In early April, the time of our visit, the farmers were preparing the land for planting and we were very interested to note some antiquated plows with teams of horses working the soil. We had a wide-ranging discussion with Chairman Li in the car and reached our hotel in Dunhua in about 2½ hours. We had a very enjoyable dinner with the Aodong executive team and were treated like VIPs. We started the meetings early the next morning.

There were a lot of people in the meetings and it was obvious that we were being taken very seriously. No one from Aodong spoke English but we had anticipated this with bilingual slides which Dar had painstakingly prepared beforehand. We presented the structure and functioning of ELAD and the results of the clinical trials. We also gave the business presentation and our concept of the agreement between our two companies. All of this was received with enthusiasm by the Aodong audience and you could tell from the questions that they had a good understanding of the subject. The meeting went on all day with a break for an excellent lunch where a young employee joined us because she spoke English very well. She looked somewhat like Kate Middleton, the soon-to-be wife of Prince William since this was the time leading up to their marriage. There was a lot of good-natured banter about the imminent Royal wedding.

We toured the manufacturing plant and the administration buildings and were impressed with their cleanliness and well-ordered appearance. They seemed to have a lot of modern equipment and knew how to use it. We also toured the deer farm which was fairly close to the HQ buildings. However, all of the products that we saw were mundane and would be classified as health foods in the US and Europe. It was obvious that they needed to upgrade their game into sophisticated pharmaceutical products, as Chairman Li had already told us.

We finished the day by drafting a memo of understanding about our cooperation which was in line with our prior discussions. Chairman Li wanted to insert a paragraph about the necessity for PR releases to give full disclosure to the public shareholders about what we were doing. We had no problem with that and so we signed it and said that we would use it as a basis to draw up a formal agreement which we both wanted to be as short as possible. Chairman Li said that he would like to get to know some of our board members and I promised to bring at least one of them to Dunhua with me next time since it was difficult for him to travel outside China. He also expressed an interest in meeting all of our management team and I undertook to bring as many of them as I could to Dunhua in the near future. After a really nice dinner, we had time to ourselves and all of us agreed that there did not seem to be any showstoppers that had emerged from the meeting and that we were developing an excellent relationship with Chairman Li and the Aodong team.

We flew back to Beijing from Yanji, a city about 100 miles east of Dunhua. Although Yanji is in China, it has a Korean culture and it is close to the spot where Russia, China and North Korea meet at a single point, not far from Vladivostok in Russia. We could tell that most of the signs in the city were in Korean and were informed that the local specialty was dog meat in various forms such as roasted, curried and boiled. Before our departure, we had lunch in a Korean restaurant in Yanji, but we did not order dog dishes. We were entertained by North Korean singers and musicians. They were competent performers but they did not smile! We were only 10 miles from the North Korean border when we were in Yanji.

The Aodong $2 million arrived in our account on May 3, 2011, about on schedule with Chairman Li's estimate, and so we began an energetic campaign, under Chairman Li's direction, to interact with SFDA to get approval for our application to market ELAD in China. This application was now almost 4 years old, having been filed originally in July 2007. Here is the news release that Aodong issued to announce the agreement:

证券代码：000623 证券简称：吉林敖东 公告编号：2011- 007

Stock code:000623 Stock Name: Jilin AoDong Announcement# 2011 − 007

吉林敖东药业集团股份有限公司
JiLin AoDong Medicine Industry Group Co., Ltd

关于拟投资美国生命治疗公司并签订意向性协议的公告
Announcement of Investment in Vital Therapies Inc and LOI

本公司及董事会全体成员保证信息披露的内容真实、准确、完整，没有虚假记载、误导性陈述或重大遗漏。

All members of the Company and the Board ensure that the information disclosed is true, accurate and complete and contains no false, misleading statements or material omissions.

2011年4月2日，吉林敖东药业集团股份有限公司（以下简称"吉林敖东"或"本公司"）与美国生命治疗公司（英文名称：Vital Therapies, Inc.）在吉林省敦化市就生物人工肝（ELAD）项目签订投资意向书。

On April 2, 2011, JiLin AoDong Medicine Industry Group Co.,Ltd ("JiLin AoDong" or "Company") and Vital Therapies, Inc ("VTI") signed the Letter of Intent for investing the ELAD project in DunHua JiLin province.

1、美国生命治疗公司及生物人工肝（ELAD）项目简介

Vital Therapies, Inc and Bio-artificial Liver (ELAD)

1、境外企业名称：Vital Therapies, Inc.

Name of overseas company: Vital Therapies, Inc.

2、注册地址：美国特拉华州

Registration address: Delaware State, U.S.

3、注册资本：$ 3,500 以万美元为单位

Registered capital: $35million US$

4、经营范围：生物人工肝研发

Business scope: Research and development of bio-artificial liver

5、经营年限：永久存续

Operation time: permanent

美国生命治疗公司拥有多位博士，医学博士及专家，具有丰富的专业经验，研制生产的生物人工肝（ELAD）是世界上首例以人体肝细胞为基础的体外人工肝，其设计理念是为严重肝衰竭的病人提供持续的肝脏支持（如合成、代谢、解毒、分泌等），给病人足够的时间使其自身肝脏得以恢复，或稳定病情直至找到可供移植的供肝进行肝移植。

Equipped with a number of doctors, M.D.s, and experts with rich professional experience, VTI is developing the first human liver cell-based ELAD® which has been designed to stabilize liver function in patients with life-threatening liver failure by processing toxins and synthesizing proteins that are key products of normal human liver function, possibly enabling a bridge to transplant or liver recovery.

2、投资意向书主要内容

Main content of LOI

1、本公司拟初步投资200万美元，持有美国生命治疗公司5-6%的股权。

The company intends to initially invest 2 million US$ for exchange of 5%-6% of VTI's ownership.

2、如生物人工肝（ELAD）项目获得中国药监局或美国食品药物管理局批准，则吉林敖东将第二次投资2500万美元，成为美国生命治疗公司的第一大股东。在本意向书签订之日起六个月内生物人工肝（ELAD）项目未获得中国药监局或美国食品药物管理局批准，则双方就合作事宜另行协商。

If ELAD is approved by SFDA or FDA, JiLin AoDong will make its second investment of 25 million US$ and become the largest shareholder of VTI. If the approval of SFDA or FDA is not obtained within 6 months after the signature of LOI, both Parties will discuss the cooperation separately.

3、该项目需获得吉林省商务厅批准，本公司现已启动向吉林省商务厅申报程序，一旦获得吉林省商务厅批准，则双方立即签订正式合作协议。

This investment requires the approval of Department of Commerce of JiLin province. The company has initiated the application procedure with Department of Commerce of JiLin province. Upon the approval of Department of Commerce, both Parties will sign the formal cooperation agreement.

公司将依据《深圳证券交易所股票上市规则》的有关规定，对投资进展情况及时履行相关信息披露义务。

The company will disclose the project status timely in accordance with "ShenZhen Stock Exchange Listing Rule".

由于该项目存在较大的不确定性，敬请广大投资者注意投资风险。

Since there is big uncertainty in this project, we would like to remind the investors of investment risks.

特此公告。

吉林敖东药业集团股份有限公司董事会
Board of JiLin AoDong Medicine Industry Group Co.,Ltd
二0一一年四月六日
April 6, 2011

The reaction of the Chinese stock market to this news release was immediate and the price of the stock shot up to increase the market valuation of Aodong from about $3 billion to $4 billion, or about 33%. We got copies of several Chinese analyst reports that clearly showed that investors knew that there was a very large potential market for a therapy approved by SFDA to save the lives of people in liver failure from hepatitis B.

So, we now had our funding and our agreement with a credible and seasoned company to help us with SFDA approval. Now we had to deliver.

CHAPTER 27
Chairman Li Directs the SFDA Program

The next six months were a constant flurry of activity driven by Chairman Li's initiative to secure SFDA approval for ELAD. I spent a lot of time in China, making 9 more trips to China in that period, with each of them being about 10 days duration and so I spent about 50% of my time in China during the rest of 2011. I was mainly in Beijing, Shanghai and Dunhua; Kameron had to handle the San Diego operations.

Chairman Li was a gracious host but hard-driving in his efforts to secure SFDA approval. We followed his instructions as closely as we could. But he could also relax and we had some stimulating dinners in some great restaurants, some with quality entertainment. A detailed description of our various activities would fill another book but I will try to summarize the main points.

He set the goal to have approval within six months of signing our cooperation agreement and he soon met with the commissioner of the SFDA and followed that up with a letter to the commissioner that was endorsed by our friends in the Commerce Department at the US Embassy. That seemed to get action and we were criticized by the SFDA for being "never seen at the SFDA" since we always worked through consultants. Of course, they overlooked the fact that foreigners are not allowed to meet with SFDA officials without special permission, which forces a foreign company to work through consultants. However, in the future, we must represent ourselves and meet with the SFDA regulators. SFDA also specified that the CEO must lead all meetings with SFDA and also take the lead in all other initiatives to gain approval. Of course, we had been doing the opposite since everyone was advising us to make Vital Therapies look like a Chinese company and so an American CEO like me needed to stay in the background. But no longer – damn the torpedoes!

He quickly confirmed that our status at SFDA was "in review and approval" and urged us to meet with SFDA frequently. This got a reaction out of SFDA that they would not meet with foreigners and so we sent our China office staff to the meetings. The SFDA device division washed its hands of the application by saying that they were ready to approve it and were waiting for the drug division to approve the use of the cells. We finally arranged a meeting with the drug division but could not make any progress and they simply pitched it back to the device division. You could call this a revolving stalemate. So, under the Chairman's direction, we sent a strongly worded letter to the SFDA drug division demanding action but it did not produce the desired effect.

Chairman Li spent time with our clinical trial physicians in Beijing and got on very well with Dr. Duan at Beijing You'An. He asked Dr. Duan to draw up a letter requesting conditional approval at about 12 hospitals and to get the letter signed by the lead liver physician at each of the hospitals. Among the hospitals that signed the letter were:

- Beijing You'An
- Beijing 301 Military
- Beijing 302 Military
- Nanjing Gulou
- QiLu Shandong
- Harbin Second University
- Dalian Sixth People's
- Tianjin First Central (largest liver transplant hospital in the world)

We discussed a possible conditional approval in one of our meetings with the SFDA device division. I thought we were making very good progress towards such a conditional approval.

In June, we took most of our management team to Dunhua to get to know the Aodong executive team. After the presentations and meetings, Chairman Li arranged for us to take a trip to Changbai National Park about 80 miles southeast of Dunhua on the border with North Korea. The feature of the park was a collapsed ancient volcano which had formed a large circular lake in the remnants of the volcanic cone. It was similar to Crater Lake on the border of California and Oregon in the US. The terrain was mountainous and very beautiful and included several large waterfalls. Unfortunately, the way up to the lake was still blocked by snow at this relatively early time of the year and so we could not see the lake. However, on the flight back from Yanji to Beijing, we had a bird's eye view since the plane flew right over Changbai. It is an impressive geological feature and apparently half of it is in North Korea. We were really impressed with the facilities in the park and the efficient way it was organized and we took a few hikes to see interesting features. On the drive to the park, we passed two theme parks that exhibited tigers and we were surprised to learn that tigers are native to the area and can still be seen.

Our relationship with the US Commerce Department at the US Embassy in Beijing was very attractive to Chairman Li and he urged us to plan some kind of event with the Department of Commerce (DOC), which the DOC had already suggested. We, therefore, asked them to set up a cocktail party soirée.

The Minister–Counselor of Commercial Affairs in the US Embassy in Beijing held the dinner party on June 23 to introduce VTI, Aodong and DOC and we also invited many of the people in China who were helping with ELAD in China. Ten of our recovered ELAD patients attended and we asked one of them to tell his story. He was a PhD in immunology, spoke English and knew how to present to an audience; he was the star of the show. His wife was also a good presenter and her endorsement of his story was a very emotional experience for all of us. The photo shows the Minister-Counselor in conversation with the recovered ELAD patient and his wife.

The attendance at the soirée was limited by a violent thunderstorm which dropped a lot of rain on Beijing that evening and made it difficult to travel even short distances. We wondered whether this was divine intervention! Chairman Li was there and worked the crowd, meeting with all the recovered patients who were there. He was so taken with the recovered patients that he asked us to arrange an "ELAD Recovered Patient Reunion" and invite SFDA and others to attend, which we did in October 2011.

The recovered Chinese patients had been successfully treated with ELAD at Beijing You'An and 302 Military hospitals. There were 16 of these patients who were so grateful that they had recovered from a terrible disease that they pledged to us, without us asking, that they would do anything to help us to move forward with getting approval for our therapy in China. After lunch in Beijing, with an impressive audience attending, many of these patients stepped up to the microphone and gave a spontaneous, unrehearsed story of the progression of the disease and their treatment with ELAD. We had simultaneous translation. Their stories were moving and brought tears to my eyes and to the eyes of many others in the audience.

These recovered patients represented a cross-section of the population of Beijing and illustrated how hepatitis B did not discriminate by class or status in the community, which explained why most Chinese families had been touched by an experience with hepatitis B in a family member or members. There were several housewives, a major in the Chinese army, several small businessmen and a PhD in immunology who was particularly impressive because he was fluent in English, understood the workings of ELAD and the devastating nature of the disease and was able to explain his experiences in language that was easy to understand. We would not have been able to do this kind of thing in the US or the EU but Dar assured me that all the recovered patients were enthusiastic and anxious to tell their stories and that this was both legal and ethical in China. They were not expecting any payment but we did give them a small honorarium in appreciation of them spending the time. There were two SFDA people at this reunion but we could not tell whether it had any effect on them.

After the recovered patients' reunion, we had several meetings and strategy sessions which resulted in several more meetings with both the device division and drug division SFDA reviewers. It seemed like we were making some progress and we were particularly encouraged when the device reviewer asked to see a brief written summary of what we expected from a conditional approval. We actually had a meeting in the SFDA building which I had to get special approval to attend because foreigners were not allowed into the building. We discussed the conditional approval proposal and we thought there was a good chance that we would eventually receive this conditional approval. After this particular meeting, we met Chairman Li in Beijing and agreed that we would step up the pace of our meetings with SFDA to try to get a commitment for the conditional approval.

During one of our strategy sessions with Chairman Li in September, we were discussing the potential for the conditional approval and debating which of the Chinese liver physicians we would like to sign the letter to SFDA. The suggestion was made that we try to get Dr. Wu Meng Chao of EHBH,as a signer. Dr. Wu is such an icon in China that we felt we needed to make personal contact with him to sign the letter requesting conditional approval.

Dar and I headed for Shanghai to try to get an appointment with him but it was not easy. He worked out of what was probably the biggest liver hospital in the world, Eastern Hepatobiliary Hospital, or EHBH, part of China's extensive system of military hospitals. EHBH is a 1,000-bed hospital that is dedicated to the treatment of liver disease and, of course, hepatitis B victims comprise a large portion of its patients. It is said to perform the largest number of liver tumor resections in the world, since most hepatitis B patients progress to liver cancer. Dr. Wu was well-known politically as well as medically and photos of him with leaders of the CCP were displayed in the lobby of the hospital. As such, he was well protected by ex-military people and so Dar had to go through them to get an appointment. His age made him even more of an icon since China, unlike the Western world, has an enormous respect for old people and especially for those that are within sight of 100-years-old. We wanted to respect these considerations and so we waited in Shanghai for 3 days until Dar succeeded in scheduling some time with him.

After we got the call, we rushed to the hospital and met his main keeper in the crowded lobby which was packed with all kinds of people. We pushed our way through and followed the keeper to a back route up to one of the higher floors where Dr. Wu was waiting for us. He greeted us like old friends and remembered meeting with me at the Shanghai conference. He began by saying that he needed new ways to treat his patients since there were so many deaths from liver disease in China and he thanked us for working to get ELAD approved to treat patients in China. I shared with him some of our latest data which obviously interested him and he peppered me with questions. He said that the potential for using ELAD to enable patients to recover from larger resections of cancerous livers was his main interest. We went back and forth for a while and then I explained that we wanted to get ELAD onto the market and our discussions with SFDA indicated that we may be able to get a conditional approval at a limited number of hospitals; we would like to include EHBH and have him sign our letter. He enthusiastically agreed to both requests and signed the letter. We parted like old friends and I had the emotional sensation that I was in the presence of a truly exceptional human being. It is a meeting that I will remember forever.

The letter was delivered to SFDA signed by 14 of the most prominent Chinese liver physicians. We decided to leave it to circulate in SFDA for a few weeks before we followed up. However, events overtook us. I returned to the US since I had arranged to host a number of my venture capitalist friends on the Outlaw golf course at Desert Mountain; they were in Scottsdale for a meeting. The night before our golf date, I got a frantic call from Dar saying that the SFDA Device Division Director wanted to meet with me as soon as possible in Beijing, preferably in about three days. I had no alternative but to make immediate reservations to go to China and left one of my good golfing friends to host the VC group on the golf course.

The nonstop Air China flight from LAX arrived in Beijing on October 13, 2011 at about 5 a.m., a day in advance of the US, of course, because of the time change of +17 hours. I was able to clean up at the hotel and then we went into the late morning meeting with the SFDA that included our main reviewers from the device division, but the Director did not show and no apologies were made. The meeting started in a very formal and peremptory way. We had assumed that it was going to be about the letter and we hoped that there may be good news on the conditional approval but it was obvious that they were leading up to something else. They raised five issues and said that if we could not respond to them satisfactorily, our application package would be rejected. Three of the issues, tumor formation, immune response and contamination had been raised before and addressed but the remaining two issues, quality control and efficacy were new. We responded about the five issues and pointed out that the application had been filed four years ago. At that point, I decided to put the letter on the table and asked whether they had received it. There were blank stares and they looked at the letter and passed it around, each one taking the time to read it.

The whole mood of the meeting changed and they started to talk in platitudes, not really saying anything. After about 30 minutes they thanked us for our time and the meeting was over. We looked at each other in disbelief and, back at our office on Chang'an Boulevard we tried to analyze what had transpired. Why had they summoned me to Beijing and why were they not familiar with the letter? The best explanation that we could come up with was that the letter had not been passed down by the Director and the purpose of the meeting was to tell us that our application for approval had been rejected and to ask us to withdraw it. Our presentation of the letter made them have second thoughts and so they did not deliver the coup de grace. But they did not have a Plan B ready, hence the platitudes and a quick end to the meeting. We speculated as to what might happen next but felt that it probably would not be good.

I decided to remain in Beijing and we did not have to wait long for something to happen. Three days later, we heard from one of our physician clinical trial investigators that he had been summoned to a special meeting in Beijing on short notice along with four other physicians who had signed the letter. The summons was apparently worded in a way that they could not refuse. We were not contacted and certainly not invited to the meeting. Although we tried very hard, we could not get any details about what went on at this meeting except that it was a high-level meeting that involved the top management of SFDA along with our clinical investigators, who had been instructed not to talk about it.

We decided to go to Dunhua to meet with Chairman Li to strategize about what to do next. We met with him and the Aodong team on October 19 but it was immediately apparent that the relationship had changed and we noted some new faces in the Aodong team who were not introduced. The relaxed atmosphere and the camaraderie were gone and the tone was austere. Afterward we speculated that the new faces were the local CCP party members, there to be sure that orders were carried out! We noted that our cooperation agreement expired on November 22 and Chairman Li said that he would have difficulty renewing it unless some tangible progress could be shown. We reviewed the status of the SFDA application and then started to talk about other ways that VTI could raise money. One way that seemed to be of interest to Aodong was for them to buy a majority interest in VTI China. We terminated the meeting with Chairman Li saying that he was going to have to issue a news release to comply with stock market regulations and he would send us a draft. We parted with him saying that the VTI relationship was still his number one priority, but it did not sound genuine. We were disappointed and distressed with the obvious deterioration of our relationship.

At this time there had also been a lot going on in the US so we will return to that subject and explain how it affected our final curtain descending in China.

CHAPTER 28
Swan Song in China

In addition to the $2 million investment from Aodong in May, we had managed to raise an additional $3.5 million in July from existing investors and some additional private China investors. We were delighted with raising this money and we are grateful to the wonderful support we received from our US venture capital investors, and from China and US private investors. All this was in a very negative climate for biotechnology investments. But with our burn rate running at over $600,000 per month for the China and US operations, this money was going to run out early in 2012. If we could not deliver the SFDA approval to market ELAD in China, we were going to have to make some major cuts in our operations or even close our doors. Therefore, we continued our efforts to get SFDA approval, even though the outlook was not promising.

We also continued our planning for the US/EU phase 3 pivotal trial in acute alcoholic hepatitis (AAH) patients:

- We made very good progress with the European Medicines Agency (EMA). The EMA actually made us feel welcome and appreciated what we were doing to try to save lives. They were based in London and had excellent offices and facilities to work with. They had recognized that they were seeing an increasing number of products that were inseparable combinations of a device and a drug, mostly cellular therapies, and they created a separate regulatory class and pathway for these called advanced therapy medicinal product, or ATMP. As our discussions with the EMA advanced, it was obvious that ELAD would be one of the first products that was subjected to this pathway. The EMA was a bureaucratic organization that meticulously portioned responsibilities among their 28 constituent countries. It thrived on the use of multiple committees that were always abbreviated to the alphabet soup of their titles. So, we went through the SAWP, CAT, BWP and CHMP. But this amazing bureaucracy worked very well and kept to its timelines, which were reasonable, and we had their green light to proceed with the phase 3 trial in October. Now, we only needed clearance from the other 3 levels of medical committees in each EU country to proceed at each clinical site.

- We did not make such good progress with the FDA. The situation with our request to use a surrogate endpoint has already been described and all we got was their agreement to collect MELD score data. But then they started to raise new objections to the trial. The two main objections were:

- The FDA denied our request for a special protocol assessment, or SPA, which most phase 3 trials now have. A SPA is an agreement with the FDA about the outcome of a trial where if the results satisfy an agreed list of outcomes, then marketing approval is assured. The FDA objected to this because our trial could not be blinded, nor include a sham treatment control arm and they felt that this introduced bias. We were blindsided by this since we had run 8 trials before with this design and you could easily prove that a sham treatment control, which is not ethical, would bias the result in the opposite direction; in other words, it would help us to achieve a positive trial result. The reason is that the sham control is an extracorporeal treatment, which involved taking a continuous stream of blood from the patient and processing it, and it could harm the patient. But they would not budge and we could not figure out why they had suddenly decided that this trial design introduced bias. We felt we were being treated unfairly.

- Their concern about bias also extended to the fact that some AAH patients would probably keep drinking alcohol through the trial once they were released from the hospital and they wanted us to isolate all patients, including the control arm, in one location for the 90-day endpoint of the trial. After several rounds of arguments, they finally dropped this unreasonable demand.

There were other issues with the FDA that made us nervous about their view of our cellular therapy but, by the end of the year, we had the FDA's allowance to proceed.

In the second half of 2011, our funding situation got progressively worse. We hated to be so dependent on our existing investors but we had not delivered in the US/EU trial and the SFDA approval looked increasingly unlikely to happen.

Pacific Growth/Wedbush, the San Francisco investment bank that has been mentioned before, helped us a great deal with our fund raising efforts, and we retained them to raise funds or find a corporate partner in the US or Europe. They had been very generous with the time of Dr. Duane Nash, their biotech analyst, who has been mentioned before, and sent him to China with us in June so he could meet Aodong in Dunhua, attend the US Embassy DOC soiree and see the trial hospitals in Beijing. Duane was a great help and introduced us to numerous investors and possible partners. But biotech was not in vogue at that time and the going was rough.

We decided to have one last try to move the SFDA on China approval and the only way was to somehow work with Aodong to either turn around the SFDA or renegotiate our agreement to gain access to the $25 million Aodong investment that was part of the 6-month agreement which was expiring on November 22.

Kameron, Dar, and I had a long conference call with Chairman Li on November 27. The translations and the quality of the line made it especially difficult. It went better than we expected and we explored several ways to renegotiate our agreement and have Aodong make the $25 million investment without the SFDA approval happening. Chairman Li was most interested in the solution where Aodong bought a majority position in VTI China and took over full responsibility for gaining SFDA approval and commercializing ELAD in China. We agreed that we needed to talk about this face-to-face and Chairman

Li agreed to meet with us in Dunhua on November 30: we caught the next flight to China.

The meeting in Dunhua was cordial with the full management team of Aodong present. We came well-prepared and presented the structure of a new agreement where they would buy a majority interest in VTI China. However, they explained that they were in a difficult situation because our six-month agreement specified that they would only go forward if ELAD gained SFDA approval. They needed government approval to make a different agreement and they had not been able to get this approval. So, the only way they could go forward would be to extend the existing agreement. But this did nothing for us. We met again on December 1 but it was obvious that neither side was going to get what it wanted and so we parted with, it seemed, genuine respect and regret on both sides. This is the PR release that Aodong issued:

证券代码：000623 证券简称：吉林敖东 公告编号：2011- 059

Stock code:000623 Stock Name: Jilin AoDong Announcement# 2011－059

吉林敖东药业集团股份有限公司
JiLin AoDong Medicine Industry Group Co.,Ltd
关于投资美国生命治疗公司进展的提示性公告
Announcement of Investment progress in Vital Therapies Inc

本公司及董事会全体成员保证信息披露的内容真实、准确、完整，没有虚假记载、误导性陈述或重大遗漏。

All members of the Company and the Board ensure that the information disclosed is true, accurate and complete and contains no false, misleading statements or material omissions.

一、 投资情况概述

公司第六届董事会第二十三次会议于2011年5月9日审议并通过以自有资金投资200万美元购买美国生命治疗公司Vital Therapies, Inc. （以下简称"VTI"）5-6%的股权，同时授权吉林敖东在6个月内追加2500万美元投资的投资权，如在6个月的追加投资的期限到期时，生物人工肝尚未获得中国国家药监局的批准，双方将对购买权合适的延期时间进行协商。该投资事项详见2011年5月10日在《证券时报》、《上海证券报》、《中国证券报》、《证券日报》及巨潮资讯网上披露的《第六届董事会第二十三次会议决议公告》（公告编号：2011-018）、《关于投资美国生命治疗公司的公告》（公告编号：2011-019）。

On May 9, 2011, the Board approved the investment of 2 million US$ with its own funds to purchase 5%-6% of VTI's ownership, at the same time JiLin AoDong was granted the option to invest an additional $25 million for up to six months after the first closing. If SFDA approval is not obtained at the end of the six-month option period, the parties will negotiate an appropriate extension of the option. Regarding this investment issue, please refer to the Announcement on Board Resolution (announcement #: 2011-018) and Announcement of Investment in VTI (announcement #: 2011-019) published in Securities Times, Shanghai Securities News, China Securities News, Securities Daily and the website of Shenzhen Securities Information.

二、投资进展情况 Investment progress

1、现追加投资的期限已到期，因生物人工肝项目没有获得中国药监局的批准，本公司为控制投资风险，保护公司利益，决定暂不追加2500万美元投资。

Now the six-month option is expired, since bio-artificial liver didn't obtain the SFDA approval, the Company decided not to invest another 25 million USD in order to control investment risk and protect the company interest.

2、作为VTI公司的股东，公司将密切关注生物人工肝项目的进展和报批情况。

As the shareholder of VTI, the Company will keep close eyes on the SFDA approval progress and status of bio- artificial liver project.

3、是否继续投资，公司将根据项目的进展情况与VTI公司继续协商。

Whether continue to invest or not, the Company will continue to negotiate with VTI based on the status of project.

三、对公司的影响 The impact on the Company

1、暂停追加该投资对公司没有重大影响。

Suspension of additional investment would have no huge impact on the company.

2、公司本着审慎投资的原则，有利于控制投资风险，保护公司利益。

The Company is very cautious in the investment, which will control the investment risk and protect the interest of the Company.

敬请广大投资者注意投资风险。

We would like to remind the investors of investment risks.

特此公告。

吉林敖东药业集团股份有限公司董事会

Board of JiLin AoDong Medicine Industry Group Co., Ltd

二〇一一年十二月十四日

Dec 14, 2011

Aodong stock sold off over the next few days, removing the roughly $1 billion premium that had been added when the deal was announced in April. The following article from the next day's China Investment Daily. Describes the situation well:

人工肝项目暂缓遭遇黑天鹅,吉林敖东成下一个重庆啤酒?

Black swan in the bio-artificial liver project, will JA be the next Chongqing Brewer?

- 投资快报 Investment Daily

　重庆啤酒(600132)式的悲剧又重演?日前,一则例行公告引来了吉林敖东(000623)投资者的担忧,由于公司投资的人工肝项目还未得到药监局的批准,致使吉林敖东对该项目的二期投资未能按时投放.正因为有重庆啤酒的前车之鉴,昨日吉林敖东是以跌停板收盘,成交量明显放大.一名长期跟踪吉林敖东的分析师告诉记者,由于人工肝项目从申请生产,小范围试点到逐渐普及需要至少几年时间,虽然对业绩影响不大,但是难免会影响到市场对该股的信心.

Will the tragedy of Chongqing Brewery (600 132) be repeated? Recently, a routine announcement drew the concerns of JA investors. Since the artificial liver project is not approved by SFDA yet, JA decided to suspend the second investment. Due to the lesson in Chongqing Brewery, yesterday JA's stock price hit its daily limit with significantly increased turnover. According to an analyst who has been following JA for long time, it would take at least several years for bio-artificial liver project to apply manufacture, conduct clinical application in a small scale and become widely used. Although it has little effect on the performance, it will inevitably affect the confidence of market on the stock.

项目投资暂缓 公司仍努力争取

Additional investment suspended, the Company still strives to obtain the approval.

吉林敖东日前公告称,因生物人工肝(ELAD)项目没有获得中国药监局的批准,公司为控制投资风险, 决定暂不追加对美国生命治疗公司Vital Therapies, Inc.(简称"VTI公司")2500万美元的投资.VTI公司所有的生物人工肝项目是世界上首例以人体肝细胞为基础的生物人工肝,但该项目能否获得国家药监局的批准还一直存在不确定性.

JA announced its decision to suspend its investment of 25 million USD to VTI in order to control the investment risks since ELAD is not approved by SFDA yet. VTI's bio-artificial liver is the first human cell-based bio-artificial liver, but there is always uncertainty whether or not this project can be approved by SFDA.

受此消息影响, 昨日吉林敖东的投资者二级市场落荒而逃.昨日盘中,吉林敖东在早盘的时候便触碰到跌停板,股价盘中几度回升,但因为大盘乏力仍然无法改变跌停的命运,最终报收22.52元.另外,成交量也急剧放大,成交量为15万手,成交总额为3.39亿元.

Affected by this news, yesterday JA investors in the secondary market fled in panic. Yesterday morning JA stock price touched the daily limit, rebounded several times, but still couldn't change the fate because of unfavorable market. The closing price was at 22.52 Yuan with dramatically increased turnover of 1500 million shares and total turnover of 339 million Yuan.

"5月份的时候,公司一期投资人工肝200万元.当时公司就给予过承诺,如果批文还没有拿到手, 会在6个月之内作出回应,现在我们只是在完成相应的义务."记者以个人投资者的身份采访了吉林敖东董秘办一位工作人员,该工作人员还表示,公司后续还会争取拿到批文.

The reporter interviewed a staff of JA Board secretary office as an individual investor. The staff said:" In May, JA invested 2 million Yuan in bio-artificial liver. At that time, the Company promised that we will respond if SFDA approval is not obtained at the end of six months period. Now we just did our job." He also said the Company will still strive to obtain the approval.

吉林敖东的公告,很容易让人联想到重庆啤酒的悲剧.曾经因为疫苗概念而股价飙升的重庆啤酒,在一则关于疫苗进展的公告出台之后,酝酿已久的泡沫已经被刺穿了.而截至昨日,重庆啤酒已经迎来了第六个跌停,市值已经蒸发接近194亿元.

JA's announcement easily reminds people of the tragedy of Chongqing Brewery. The stock price of Chongqing Brewery had risen significantly thanks to the vaccine concept, however after announcing the update on vaccine, the bubble was broken. As of yesterday, the stock of Chongqing Brewery has plunged by the exchange's 10 per cent daily limit for 6 days in a row, wiping 19.4 billion Yuan off market value.

机构市值一日蒸发3亿

Institutions' 300 million was wiped off in one day.

在包括生物人工肝在内的各种投资亮点环绕之下, 吉林敖东一直是机构资金的宠儿, 公司的前十大流通股东名单中从来不缺乏机构的捧场.截至今年第三季度末,博时新兴成长,华夏优势增长,易方达深证100,诺安平衡,银华-道琼斯88,融通深证100和诺安灵活配置7只基金和广发证券(000776)一家证券公司携手出现在前十大流通股东名单中, 累计持股约1.04亿股,占公司流通盘6.35亿股的16.5%,其中,华夏优势增长,易方达深证100等基金在三季度还进行了增仓. 如果按照前十大流通股东名单里,合共持有吉林敖东1.15亿股,占流通股本的18.12%的流通股本,昨天一天市值蒸发接近3个亿.

In recent years, highlighted by various investments topics, JA has been the favorite of institutional capital. By the end of third quarter this year, seven funds and GuangFa Securities are on the top 10 circulated shareholders list with total 104 million shares accounting for 16.5% of JA's circulated shares. Several institutions even increased their shares in the third quarter. Yesterday these Institutions' 300 million was wiped off.

人工肝项目普及需要几年时间

It takes several years to popularize bio-artificial liver project

事实上,吉林敖东的人工肝项目审批已经扰攘了四年的时间.VTI公司的人工肝项目早在2007年就已经开始向药监局申请批文,直到目前药监局都并未明确表态,我们推测可能缘于药监局对新药的谨慎态度. 生物人工肝在全球范围内尚无获得生产批文的先例, 药监局可能在一段时间内仍将处于观望状态.而目前VTI公司人工肝项目在欧美已完成二期临床.

In fact, the bio-artificial liver project has been in the process of approval for 4 years. As early as the year of 2007, VTI filed the application with SFDA. So far, SFDA hasn't shown clear attitude. We think it is probably because SFDA is very cautious on new drugs. There is no such precedent that bio-artificial liver is granted the approval of manufacture, probably SFDA will still wait and see over a period of time. Now VTI has completed the phase II clinical trials in the U.S. and E.U.

在VTI公司人工肝项目获得国内生产批文之前,吉林敖东于今年5月份投资的首批200万美金主要是用于锁定项目.在经历半年时间申请批文尚无明确消息的情况下,公司暂停追加投资主要是出于风控和谨慎性的考虑.

Before obtaining SFDA approval, JA's first investment of 2 million Yuan is mainly to lock the project. Without certain news on SFDA approval after six months, the Company suspended the additional investment out of consideration for risk control and conservatism.

目前吉林敖东对VTI公司的持股比例仍将维持在5-6%(如果追加投资, 对应持股比例在30%以上).一名长期跟踪吉林敖东的分析师认为,由于人工肝项目从申请生产,小范围试点到逐渐普及需要至少几年时间,目前市场上对于公司的最近三年盈利预测均未体现该部分业绩贡献,所以暂停追加投资对公司的短期业绩影响并不大,但是可能会降低市场对公司长期业绩增长的预期.

At present JA has 5-6% of VTI ownership (if additional investment is made, the ownership should be over 30%). According to an analyst who has been following JA for long time, it would take at least several years for bio-artificial liver project to apply manufacturing, clinical application in a small scale and become widely used and the 3 years' profit forecast on JA doesn't include the contribution of artificial liver, therefore the suspension of additional investment would not have big impact on short-term performance of JA. However it may lower the expectation on long-term performance growth of the company.

华泰联合的研究认为,在VTI公司正式完成欧美市场的三期临床并获得当地监管部门批文之前,国内药监局可能都将处于谨慎和观望的态度,而欧美市场的三期临场至少需要1至2年时间才能完成,依此推断,未来人工肝项目在国内申请批文的过程可能还需经历较长时间.

According to Huatai Securities, SFDA may continue the wait and see policy before VTI completes the Phase III clinical trials and obtain the US/EU approval. It takes at least one to two years to complete the phase III clinical trials in the U.S. and E.U, therefore it would take long time to obtain SFDA approval in China.

不过, 也有投资者对吉林敖东显现出信心.有个人投资者在上说道,吉林敖东还是很谨慎认真的, 只用了1000万元投资人工肝项目."今天的公告只是告诉大家继续等待国家药监局审批,基本面无任何变化,有什么好慌乱的?人工肝项目,公司早就公告,对2011业绩无影响,也未被炒作.今天的公告是例行公告,原计划半年审批后再增资控股, 现在继续等待审批结果而已,公司投资谨慎,需要等待确定审批再投2500万美元,是对股民负责任的行为.今天完全是黑天鹅事件!"

However some investors still show confidence in JA. An individual investor posted its comments online as follows: "JA is so cautious that they only invested about 10 million Yuan in the bio-artificial project. Its announcement just informed us to continue to wait for SFDA approval. There is no substantial change in the Company. We have no reason to panic. About the bio-artificial project, the Company has announced that it has no influence on its performance in 2011. The announcement is just a routine one. Its original plan was to make additional investment after approval. Now they will continue to wait for approval. JA is very cautious in the investment, so they will make the 25 million USD after SFDA approval. They are responsible for shareholders. Today it is definitely black swan event!"

This was a sad ending to our adventures in China but we had to face up to the reality that there was probably no way we were ever going to get ELAD approval in China. We did not know the reasons why we were having a problem but we did know there had been a sea-change in the way China was being viewed by the US and the rest of the world. We heard this from several of our potential investors who said that, if they invested, withdrawal from China would be a condition of their investment. Viewed from our perspective this was regrettable but was caused by too many cases of IP theft by the Chinese and other actions that changed the perception of China to US investors. We understood this but we were crushed that our life-saving product would not save any more lives in China and with the 8 years of fruitless time and effort we had expended there.

There is one more postscript to the China story. I had made arrangements to take our family to China over the Christmas period in 2011. But when I returned to the US after this last trip to Dunhua on December 3, there was a nasty surprise waiting for me. It goes back to the patient who died due to the unavailability of plasma while being treated with ELAD in the trial at You 'An Hospital in 2007. There had been a lawsuit that the hospital had successfully defended after we had offered to settle the claim, which the hospital refused to accept. The family had not given up and won a civil suit for a settlement of about $50,000. We knew nothing of this until I received a letter from the hospital asking us to settle it. I had refused to pay it because the hospital had clearly taken the responsibility for it when they refused our offer to settle it. Now, I had a nasty letter from the hospital threatening all kinds of things, including arrest the next time I visited China, if we did not pay up. I nearly had to cancel our Christmas trip but our clinical trial insurer stepped up and paid the bill. It is one more example of why you need really good clinical trial insurance to sponsor a clinical trial!

Were there other factors in play that caused us to be denied SFDA approval? The answer is probably yes. Top of our list is that we had steadfastly refused to make any payments to lubricate the system, otherwise known as bribes. We had never been asked directly for these kinds of payments but it was well known that the practice still existed at SFDA, even though the execution of the Commissioner in 2007 had sent a chilling message to the SFDA management. I was proud of the fact that our people had not engaged in this practice and that we could hold our heads up high.

We were originally invited to come to China by some of its leading physicians and by the SFDA and they clearly knew at the time that ELAD was still under development and was not yet approved in the US. However, when the SFDA bribery scandal hit, that was all forgotten and we were accused numerous times by several SFDA reviewers and others of trying to get approval in China before we had approval in our home country with the innuendo that there was some-thing wrong with ELAD. These accusations hurt, but it was true that, at the invitation of the Chinese, we were trying to do something that had not been done before: gain approval for a high-profile product in China before we got approval in our home country. The SFDA bribery scandal had up-ended all that and, despite repeated assurances that we were grandfathered in through having started the process before these new rules were issued, this was now a reprehensible thing to do and made us suspect. The Chinese are well known to be xenophobic and we were probably seen as foreign devils, which did not help our cause.

We stand by the clinical trial results that we created in China. The SFDA was never able to find any safety issues with ELAD, nor anything wrong with the trials. I don't think that the ELAD approval application has ever been rejected and it is probably still on file, since 2007! The eventual Chinese buyer of the ELAD assets is still trying to get China approval and they may well succeed.

But these are excuses and the real blame lies with the CEO, namely yours truly. The first error was that we were a year too late. If we had just been a little earlier, we would have probably got approval before the SFDA bribery scandal burst into the open and caused all the problems. Plus, I am sure that I made many wrong calls on how to proceed with the SFDA relations. But with many different voices giving us conflicting advice, it was a crap shoot as to who was correct, if anyone.

The outcome was that we did not get SFDA approval and we had to return our focus to the US and EU. But working in China for those 8 years was an experience that I really appreciated and enjoyed, in spite of the problems.

My big regret is that we did not get to save any more lives in China or elsewhere. That weighs heavily on my conscience.

Finally, to address the elephant in the room: were there any overriding political issues that prevented ELAD from getting approval in China? It is an issue that I could argue for or against with equal conviction.

We were operating in China from the peak of their love affair with the West in 2004 when it seemed that everyone in the US wanted to get in on the China business game. But, at the end of our China "trials" in 2012, the US/China relationship had deteriorated with several scandals (the heparin scandal was probably the worst, where the blood anti-coagulant was isolated in China from pigs' intestines under less than sterile conditions, exported to the US and killed several people), multiple exposures of IP theft by the Chinese, several successful FCPA prosecutions by the US Justice Dept and more. In 2011/12 it had reached the point where potential US investors in our company insisted that we withdraw from China if they invested. Quite a turn-around from the 2004 love affair! None of this helped our prospects of getting approval to market ELAD in China.

The execution of the SFDA Commissioner in 2007 for corruption was a severe adverse event and the situation with our ELAD marketing application went downhill from there, in spite of our verbal commitment from the SFDA to give us a decision on our marketing application within 120 days of filing. But was there more to it than that?

I could make a case that someone in the CCP ran the numbers and concluded that, if ELAD was approved, the only efficacious therapy for hepatitis B flares would be owned by a foreign company and could well end up repatriating billions of dollars in profits to the US. Even though it would save thousands of Chinese lives, the shame of it being a foreign innovation would be unbearable. Better to try to steal the technology and set up a Chinese company to make and sell it.

We know that this was in fact tried by the company in Guangzhou, described in Chapter 17, which stole some of our cells and also stole the full application that we made to SFDA which contained information on how we grew the cells. Was this company set up by the CCP with the express purpose of stealing our IP and getting a Chinese version of ELAD on the market while we withered and died from the neglect of our application? We don't know, of course, but we do know that the Guangzhou company raised a lot of money from somewhere and spent it on a fruitless effort to grow the cells. We also know that this former FDA reviewer was not punished for his activity in spite of China being a very strong law and order place and theft of a SFDA marketing application being a high-profile crime. It is possible that this whole effort was set up and financed by the CCP. When it failed, they simply decided to punish us and forgo this product for China's fourth largest cause of death. What better way to do it than to simply stonewall the foreign devil US company so that they died on the vine, which is what happened. The circumstantial evidence here is quite strong.

Now that we had decided to withdraw from China, we had to focus on financing the company and running trials in the US and EU to secure ELAD approval. In the rest of the story, the events are a bit too controversial and too recent for a detailed telling of the story. The final seven chapters now revert to our US and EU work to gain ELAD approval.

CHAPTER 29
Return to the US: Bankruptcy Avoided

I had kept our Board and investors well informed about the China and US/EU situation and we received excellent understanding and support for our actions. Now that China was moribund and we were low on funds, we needed another loan from our investors to keep going while we worked with Pacific Growth/Wedbush on funding from new investors. When I returned from the family trip to China in early January 2012, we were confident that the shareholder loan would be available. But it did not happen and our key investors withdrew their support.

This was disastrous and we were staring bankruptcy in the face. We had to lay off most of our employees and we had a miserable January. Giving them this news and then working on the layoffs was difficult. But it had to be done and we retained about five people to work on shutting down the company. The most precious asset was the cells and we made quite sure that they were kept healthy and safe and that the manufacturing facility could be restarted if needed. All the employees took things in a very mature way and most of them said that if we were able to restart the company, they would be very interested in rejoining us. None of us realized that this would in fact happen.

Within a week, Wedbush came through when Duane Nash introduced us to one of his clients who was a high net worth former Goldman Sachs investment banker. Muneer Satter visited our main office and manufacturing plant in November 2011 while I was in China and he expressed interest in learning more. After we had been abandoned by our US investors, in late January 2012, I met with him at one of the upscale hotels in Los Angeles on Wilshire Boulevard. I saw no point in trying to polish the situation and was very candid with him about withdrawing from China and about the significant risks in continuing to try to get approval in the US/EU. I emphasized that we were trying to do something that had not been done before which was to save lives by using a cellular therapy.

Muneer initially wanted to work with our investors to restructure the company to drive to approval in the US with our planned clinical trials. However, he met with a cool reception from our investors and I thought that was the end of it. However, this only seemed to motivate him and he came up with a plan which would purchase our former investors' shares and restart the company. He proceeded very prudently and invested about $2 million in two separate financings over 3 months to give us funds and time to complete our team, plan the clinical trials and allow him time to do detailed diligence before he made a decision on whether to lead a much larger investment of about $45 million. What a diligence it was! He hired the best people and they spent a long time scrubbing every detail from our ownership of the cells, through the intellectual property and the strategy to gain approval and get to market, including a careful look at the market size, pricing and characteristics.

Muneer was very fair to our former investors and gave them all the opportunity to invest additional funds alongside his investment at the same price and pro-rata to their prior ownership. This was a very low price reflecting the restructuring that he had implemented. None of the VC investors took up their pro-rata shares but a surprising number of our smaller, individual investors did invest their pro-rata amounts and therefore preserved a significant amount of their prior ownership. This included one China investor, our largest US individual investor and several members of management. All of these continued to take their pro-rata shares of future private financings which turned out to total about $108 million prior to the IPO in 2014. If they sold their shares after the IPO, they would have done very well!

All of this took about six months and we had some nervous moments during the diligence since Muneer's experts uncovered several things that we had not thought of. However, by June 2012, he was ready to proceed. We had already hired back about a dozen of our people and we were gratified that we were able to get everyone we wanted. I don't want to single out anybody for special mention since this was very much teamwork and required the support of everyone. However, Muneer had great respect for Duane Nash and wanted us to hire Duane into the management team. We were able to do this without offending Wedbush and brought Duane into the team as the Executive VP of Business Development. Muneer had also come to respect Rob Ashley who was our COO since 2008 and we kept him in that position. Kameron took advantage of the upheaval to retire since he was well over the age but we still had access to his wisdom and experience, which were both considerable.

That left me and I was fully expecting to be asked to step down as CEO. I was actually welcoming the prospect since I had now turned 70 and had put my life on hold during all of the China adventures, as had the rest of the management team. There was a lot of golf to be played to catch up on the opportunities missed! There were also some philosophical and strategic differences between myself and Muneer that I did not think could be resolved. However, we had several open discussions and he decided that I should stay on for now, which was fine by me.

Muneer was one of the finest human beings that I have ever met. He was a remarkably hard worker, scrupulously honest and ethical, and never tried to profit personally out of the difficult situation the company was in except for driving a hard bargain on his investment, which I expected and which was appropriate. In my career as a venture capitalist, I have met many of these high net worth people and they normally try to take as much out of the company as they can to cover their expenses and to get back their investment as fast as possible. However, I was gratified to see that Muneer never took a penny out of the company for any expenses and never even submitted an expense report. He even used his private residence in Chicago for meetings and dinners and his private jet to help us with never a word about payment. This is extraordinarily unusual and told me a lot about him. I was also blown away by the foundation that he had set up and by the really good causes that he supported. It is what I would have liked to do if I were in his position.

Where we differed was in the backgrounds that we brought to the company. I was a scientist, a risk-taking VC and an entrepreneur. I am very comfortable with the kinds of risks that came with the territory and that you had to take in the biotechnology field. Muneer's background was very different. Although he had been in the very dynamic and risky field of investment banking and had run Goldman Sachs' largest private equity fund, he was used to hedging every risk that he could identify and had dealt mainly with profitable, stable businesses. This was anathema to me since hedging our risks meant spending lots of money and I prided myself on getting things done on tight budgets. These differences were to lead to some significant disagreements in the future.

Muneer took firm charge of the fundraising efforts and we started out in June 2012 by visiting many of his friends and acquaintances to raise the rest of the $45 million targeted funds. But as Muneer got to know the team and the company better he decided to change the strategy and called me up one night when we were in New York City on a fundraising trip to say that he had decided to commit $60 million to the company so that we could immediately start the clinical trials and implement our plans and then he would sell off parts of this investment to others who wanted to join us. I was stunned but I did manage to say that we were on a very risky venture and he should only do it if he could afford to lose that investment. He assured me that it was not a problem and so we agreed to proceed. He announced this to Duane and Rob at breakfast the next morning and the stunned looks on their faces were a sight to behold! Needless to say, the rest of the fundraising went smoothly. When I announced this at our employee meeting a couple of days later, they all had a similar reaction. I should point out that this was about July 2012 and the biotechnology market was still not popular. The boom in biotechnology did not start until about 18 months later. At the time the $86 million investment that we announced in a PR release was one of the largest financings that had been done in biotechnology for a while. We were determined to make this successful and to justify Muneer's faith in us. The funds were taken down in four tranches over a two-year period.

The way that Muneer carried out this restructuring was a master lesson in the art of investing in private companies. It set us up for success. Now, all we had to do was to get the requisite good clinical trial results!

CHAPTER 30
Rebuilding

Until this point in late 2012, the company had never had sufficient funds to do everything required to make progress and comply with all of the regulations. We had to economize on everything to make our money go as far as we could and stay within the rules. We never knew where our next financing was coming from. Management was on the low end of salary compensation, which was made up by more stock options. But now we suddenly had more than enough money to do the job. The dog had caught the car and now we had to figure out what to do with it. Many times, I had fantasized with Rob Ashley and the other members of the management team about what it would be like if we actually had enough funding to do the job properly. An $86 million financing was beyond our wildest dreams. Now, that dream had come true and we had to figure out how to implement it. A very nice problem to have but it presented challenges.

We spent the next few months in constant planning exercises to design the US/EU clinical trials and to position ourselves with the regulatory authorities for the best chance of approval and commercialization. Fortunately, this was one of Rob's skills and our CFO, Aron Stern, was a whiz with Excel financial spreadsheets. Muneer took a hands-on role in the planning process and was a great help.

However, old habits are hard to break and we were constantly aware of the high-risk business that we were in and reluctant to spend money. This put us in conflict with the board and Muneer who wanted us to expand the management team and spend money to do the very best job possible to get ELAD approved and commercialized. We had a small management team of five people and we wanted to continue to keep the executive team small and focused. The board had other ideas and wanted us to hire specialists in the key functional areas. I was uncomfortable with this and it was very difficult to tell Rob that he had to give up his responsibilities in manufacturing, clinical operations and regulatory to specialist VPs hired for those areas with Rob becoming VP of R&D. But it had to happen and we brought on specialists in those three areas and in several other areas which expanded the management team to 11 people. We hired some very good new people and we were also thrilled that we were able to hire back all the former employees that we had been forced to lay off in January 2012.

It seemed that the only person who was getting his role expanded was the CEO, namely me, and I tried very hard to off-load some of these positions reporting directly to me. But that was simply not appropriate since, unless these positions reported to the CEO, the incumbents felt that they were much lower in the pecking order and we could have lost some good people. So, I formed one large executive committee of 12 people and developed my own systems for managing this large number of people reporting to me. It seemed to work well but I was uncomfortable with the amount of money we were spending. My philosophy had always been to keep the spending down until we were sure that we had a product we could take to market and we were still two or three years away from that point. There was still high risk in our clinical projects and we had to satisfy the regulatory authorities not only that ELAD was safe but also that it saved lives as proven by a statistically significant survival trial.

Muneer proved to be generous and increased everybody's compensation up to industry standards. However, he demanded commitment and good performance, which was fine with me. I insisted on interviewing all of our candidates one-on-one before we hired them. I told them that I wanted to satisfy myself that they wanted to join us more than any other opportunity, that they were dedicated to saving patients' lives and that they were committed to the company, not just involved to get a paycheck. I used the example of the plate of ham and eggs where the chicken was involved but the pig was committed. It made the point and several decided not to join us but those that did come on board were excellent additions to the team.

After spending a long time looking at the clinical trial options, we decided to initiate three phase 3 trials. These were:

1. VTI-208. 200 patients with acute alcoholic hepatitis (AAH) with a survival endpoint. This has been covered earlier in Chapter 24. This was targeted mostly for US clinical sites.
2. VTI-210. 100 patients in AAH who had not responded to the current clinical standard treatment with steroids. These are anti-inflammatory drugs and were administered to AAH patients on the basis that it is an inflammatory disease. There were no clinical trial results to prove that steroids were efficacious but no one seemed to worry about that. This was a trial that the EMA in Europe had requested that we run and they were very pleased that we were planning to do so.
3. VTI-212. 120 patients in fulminant hepatic failure (FHF) which has been described in Chapter 3. We decided to run this trial even though we knew that the patients would be difficult to find since there were so few cases. But the good results that we had achieved in the Hepatix days made it an obvious trial to run.

We hired some really good people to join our executive team and I would like to highlight two of these:

Dr. Dr. Jan Stange. Yes, you read that right, he had two doctorates and under the German system was entitled to the double prefix. First was his MD degree, after which he specialized in nephrology, the specialty focused on kidney and bladder problems, and worked his way up to a senior clinical position at the University of Rostock hospital, one of the leading German hospitals in liver and kidney disease. Second was his PhD in liver therapy which was obtained in his spare time at U Rostock.

Rostock is a large city on the Baltic Sea about 100 miles east of Hamburg and 150 miles north of Berlin, in the old East Germany. Jan had been born into this communist country and knew nothing of the Western capitalist world until the wall came down in 1990. But that did not stop him from innovating a very interesting product to treat liver failure which used dialysis against a countercurrent of albumin to remove toxins from the blood of liver failure patients. This was called the MARS system and it had some remarkable results in liver failure where it could bring patients out of their encephalopathy, or coma, and relieve many of the other symptoms of liver failure. However, it did not give any long-term survival benefit even though there was a significant short-term survival gain of about 4 weeks which could prove to be long enough to bridge patients to a liver transplant.

Rob Ashley was very impressed with Jan and he had been pushing me to meet him, which I finally did when my wife and I spent a few days with him and his wife in Paris in November 2008. We got along very well and I resolved to hire Jan if ever we got the resources to do so since he knew the liver failure world better than anyone and would make an excellent Chief Medical Officer (CMO). He knew all the leading liver docs in both the US and EU and that is the key to running successful clinical trials. So, we talked with Jan and brought him on to join our team as CMO in late 2012. I made it clear to Jan that he only had two key responsibilities: to sign up clinical sites and to keep our relations with the PIs (Principal Investigators, the lead physician at each site) on very good terms; and to ensure that all patients enrolled into our trials met all of the entry criteria. Since we planned to have about 60 clinical sites in US, EU and Australia, Jan was constantly traveling and did a great job. We are still good friends and are planning a new company with an interesting liver product as I write this book.

Andrew Henry came on board as our VP of clinical operations. He had great experience with being in charge of running clinical trials at several large pharmaceutical companies, most recently at Astra Zeneca. Andrew wanted to experience life in a small pharma company and so it was a good fit.

The position of VP of clinical operations is generally not filled in most biotechnology companies since they do not manage their own clinical trials. They use companies known as CROs, or clinical research organizations, to design and manage their clinical trials. However, this is very expensive and also means that you lose control of the conduct of your own trials. This trend, to outsource the operation of clinical trials, started in the 1990s and was embraced by the big pharma companies. A cynical explanation is that this off-loaded the most difficult and distasteful part of drug development, the design and operation of trials, and so made life easier for big pharma employees. The problem is that this is the most important part of drug development and contracting it out to others means you lose control and contact with the most important people namely the physicians, nurses and others responsible for patient care at your clinical sites. It also significantly raises the costs of the trials and is one of the main reasons that the cost to take a drug through the clinical trial process to approval has ballooned recently to over one billion dollars per drug. I saw no merit in using CROs and was determined that we would run our trials ourselves. Fortunately, our executive team and our board agreed with me.

So, we decided that we would manage our own trials and hire an appropriate person to do this. Andrew was perfect and joined us in 2013. He was the only new executive hire that we had to relocate to San Diego. In the next few years, we got into some difficult situations with clinical trials and especially with the regulatory side but I came to learn that Andrew was always right. He had a perfect record and I respect that a great deal. He had the largest department in the company and managed his people very well.

Of course, all of these new people needed to hire their own teams, one of the drawbacks of having a large executive team. Before we knew it, we were very close to 100 people in the company which made me uncomfortable. However, we were finally doing it correctly and getting everything done.

We outgrew our old facility very quickly and moved everybody except the manufacturing team into a new building about 300 yards down the street. It was a nice modern building, not a palace, but good enough to give our visitors the impression that we were a company on the move. I was delighted that Muneer and the board agreed with this HQ philosophy.

The added bonus was that our move down the street left additional space for the manufacturing group in our old building. They now had plenty of space and we could make all of the changes to the manufacturing process facility that we had been postponing for a long time. We were doing our own manufacturing of the key component of the product namely, growing the human liver cells in the cartridges that was the crucial part of the treatment. The situation with manufacturing was similar to that with the use of CROs for the trials: most biotech companies contracted out their manufacturing to a contract manufacturing organization, or CMO. Again, this cut you off from all of the issues with manufacturing a drug product and, since this was the most common reason for drugs to fail to get approved, it obviously increased the risk.

Since we were breaking new ground with a cellular therapy, the FDA had not yet made it clear exactly what regulations we had to comply with and so we had differing internal views that had to be resolved, sometimes after heated debates. I will not go into detail about the regulatory and quality control people and procedures that we had to follow except to say that because of the fuzzy guidelines, there was a lot of disagreement. We resolved these issues by simply asking the FDA to give us guidance and we were pleasantly surprised at the good cooperation that we got from them. The FDA made it clear that we were regulated by the biological division, known as the Center for Biologics Evaluation and Research, or CBER, even though we had a device incorporated into our product. But CBER said that they were making the decisions on the device and not the parallel device division (CDRH) of the FDA, although they did invite CDRH representatives to our meetings, as a courtesy.

We were fortunate to be able to attract Rich Murawski as our VP of manufacturing. Rich was a unique individual with a style all his own. He had run one of the manufacturing plants of Dendreon which was one of the first companies to get a cellular therapy approved, this one being for prostate cancer. While the process was different from growing our cells, and it also differed by being autologous and not allogeneic like ELAD, there were enough similarities that Rich was able to fit right in and bring our manufacturing into compliance while keeping an eye on the manufacturing costs.

We also started to look at the product pricing and initiated a separate trial known as VTL-209 to gather all of the costs of treatment with ELAD.

We began the process of signing up the clinical trial sites in the fall of 2012 and treated the first patient in VTL-208 in March 2013. At that time, we had sites in England, Scotland, Spain, Germany, Austria, Australia and the US. Over the next year we built up to a total of 60 clinical sites which was a formidable number but complied with the board's directive to make this one of the best trials that had ever been run in this field.

Our therapy involved the use of a large bedside device to which were attached 4 cartridges with a total of about a pound of the human liver cells we used to treat each liver failure patient. It had to be implemented in a room in the hospital's intensive care unit, or ICU. We needed to monitor the progress of the therapy over the 3 to 5 days that it was continuously in operation and make whatever changes were necessary based on the in-line measurements that were continuously taken. However, we could not treat the patient and we had to allow the hospital personnel to do that. But we did need to have our own nurse in the ICU room all the time, 24/7. We called these nurses our specialists and we had tried numerous ways of hiring and managing them in our past trials, from using them as employees to using them as consultants. Nothing worked and the specialists were always unhappy. So, Julie Magnuson, our VP of human resources, and Teresa Shafer, our head nurse, jumped in to change the way we handled the specialists and make them feel like they were part of our team. This turned out to be very successful and we had virtually no problems with the specialists going forward. I salute the work that Julie and Teresa did since it required a lot of time and effort to make the specialists feel like they were integral to our success, which they most definitely were. Theirs was a difficult existence since they had to be ready to go to the US, EU or Australia on 24-hour's notice, but Julie and Teresa worked to make it an enjoyable position to hold. At our peak time, we employed about

20 of these specialists and they were truly very special people. I got to know many of them very well and really enjoyed listening to their stories. They helped to educate me and to keep me informed and in contact with what was happening at the level of the patients we were treating, which was very important to our potential success.

I have to mention our VP of human resources since I belong to the school that said I would never have such a position in any company that I was running. I got to this point from my experience as a venture capitalist where I watched numerous human resource specialists ruin several companies, after building their empires. Our long-time CFO, Aron Stern, who specialized in keeping me out of financial and legal trouble, well knew of my strong opinion about HR and he had suffered through being our de facto HR person. One day, he gingerly raised the HR subject with me saying that he had found someone who could probably meet my HR standards and he introduced me to Julie Magnuson. We got on very well and after a trial period, we hired her because you can't have over 100 employees and not have a professional HR person to keep you out of trouble, especially in California! Julie and I shared similar opinions on how to treat and manage people and she did the job efficiently and without a huge empire. I came to rely on her judgment and we worked together on things like defining the company's culture, which was a very rewarding exercise.

The successful design and implementation of our clinical trials depended on the lead physician at each trial site who is known as the principal investigator, or PI. These were all very hard-working and incredibly dedicated physicians whose first priority is the treatment of their patients. They included a range of physician specialties including hepatology, nephrology, intensivists and more. Treating liver failure patients is a very frustrating task for a physician since the mortality rate from liver failure is so high and the only real cure is liver transplantation which is severely limited by the shortage of livers and the very high cost of the procedure.

We had a clinical advisory board which consisted of about 10 of these physicians and they were extremely helpful in the design and implementation of the trials. I made it one of my priorities to get out into the field to meet with as many of our PI's as I could, thereby learning a great deal about our target patient population. Most of what you learn about these patients is not very encouraging since we were focusing on serious alcoholics. I was amazed at the amount of alcohol most of these patients habitually consumed, 2 bottles of vodka per day was not uncommon, and, if I had not already given up drinking, I would've gone on the wagon based on what I learned. But our PIs had one very important thing in common and that is that they all wanted to see a simpler, lower-cost therapy that could save the lives of patients in liver failure and therefore they welcomed us into their hospitals.

So, by the middle of 2013, we had started to treat patients in the first of our clinical trials, VTL-208 in AAH in the US. The second trial was delayed in starting by the stifling bureaucracy in the EU, but it got underway in the fall of 2013. And the third trial, VTL-212, in FHF, got a slow start and enrolled an occasional patient mostly in the US. By the middle of 2013, our burn rate was up to about $1.8 million per month primarily because of our headcount at over 50 employees and the fact that these liver patients were very expensive and averaged about $60,000 each in actual hospital costs, not counting the high cost of the treatment and the team necessary to implement it. We had high hopes for successful clinical trial results.

By the end of 2013, we had about 40 clinical sites up and running in the US, England, Scotland, Spain, Germany, Austria and Australia. Each of these countries had a story about what we had to do to actually get sites open and enrolling. We also were in a very strong financial position with both cash and committed capital. And we had started to look at the marketing situation in the US and EU to determine how we should proceed with preparations to get insurance reimbursement in these countries. It was a complex situation and I will not bore you with the details.

And then, the US initial public offering, or IPO, market for biotechnology companies started to wake up. We found ourselves very well positioned, and so………..

CHAPTER 31
IPO!

We had been watching the US public stock market for several years but it was slammed shut for companies like ours and had been that way for the whole time we had been in China and going through the recapitalization. However, suddenly in mid-2013, the market seemed to wake up and several biotechnology companies were able to successfully complete initial public offerings, or IPOs, raising amounts in the $50-100 million range. We had several meetings with prominent investment banks who specialized in biotechnology and medical markets and it was obvious that we were well situated. The quality of our investors helped a great deal. The market was still not wide open but investors were beginning to realize that biotechnology could build highly valued companies and that in the years since the last biotech boom at the turn of the millennium, there had been some significant things happening.

The most significant development was the success of the Orphan Drug Act which had been passed by Congress, in a rare display of bipartisanship, in 1983. This provided significant benefits to companies developing drugs for orphan medical conditions, defined as affecting less than 200,000 patients per year. It enabled companies to get 7 years market exclusivity for an orphan drug, from approval by the FDA. This was almost as good as a patent since, although patents run for 20 years, they are issued on the application date and it generally takes at least 10 years to get a drug through the FDA regulatory hurdles which leaves less than 10 years exclusivity for the patented drug.

We applied for and were granted orphan drug status for ELAD for all indications in acute liver failure in the US and in the EU. The EMA in the EU was more generous than the US FDA and increased the marketing exclusivity period to 10 years.

There were other benefits but the one that was not specifically in the orphan drug act and that took quite a long time for companies to discover was the fact that the orphan drug exclusivity enabled them to charge very high prices for drugs that addressed very small markets, some as small as several hundred patients per year. In other words, there are other ways of creating a big market than serving more patients - you simply raise the price of the drug. The Orphan Drug Act made the development and marketing of drugs for orphan diseases profitable whereas prior to the Act, diseases that affected only small numbers of patients were usually ignored since they were too costly to develop.

I remember that when the first orphan drug was marketed for over $100,000 per year per patient, in the mid-1990s, we all thought the company was crazy and it only slowly penetrated that this was a great way to go. There were several companies that then got drugs approved and priced them well over $100,000 per year per patient. Surprisingly, the insurance companies were willing to pay these prices since, in many cases, it actually decreased their cost of providing for these very sick patients. Further, the adverse publicity generated by an insurance company refusing to pay for drugs for patients with serious orphan diseases was simply not worth it. This enabled the creation of several companies which achieved market valuations of over several billion dollars from developing and marketing orphan drugs, which made investors really take notice. They took even greater notice when this kind of drug pricing spread to other drugs as well. This is the main reason why the United States leads in drug development and why efforts to control drug prices, if successful, will result in significantly reduced new drug development, which is exactly what has happened in Europe.

As an example, the UK used to be a powerhouse of drug discovery and development (penicillin, insulin, DNA, monoclonal antibodies, viagra) but now it is a shadow of its former self and the once dominant UK drug companies have mostly been acquired or moved to the US. Why?

Because the UK National Health Service has worked with a quasi-government body called NICE (National Institute for Clinical Excellence) to throttle down the price of all drugs to the point where it is not profitable to develop or market drugs in the UK. NICE must be one of the most inappropriately named institutions in the world!

When this revolution in drug pricing was combined with the abundance of capital and the creation of very highly valued companies, the market started to ask for more of the same and therefore the IPO market came back to life for biotechnology. It created the greatest and longest bull market in biotechnology stocks and the related IPO market, which lasted from 2013 to the end of 2021.

We decided to take advantage of it in 2013.

After meeting with several investment banks in June, we selected one, Credit Suisse, as our lead banker and then started to get to work with all of the administrative bureaucracy necessary to create and file the requisite documents to move forward with the public offering. This is when all of the support people suddenly multiply and start going through the company's records in minute detail. And the expenses start to build very fast. Some of the meetings had up to 30 attendees, most of them being lawyers, accountants and auditors. I wanted to get our documents done expeditiously because we were concerned that the bull market in biotechnology IPOs would cool off. I had experienced this numerous times with prior biotechnology booms. Things went very well until we encountered an intractable auditing issue that slowed us down by about six weeks. It was trivial and I can't even remember exactly what it was but it delayed the filing of the requisite documents until about the beginning of October and we couldn't start the full process of raising the IPO funds until around mid-November. This proved to be a fatal delay.

As the CEO, I had to take the lead in the fundraising "road show" meetings but Duane handled the actual presentations. Our team was me, Duane, Jan and Rob - we got to know each other very well and made a good team, feeding off each other in the discussions and mostly avoiding the usual error of stepping on each other! This was exhausting and I was away from home for 3 weeks straight, including almost a week in Europe (UK, Germany, Switzerland). We used a private jet to keep to the schedule in 5 US cities. It was grueling and would have revealed any physical weaknesses that any of us had (fortunately, none). There were, of course, some light hearted moments along with some others worth noting:

The funniest moment was at a dinner in Chicago with the Vice Chairman of Credit Suisse. We were sitting opposite each other and struck up a conversation during which he noted my English accent and said that he spent several years in England at University. I asked whether he had played rugby and he immediately said yes and he loved the game, so I pressed further and asked if he knew any rugby songs and he said, of course, he knew them all. So, I moved in for the kill and said OK let's do a chorus of "The Sexual Life of the Camel" right now. He readily agreed and we started singing in this upscale restaurant. I was impressed that he knew every word, as did I. A respectful silence descended on the restaurant while we sang the whole song, and then at the end, laughter and thunderous applause! This particular song was raunchy but not so bad as to give offense and so we got away with it and became friends. Rugby does that to you – it is an incredible socializing game. I am tempted to reproduce the words of the song here but it is probably inappropriate. Anyone wanting to know the words, please contact me directly and I will oblige.

On the weekend of November 11, 2013 Duane and I were in London and we were in a hotel close to Trafalgar Square and Whitehall. This Sunday was Remembrance Sunday in England where those who sacrificed their lives in the two world wars were remembered: the eleventh minute of the eleventh hour of the eleventh day of the eleventh month, when the guns fell silent in the First World War. We stepped out of our hotel, walked down the street a little way and could clearly see the Cenotaph in Whitehall which was the center of the service of remembrance. There were crowds of people and we were moved just watching from a distance of about 200 yards. Since this was a time of terrorism in Europe, we could clearly see the armed police presence on the rooftops of the buildings in Whitehall. It was impressive. The British really know how to put on a show.

This was an emotional moment for me since my father had been of the age to be in the British Army for both world wars, serving as a sergeant in the Royal Horse Artillery in Egypt in WW1 and in the British Expeditionary Force in France in WW2. In 1940 he was at Dunkirk where he survived and was evacuated across the English Channel on the Royal Daffodil. This large pleasure steamer actually made six round trips under fire and was only damaged on the last one. What bravery! He and my mother and my foster parents also survived the brutal blitz on London during the Battle of Britain and the rest of the war including the V-1 and V-2 rockets.

Finally, the road show was over, we returned home and it was time to price and sell our deal to complete the IPO. But in the week before the pricing, the financial markets had a tantrum resulting in a significant downturn and we simply could not get the deal done on a basis that seemed reasonable to us. We would have had to cut our price by about 40% in order to get the deal done. Since we were in a good financial position, we did not think that it made sense to raise money in the IPO at about the same price that we had raised the last private money and so, after reviewing the situation with the board, they agreed that we should decline to do the deal at this low price and wait for more favorable conditions in the financial markets. This was not a popular decision, especially with our bankers, but we believe it was the correct decision. Management and the board were unanimous.

The good news is that by the spring of 2014, the markets had recovered and we tried again to get the IPO done. This meant we had to refresh all the documents and go through the roadshow again. By this time, we were much further along in the clinical trials and this helped our story so that we raised about $61.5 million at a good price and finalized the IPO on April 17, 2014. The net proceeds to the company were about $51.9 million after deducting all of the expenses which were close to $10 million.

We owe a huge debt of gratitude to Muneer who worked with us every step of the way and also to our other investors who were incredibly supportive and bought a significant amount of the IPO shares. Now we had over $100 million in cash and were about halfway through the main VTL-208 clinical trial.

Being the point person for implementing the public offering was a unique experience. It was grueling, involving about 30,000 miles of travel, not much sleep, and expenditure of a lot of energy. I had been the lead investor and lead board director for several companies in our VC portfolio who had done IPOs but actually being on the other side and responsible for making it happen was a different proposition. Fortunately, I had incredible support and a superb team which made it a lot easier. I'm sure that the astute reader has already noticed the rather large IPO expense number, close to $10 million. These consisted primarily of the investment banks' commissions, since we had four banks in the syndicate, the legal and audit fees, and the travel and roadshow expenses. We were higher than most since we had to make two tries to get the IPO done. However, it was well worth it and there were significant benefits to being public with the main one being that it was relatively easy to raise additional money providing you were close to your plan. We took advantage of this 3 times in the future to do additional fund raisings. It also gave some of our early investors the opportunity to sell their shares and exit the company but, surprisingly, few took advantage of this. Even though I had considerable ownership and had exercised a lot of my share options for cash, I did not sell any shares at any time and still hold onto them in the successor company.

CHAPTER 32
Disappointment

Being a public company was quite an adjustment from being private. Here are some of the things that changed:

1. We could no longer communicate directly with our earlier shareholders. I found this to be a really difficult adjustment to make since I had developed very good relationships with many of the shareholders. But, to comply with Securities and Exchange Commission, or SEC, regulations, now I had to be very careful what I said and make sure that I did not release any insider information to anyone. Everything had to be released at the same time, usually in the form of a news release or a shareholder call. These calls were generally every quarter unless we had something very special to announce.

2. The potential legal traps were many and serious. I developed a very good relationship with our outside corporate counsel and we also brought on an internal legal counsel as well. At the end of every quarter, our CFO and I had to personally validate the financial information that we released. We could not insure against the liability of this and therefore our personal assets were on the line. This was sobering but it was a product of the Sarbanes-Oxley legislation spawned by the Enron disaster.

3. We had to add a significant number of employees to our financial department and in several other areas of the company, notably shareholder relations. I never added up all the additional costs to being public but it probably approached $5 million per year.

4. I found that I was spending almost half my time on communications, administration and bureaucratic matters

related to our public status. I tried to delegate these additional responsibilities but with the personal liability heaped on the CEO by the Sarbanes-Oxley legislation, there was a limit to what could be prudently delegated.

As 2014 progressed, the clinical trials were proceeding very well, in the case of the main 208-trial, and not very well with the 210 and 212-trials. The 210-trial continued to be delayed by the EU bureaucracy and we finished the year only enrolling five patients. There were similar problems with the 212-trial but this was due to the very low patient availability to enroll in this trial. Out of frustration, we converted it to a phase 2 open-label trial, which meant that we did not have a control group. I was very comfortable with this since it meant we were not withholding treatment from the control group and so we were not put in the position of needing to have a large death rate in the control group for us to succeed. I have already opined on the use of a control group in survival trials in Chapter 24.

In addition to the clinical activities there were two other significant happenings in the second half of 2014:

1. We raised an additional $35 million in a follow-on public offering to supplement our IPO funds. This is one of the major advantages of being a public company in that, if things are going well, it is much easier to raise additional funds. The reverse of that is also true.
2. The results of a very interesting trial in the UK were released. Earlier, I discussed the use of steroids as a therapy for acute alcoholic hepatitis and noted that their efficacy had never been demonstrated in a controlled clinical trial. Such a trial had now been run in the UK and the result is very interesting. Here's a quote from our PR release at the end of 2014:

"In related news, the Company would like to note the recent release of the STOPAH (Steroids or Pentoxifylline for Alcoholic Hepatitis) trial results. STOPAH, which enrolled 1,103 subjects at 65 sites in the United Kingdom, was sponsored by the UK National Institute for Health Research Technology

Assessment Board and evaluated the effect of steroids and/or pentoxifylline, two anti-inflammatory drugs that are often used in the treatment of acute alcoholic hepatitis (AAH), on the survival of patients suffering from the condition. The results highlight the unmet need for AAH patients since there was no statistically significant impact on patient survival at 90 days or one year by either drug, although there was a short-term benefit on survival at 28 days in the subjects receiving steroids."

This was a truly remarkable trial that could only have been done by a government health organization because, with 1,103 subjects and 65 sites, the cost would have been far too high for a private company and the pay-off, if the drugs were efficacious, would have been minimal since they are both generic drugs with very low profit margins and the sponsoring company could not have got any exclusivity or price increases for marketing the drug from spending this kind of money. I estimate that the cost of this trial for a private company would have been more than $300 million, including the cost of the patients In the hospital and the hospital and company overhead costs of running the trial.

The short-term survival benefit with the steroids was minimal but is very interesting and confirms that AAH is an inflammatory disease. The fact that the survival benefit does not extend past 28 days is attributed to the initial anti-inflammatory effect of the steroids which is then overcome by the immune suppression effect of these drugs which makes the patients more susceptible to infection, which is what most of them died from. Several eminent liver doctors remarked to me that their liver failure patients don't die of liver failure, they die of infection caused by the liver failure, a view which supports these results.

Our reactions to the results of this trial were mixed. First, we were overwhelmed by the size and scope of the trial and disappointed that there was no real benefit for AAH victims. Second, we drew comfort from the fact that many people in the UK government health system must have felt that AAH is a serious problem there to justify such a trial and that there is an ongoing need for a successful therapy, where we felt we were now in the lead. This UK trial indirectly benefited us because there were now a lot of physicians and nurses in the UK who were experienced in handling AAH patients and who were delighted to participate in our trials. It was a lot easier to recruit sites and patients after the results of the trial were published. But it remained a serious administrative and bureaucratic challenge to get approval to run our trials in the UK with their onerous four levels of trial approval. We never really gained a lot of traction there because of this, with the exception of a couple of sites that had exceptional physician investigators such as Aintree in Liverpool.

We finished the year 2014 having enrolled 194 patients in the 208-trial, with 50 clinical sites open and with a burn rate of about $4 million per month. The burn rate had increased because we were now over 90 people and we were enrolling expensive patients at the rate of about 10 per month. The trial was fully enrolled with 203 patients by the end of January 2015 and we then had to wait 90 days to record the survival data on all patients and then another three months to fully analyze the data so that it was clean and reliable. We therefore announced that we would release the top-line results in the third quarter of 2015. The excitement was building in the company; just about everybody expected to get good results.

It took us over six months to analyze the data to get the preliminary results. The main reason was that the FDA was paranoid about bias in the trial and would not let us begin the analysis until the results of every patient had been recorded and locked so that they couldn't be changed under any circumstances. This is called data lock in clinical trial parlance. So, we could not start analyzing the patients as a group for over three months. And then we had to take special precautions to make sure that there was no bias in this analysis. The only way we could do this was to hire a third-party CRO to handle this analysis for us and, fortunately, we had one very close to us in San Diego.

Finally, we were ready and all the management team and Muneer gathered at the CRO in San Diego on Wednesday, August 19, 2015. It was a tense time even though we were all expecting a good result since we were aware of the consequences of failure. The way it was handled was that Rob Ashley, our VP of R&D, went in first to look at the data and make sure it was what we wanted. Then the rest of us were shown into a large conference room. As we entered, Rob was not looking at me and I could tell from the expression on his face that it was bad news. Unfortunately, I was correct. On the primary endpoint, survival at 90 days, there was no difference in survival between the treated and the control group at any point on the Kaplan-Meyer survival graph. We were devastated and a deadly silence fell over everyone. There was some good news, namely that the safety data looked good with the control patients doing slightly worse on the safety parameters than the treated patients.

I broke the silence by remarking to Muneer that we would probably have to close the company down and liquidate and his look told me that he agreed with me. However, then the CRO presenter went through the secondary endpoints and some of them looked very encouraging, notably the significant difference between the survival curves for less sick patients that, along with other secondary endpoints, had been pre-specified in the data analysis plan. The mood changed and our VP of regulatory affairs remarked that if this were a phase 2 study, we would all be delighted with these results since it would guide us on future trials. Some smiles broke out and we all agreed that we needed to lock ourselves up for the next 2 days to decide what we needed to communicate to our investors and create a plan for a possible new trial. Time was crucial since we must legally, by SEC regulations, release significant information within 48 hours. Anticipating this, we had purposely convened to learn the results on Wednesday and made reservations in an appropriate local hotel for 2 days; we had to make a public relations release of the results by Friday immediately after the market closed at 4 p.m. ET.

In summary, as shown in the two Kaplan-Meier graphs in the PR release and in Figure 3 in this book, there was no difference in survival between treated and controls for the group of 203 patients, the primary endpoint, but there was close to a statistical difference, p=0.077, between the two groups in 120 patients with a less severe form of AAH as defined by a MELD score of 28 or below, a pre-specified secondary endpoint. If there had been more patients in this subgroup, we would probably have reached statistical significance, defined as a p-value of less than 0.05.

As we dug into the data further in those 2 days, it became clear that there were numerous other conclusions to be drawn from an analysis of the subgroups such as the fact that we did not benefit patients who had severe kidney disease in addition to their AAH and so they should be eliminated from any further trials. By Friday morning, we all felt that we had enough understanding of what happened to issue a comprehensive news release and I retired to my room to write it. By Friday afternoon, we had something we could all agree on and issued it after the market closed on Friday, August 21.

We watched the trading of our stock on that Thursday and Friday with trepidation to see whether any hint of the results had leaked out but it stayed steady and we were reassured that our security was tight. Muneer surprised us all by staying with us over the weekend and arranging multiple calls with our big investors to explain the results. He worked incredibly hard. However, the reaction on Monday morning, after the PR was issued, was swift and our stock traded at a very high volume and lost over 50% of its value, which was not unexpected.

CHAPTER 33
Designing a New Trial

The next six months were a whirlwind of clinical data analysis and planning the design of a new trial. We engaged several experienced statisticians and other experts to dig into the VTL-208 clinical data to help us to define exactly the kind of patients who we should enroll in a new trial to maximize our chances of a successful outcome. We encountered a lot of skepticism since we were doing what is known in the trade as a "post hoc" analysis, defined as trying to find positive data in groups of patients that had not been specified before the trial started. However, each individual parameter had been pre-specified but the result of the four of them together had not been, except that three of the parameters together comprised the MELD score, which had been pre-specified and so it was not a stretch to do this. This may seem to be splitting hairs but it is a big deal to statisticians.

Many people in the business are very skeptical of all post hoc data. I still cannot understand this view of data analysis since the data remains the same whether it was pre-specified or not and how else are you going to make progress on these very difficult diseases than by teasing out all of the information you can from these very expensive clinical trials that we had run. After all, we had agreed to be judged by the gold standard endpoint of survival, using death from any cause, rather than using biomarkers as they use in many of the cancer clinical trials where the bar for approval, in CDER, the drug side of the FDA, is much lower than in the biologic side of the FDA where we were regulated. We would have loved nothing more than to have done this work with animals but unfortunately there was no good animal model and we had to have the human data in spite of the expense and the difficulty of creating it.

Our team of experts looked at the data from the point of view of the survival outcome with various combinations of the analytical results that defined these AAH patients. The main defining factors were the MELD score and its components, namely bilirubin, INR (blood coagulation ability) and creatinine (kidney function), to which we added age. We were surprised to learn that there was a strong correlation of survival with age in our trial data and that our AAH patients below the age of about 45 years old had a much better outcome than those above this age. This should not have surprised us since age had originally been shown to be a significant factor in the Mayo Clinic studies which developed the MELD score. However, age was not included as one of the factors of MELD, it was rumored, due to fear of being accused of age discrimination.

We finally teased out the optimum combination of these four parameters that gave the best survival outcomes in our trial. We identified 60 patients in the results of the trial, a mix of treated and control patients that met the criteria of all four parameters and when the analysis was run on these 60 subjects, the p-value was 0.006, well within the definition of statistical significance of 0.05 required by the FDA for approval. This Kaplan-Meier curve is shown in Figure 3, taken from the August 21, 2015 PR release. It was impressive that we got statistical significance with just 60 patients although this met with great skepticism from a number of statisticians and from the FDA because of its post hoc source. However, we proceeded to design the new trial based on these 60 patients and the FDA allowed it to proceed. Importantly, we used a new control curve in this analysis using 31 control patients that had exactly the same patient entry criteria as for the 29 treated patients. This is yet another illustration of how stable the control results had always been across all our trials and makes the outcome of the second phase 3 trial, which was trashed by the control curve, even more suspect, as described in Chapter 35.

We still had over $60 million in cash, enough to complete the trial, but we wanted to get a safety cushion and so raised an additional $30 million in another secondary offering. At the end of 2015, we had over $83 million in cash, more than enough to complete the trial providing we did not start spending on other things. Fortunately, there were a lot of people who were impressed with our analysis and our plans which enabled us to raise the additional capital. We also leaned very heavily on the expert liver physicians who comprised our Clinical Advisory Board, or CAB, to review the data and the new trial plans. There was unanimous agreement from the CAB that we should proceed which, coming from the experts in the field of liver failure, gave us great encouragement.

We had managed to avoid layoffs which kept the company together and enabled us to start recruiting clinical sites and to start the trial, known as VTL-308, with the first patient treated on May 10, 2016, at which time we had 10 clinical sites open for enrollment out of a planned 40.

One of the things I regret is that we did not pull out of the EU and focus on running the VTL-308 trial solely in the US. We had had a lot of problems with the bureaucracy in the EU which resulted in a lot of time wasted and increased expenses, in addition to the high cost of trans-Atlantic travel, the ground staff needed in the EU and the management time that was spent on EU travel and support. I tried hard to pull us out of Europe but I was in a minority of one and felt that I had to concede. That was an error. Continuing in the EU cost us a lot of time and money and I should have insisted that we focus on the US only. I found myself as the only voice calling for getting a successful trial completed in the best way possible and not diluting our efforts with many other things. My argument was that unless we got a trial successfully concluded, all of our other efforts were irrelevant but, as I will relate, I remained in a minority of one. The counter argument from everyone else was that we needed EU trial results to get speedy approval there. That reasoning was soon expanded to the fact that we needed to start writing the approval documents now and actively prepare for commercialization and manufacturing in higher volumes to support marketing, all of which was fast depleting the company's cash.

I started to think about retirement. At 75 years old and with a seriously ailing wife, it was time. I think that, at that time, I was the oldest active CEO in the biotech world.

In addition to designing and implementing the new VTL-308 trial, there were many other things that transpired in 2016:

Shareholder Lawsuit. We were served with the ritual lawsuit for causing the large drop in our stock price after the announcement that the trial had failed to meet its primary endpoint. We joined many other biotechnology companies in being sued by these reprehensible law firms who then trolled for plaintiffs. We had been aware of the risk of such a lawsuit and we were well insured but it was still an enormous time sink for me, the board of directors and members of our management team. The basis for the lawsuit was that we had not warned everybody that this kind of thing could happen but nothing could be further from the truth because we had pages of risk factors in our public disclosure documents including a very prominent one saying that the trial could fail for reasons not of our causing. The plaintiff lawyers didn't worry about that, of course, and the filings of the lawsuit made us out to be the most horrible people who had misled these innocent shareholders.

We searched all of our documents relevant to the trial and its result just to make sure that there was no smoking gun that we did not know about. I was quite sure that there would be no incriminating evidence because I was constantly warning our employees to be very careful what they put in their written communications since a careless remark could be interpreted in a negative way and cost us a lot of money. But it was obvious that we had not done anything wrong and that we had proceeded in a way that followed all the rules. The main question that the plaintiff lawyers wanted answered was the amount of our insurance upper limit and then they tailored their demand to this limit. This did not seem right to me and we had a very interesting session of the board where we decided to actively fight the lawsuit. We had great litigation lawyers and they came up with documents that were simply superb so that, after what seemed an eternity of back-and-forth filings, the plaintiffs threw in the towel and we did not pay any damages.

This was an unusual result since most biotech companies simply let their insurance company pay out the limit of the insurance without fighting it. And many of them had a good reason to do so since the usual cause of the payout was potentially incriminating emails that were always interpreted negatively. Nonetheless, it still cost us a lot of time and money, over $1 million in legal and other expenses, and executive time, which ate into our productivity. Oh, the wonders of the trial lawyer system! My opinion of these trial lawyers is not printable.

Citizens' Petition. At the same time as the shareholder lawsuit was active, there was another shocking development on the quasi-legal front involving short-sellers. Most people do not understand short selling and so I will explain. These are stock traders who, instead of buying your stock and wanting it to go up, do the reverse and first sell your stock wanting it to go down. Of course, in order to sell the stock, they have to borrow it from someone who already owns it, and that usually costs them a borrowing fee. Then, if the stock does go down, they can buy it back at a much lower price than they sold it for, return the stock to the lender and they have made a profit. This has led to the old Wall Street jingle:

"He who sells what isn't his'n

Must buy it back or go to Prison"

There are several problems with this, the first being that, having sold the stock, the potential losses if the stock goes up a lot are unlimited (if you buy and then it goes to zero, your loss is limited to the price you paid for it) and many of these short sellers have been bankrupted with the most well-known cases being Porsche and Volkswagen stock a few years ago, and the meme stocks on Robin Hood creating short squeezes more recently.

The second problem is that the short-sellers have a habit of doing anything that they can to force the price of the stock down including some questionable legal tactics. It seems that the possibility of unlimited losses, if the stock goes up, concentrates their mind in a way that they lose their sense of fair play and legality. This is what happened with Vital Therapies.

We had known that short sellers were active in our stock in 2015 and that they did very well when our trial failed and the stock fell. In fact, they were so thrilled about it that an infamous stock manipulator, who shall be nameless, couldn't resist boasting about how he had made a killing selling VTL stock short. He didn't care that the result was a disaster for the patients in that they continue to suffer. This tells you a lot about the nature of short-sellers. They don't care if a company makes drugs or widgets. This put us on our guard but we were totally unprepared for the underhanded actions that the short-sellers would take as we prepared to initiate VTL-308.

The first hint that something was wrong came from our interactions with the FDA in January 2016. We had several meetings and telephone calls with our FDA reviewers while we were in the planning process for the VTL-308 clinical trial. These interactions were constructive and cordial even though we did not like some of the decisions that were rendered by the FDA. However, in January, it seemed like the FDA reviewers suddenly had gone silent and the meetings were very icy. We couldn't figure out what was wrong until one of our clinical trial site physicians in a routine contact in February asked for an explanation of the Citizens' Petition. We had no idea what he was talking about but we promised to investigate and respond. What we discovered was unprecedented and shocking.

We got a copy of the Citizens' Petition which is a public document and a legitimate route for an individual or an institution to present their arguments to the FDA about some issue that is being considered for a decision. It is usually used to present arguments about generic drugs and other commercial questions but we were amazed to see that this one was a diatribe against Vital Therapies and ELAD, basically saying this was dangerous to patients and that the trial should be stopped. The arguments were erroneous and would have been funny if this were not such a serious matter. When we started calling around our clinical sites, we were startled to find that this petition had not only been filed with most of our clinical sites but that the filer had requested to meet with the hospital staff at many of our sites. To our knowledge, this is the first time the Citizens' Petition route had been used in clinical development to try to stop a trial in progress. And certainly, this was the first time hospital physicians had been lobbied to stop a trial.

When we informed the board of this, we came in for some harsh criticism that we did not have the systems in place to alert us of these things much sooner. We thought this was a little unfair but we soon got everyone working together.

The first thing we did was to call the FDA to request an urgent meeting, which they granted us quickly. But they said nothing in the call, they just listened as we described the situation, which we thought was very odd. However, we learned later that the FDA was under instruction not to respond in any way to Citizens' Petitions and so that explained their behavior and also why they suddenly became silent and icy in January. But it also deprived us of the Agency's help to handle this disgusting development.

We did some investigation and forensics on the Citizen's Petition and found that it had been filed by a person we had not heard of in Canada. We suspect that this was by design since what they were doing was so close to legality that if the US government decided to take action, the filer was in Canada and beyond the reach of the US law. We also found several typos and errors in the wording and had the bright idea to compare it with the Citizen's Petitions that had been filed before by the infamous stock manipulator referred to already. Bingo! The typos and errors were identical. To give himself some legal cover, the filer had inserted a short paragraph to declare that he was a short seller and stood to gain if the stock lost value but, crucially, he had not added that if the stock gained value, he would be on the line for unlimited losses.

Over the next few months, we talked to a lot of our physician investigators at the hospital sites. We found that the lobbying by the short-sellers of the trial physicians and the committees that regulated the hospital trials was getting more intense rather than diminishing, especially in the EU. We even had some requests from some of the EU clinical sites to meet with them to explain what was going on. The question was what to do about it. I wanted to go public with the whole situation but the board did not agree with that. However, it was obvious that we were going to have to address the subject in some way and so we decided to arrange a shareholder call and address the issues that were raised in the Citizens' Petition. The call went very well and we addressed all the issues. The lobbying of the clinical sites continued but it seemed to slowly become ineffective and so the issue faded away. I was not happy with the way that we had handled it but it did not seem to be hurting us anymore, although a lot of damage had been done and a lot of time and money had been wasted.

Accelerated Approval. During the AIDS epidemic, the FDA received a lot of criticism and lobbying about their slowness in approving new drugs. They were doing their job as prescribed by Congress but it was felt that for serious and life-threatening diseases, such as AIDS, there should be a faster way of getting these drugs on the market because people were dying in the years that it was taking to get approval. Therefore, the FDA developed a new approval route called accelerated approval where a drug's marketing approval could be granted based on the impact of the drug on known and validated markers of the disease, such as in measuring the levels of markers in the blood. In the case of AIDS, the marker was the viral particle count rather than the actual progress of disease recovery, which could take years. The caveat was that this approval would be conditional on running a full trial with clinical endpoints, preferably survival, in the future and that, if this trial failed, the drug could be removed from the market. All this work was done in CDER, the drug division of the FDA, which embraced accelerated approval, especially for cancer drugs, which could now be approved based on so-called surrogate markers. Today, most cancer drugs are approved by this route. But few have been removed from the market because the companies learned that there was no time limit to run the validation trial. And since the required validation trial uses survival/death as the endpoint, and few drugs can meet this gold standard, there is naturally a reluctance to run these survival trials.

However, the biologics division, CBER, where we were regulated, had not embraced accelerated approval in the same way as CDER. Therefore, Rob Ashley, our VP of R&D, felt that we should try to see if we could make an argument to use either the MELD score or bilirubin as a surrogate marker to gain approval for ELAD under this accelerated approval route. It made sense to me since we were definitely developing a therapy for a life-threatening disease, we had good data for both markers and our existing endpoint of survival was agreed to be the gold standard and therefore the most difficult to meet.

We went back and forth with CBER at the FDA several times but we were not able to convince them to accept MELD or bilirubin as a surrogate marker that could be used for approval. Their explanation to us was that our survival period of 90 or 180 days was so short that we did not need accelerated approval. But this ignored the inherent difficulty of the survival endpoint where deaths were counted from any cause, even if the cause had nothing to do with the disease the trial was studying. In addition, the control group had to die at about a 50% rate in 90-180 days to give the trial a chance to succeed. Either of these factors could have caused an effective drug to fail in its trial. We felt that this was just the inertia of the CBER and that we were disadvantaged compared to those regulated by CDER because the same arguments could be used against cancer drugs. But there was nothing we could do about it and we simply had to proceed with the wretched survival endpoint which was very unfriendly to the patients and, in my opinion, unethical since it denies a potentially life-saving drug to the control patients and needlessly extends the time and expense of the trial by doubling the number of patients needed.

Donor Liver Preservation. This was a project that was suggested to us by one of our clinical trial physicians: Dr. David Reich at Drexel University Hospital in Philadelphia, one of our trial sites. Dr. Reich is a liver transplant surgeon who had been working for years on the problem of preserving livers that had been harvested for transplant. The problem is that they begin to deteriorate very rapidly and after 12 hours they are of questionable use. He suggested that we perfuse these livers with the output from running blood plasma through our cartridges that contained the live C3A cells. He felt that this had a very good chance of preserving these livers for transplant. He brought in the liver research people at the University of Birmingham in England since they had excellent facilities, people and equipment to do this work. U Birmingham was also one of our clinical trial sites, specifically Queen Elizabeth Hospital which is one of the showplace hospitals of England. This 3-way location project got underway and we were starting to get some very promising results when we had to terminate it in 2018. We hope that someone continues this work since there is a great need to increase the number of viable livers available for transplantation.

CHAPTER 34
Irrational Exuberance

(With acknowledgment to Alan Greenspan)

By the end of 2016, we had the VTL-308 trial under control with 38 sites open out of a target of 50 and 38 patients enrolled out of a target of at least 150, primarily at the US sites. The EU sites were slowly opening and we felt confident enough about progress to say that we expected to announce top-line results in mid-2018. This required an average enrollment rate of about 10 patients per month to complete the enrollments by the end of 2017. Data lock by the end of March 2018 and analysis for 90 days gave us our mid-2018 results release date.

This trial had a particularly narrow spectrum of patient enrollment criteria and so it was essential that Dr. Dr. Jan Stange, our chief medical officer, stayed in close contact with every site and approved the enrollment of every patient. We could not take the risk of enrolling patients that were not within the specifications of the enrollment criteria. This caused a few friction points with the clinical trial physicians since they were mostly very independent but Jan did a good job of keeping them satisfied.

My concern was that everybody was too bullish on the prospect of getting good trial results and they wanted to charge ahead and spend money now to shorten the time to commercialization, such as preparing the BLA filing documents, ramping up manufacturing along with QA/QC and preparing for commercialization with marketing and sales people and reimbursement studies. I felt like the Dutch boy who prevented flooding by putting his finger in the hole in the dyke!

My argument was that spending a lot of money on commercialization issues prior to getting good trial results and product approval was one of the oldest mistakes in the biotech book and it had tripped up many companies before us. I pointed out that good results and a smooth approval were by no means certain and there were likely to be significant issues with the trial results that may need a lot of work to resolve, hence the need to be well financed. We must ensure that we kept enough money in the bank to be able to work on any issues and to handle delays because it would not be possible to raise more money if the results were in doubt. I think that most people thought that I was Cassandra personified and they still wanted to spend on commercialization. I had to give a little and agreed that we would form a commercialization committee consisting of board members with experience in that field. But I set a goal of having at least $20 million in the bank when we announced top-line results, after payment of accrued expenses. As 2017 progressed, this became a tough target to defend.

My thoughts of retirement were getting more serious and it was obvious to me that the board would like to see someone installed with significant commercialization experience as the CEO. I did not have that on my resume. Muneer and I had a conversation about this in the summer and we agreed that I would step down at the end of 2017. With my wife's health making for a difficult situation at home, this suited me very well and so plans were agreed and all thoughts turned to hiring an appropriate CEO. I was happy to work with the board to hire the right person. Frankly, I thought it would be very difficult since any candidate would have to take the risk of an adverse result in the phase 3 clinical trial and it could be a short tenure as CEO and a not very attractive wind down of the company. This is something that sales and marketing people are usually not comfortable with.

But I was wrong and Russ Cox, a good friend of one of our board members, was hired as CEO. Russ and I spent several long sessions going over every aspect of the company and I was very open and frank with him about the good and the problematic issues including the possibility of a bad trial result. He was comfortable taking that risk. I grew to like and respect Russ and we did a flawless handover of the CEO reins at the end of 2017. The board was fair and generous with my departure package but I declined the offer to stay on the board. I had seen the situation so many times as a VC and having the prior CEO stick around always caused problems. So, I made a clean break and retired to Arizona where I had always been living. With the subsequent political events, I am so glad that I never succumbed to moving to California and I never want to do business there again. The only problem is that my Arizona fortress is now being invaded by California refugees. Wait until they experience an Arizona summer, which is our best weapon to keep the Californians away!

The only person that did not like the situation was my wife. Although she had significant health problems, she was furious with me for stepping down from the CEO role and was very concerned with what might happen if there were some problems with the clinical trial results. Even though she did not know Russ she felt that a new person would not have the same commitment to the company and may simply give up if there was a difficult problem to resolve. She had a point and she was relying on her observation of my commitment through all the problems that the company had since I took over in 2003. It turns out that she was prescient in her analysis of the situation!

When I stepped down as CEO at the end of 2017, we had enrolled 130 patients and had 43 clinical sites open in the VTL-308 trial. This was a little behind our projections and we had extended the time for the announcement of top line results until the third quarter of 2018.

I retired to Scottsdale, started to read more books and play more golf and kept my promise to leave everything to Russ from now on. He invited me to the EASL meeting in Paris in April 2018, which I accepted, but I did not maintain any of my contacts at VTL. Apart from one trip to pick up my artwork from the office, I did not return to California and did not miss it. I enjoyed living in Arizona, free of paying CA income taxes, the high prices and the bureaucracy.

I did not sell any VTL shares at this time nor at any other time. I had exercised most of my stock options (and paid the taxes for doing so) and I was in this until the end, come what may. I had resisted the temptation to put a lot more money into VTL and kept to my diversified financial plan for retirement which would be fine irrespective of the outcome at VTL. But I had a significant amount of my net worth tied up in VTL stock and I obviously was vitally interested in a positive outcome, which I could no longer influence.

The golf and reading morphed into book writing and I resolved to write a book about VTL when the outcome was clear. Meanwhile, I worked with a co-author to write the first book about one of our companies from my VC days which developed a drug that induced a natural tan. It is a fascinating story and the book is now published. In the process, I learned a great deal about book publishing and will put that to good use in this book about VTL.

CHAPTER 35
Disaster!

The call came when I was not expecting it, at dinner time in August 2018. I had expected the results a week later. Russ informed me in a very businesslike way that the trial had not met its primary or secondary endpoints. I assumed he was busy analyzing the data every and which way so it was a short call. I explained the situation to my wife and we consoled each other with the knowledge that the team was going to go through the results to see if there was anything that would merit further clinical investigation. And then we waited.

The public announcement came out the next day. It was short and nothing like the detailed announcement that we had made after the first trial failed in 2015 with a deep analysis of the results and some plans for the future. This 2018 announcement indicated that the company was going to be closed down and liquidated. It did not even have the Kaplan-Meier curve showing the results. I was shocked and over the next few weeks I tried to get more information but it was difficult since I no longer had any status at the company and therefore people were reluctant to talk to me. I grew frustrated and worked with two of my colleagues to see if we could buy the cells and the IP assets of the company, including the clinical data. We were initially told that would be possible but then that story changed: they had an attractive cash offer for the IP and the manufacturing assets from a Chinese company. The public shell of VTL would also be sold by merging into another company.

We did not want to compete with this substantial Chinese cash offer since, apart from the cells, we did not want the hard assets and we did not have any details about the clinical trial results so, we would have been taking a leap into the unknown. We had to wait for two months to learn more about the detailed results when they were presented at a meeting in Germany in October by one of our leading enrollers in the trial, the lead physician at Rutgers University Hospital.

We were surprised to learn that the treated group of patients in the trial had performed about the same as we expected from the post hoc analysis in the VTI-208 trial in 2015, with about 70% of the treated patients surviving at 90-days after initiation of treatment. However, what blew up the trial results was that the control group, which was expected to show 50% survival at 90 days, also had about 70% survival. You can see 2015 results in the Kaplan-Meier curves in Figure 3, along with the post hoc analysis of the 2015 trial, the so-called "golden population." In Figure 4, note how the control group in 2015 performed as expected in the golden population but is very different in the 308-trial result. Both groups had the same enrollment criteria and should have performed the same.

This raised the possibility of something being wrong with the results in the control group. If this control group had shown the expected 50% survival at 90 days, we would have had a strongly statistically significant result and would have been on our way to filing the BLA, gaining FDA approval and marketing ELAD.

The performance of this control group strained credibility. We had used a similar control group in many of our clinical trials before this and it had always reliably given 50% survival at 90 days. The same control group in the 2015 trial had also given a 50% survival result. So, what suddenly caused this control group to show significantly increased survival and was work done to determine why the control group had gone awry? It seemed that, after getting the results, the closedown decision was made within two days and implemented immediately. I rapidly got over my disappointment and sadness, but there was nothing I could do about it if we did not have access to and control of the clinical data.

There are many possible explanations for why a control group in a clinical trial does not perform as expected. The most benign reason is that the standard of patient care changes without your knowledge and it results in significantly improved survival in the control patient population. However, if there had been such an improvement in the standard of patient care, it would have also showed up in the treated population and boosted their survival as well; that did not happen. Another benign reason is that it is possible to get a statistical outlier result that is several standard deviations away from the norm. Possible, but unlikely.

There are two lines of reasoning to explore. First, why we got significantly different results in the Chinese clinical trials compared to the US trial results. This is important to explore since there is much skepticism about the Chinese clinical trial results. And secondly, I will explore a couple of "conspiracy theories" about what could have possibly changed the performance of the control group in the final US trial, the 308-trial.

I am not questioning the 308-trial results. I have every confidence in the way the trials were run and particularly in the team that was responsible for the clinical trial operations. I know the management of this team and I'm sure that they checked every detail to be sure that these trial results were reliable.

First, the question of why the Chinese trial was so successful and the US trial failed. Here are some possible explanations:

1. Contradictory trial results in pivotal phase 3 trials are not uncommon, especially when the trials are run in different countries. Sometimes the reason is never determined and we need to remember that we are dealing with actual human patients where each one is a biological system and everyone is different. Even though we tried to standardize things like the entry criteria into the trial, there is a wide spectrum of possible results due to the variability of each patient. Further, we are dealing with a limited number of patients and trying to get a consistent outcome. We need to recognize that the statistics of the trial can always give us an outlier result. Such a result is not likely but can happen. Most trials are designed with about a 95% probability of yielding the correct result and so there is about a 5% possibility of getting an outlier result.

2. There were many differences in the design of the Chinese and US trials. The most important difference was that the enrollment criteria for patients selected for each trial were different; we refer to this in the pharma world as different indications. In China, we selected only those with liver failure caused by hepatitis B or related reasons. In the US trial, we selected only those with liver failure caused by excessive alcohol consumption. We already know that the liver is a very complex organ and so the detailed biochemistry of these two different groups may have accounted for the different results. In other words, the type of liver failure may have been very different in each group which could have resulted in very different outcomes.

3. Compared to US clinical trials, Chinese trials are run in an inefficient way and the quality of the clinical sites at the hospitals is not up to US standards. We tried to smooth out some of these differences but there were some features of the Chinese trials that make them unacceptable for US purposes. Two such differences that could have influenced the results are:

a) The China trial was not run on a blinded basis. We could not do that in the US either since it was impossible to hide the large ELAD system by the side of a treated patient's bed but, in China, the managers of the trial were not blinded and post-treatment care was not provided on a blinded basis, as in the US trials. We could also look at the results as we went along which is not allowed in the US. Personally, I do not see that looking at the ongoing results affects the outcome of subsequent patients with a serious condition like hepatitis B.

b) As described in Chapter 9, the China trial had a plasma exchange treatment for both treated and control patients before the therapy period started. Subsequent work in Denmark has shown that plasma exchange does have a small positive effect on survival although it takes a lot of patients to show it. Plasma exchange is just that: fresh blood plasma from a human donor is added to the patient's blood by infusion at the same time and rate as the patient's plasma is removed and discarded. Usually, about one liter of plasma is infused and removed which means the net new plasma substituted is about 0.8 liters. Obviously, some toxins are removed and fresh new natural, presumably beneficial, substances are added. This could have had an effect on the results in China but, since it was done for both treated and control patients, it is more likely to have increased the difficulty for ELAD to show a survival benefit.

4. In China, we had to use the endpoint of transplant free survival rather than overall survival in the US trials. This has already been discussed at length in Chapter 9. This could have affected the results although we do not think that is the case.

5. All of us, including the Chinese physicians and nurses, may have been too optimistic about the outcome in China and we may have let this interfere with our balanced judgment. This is always possible but there were many of us observing the treatments and we could see very clearly the significant improvement in the treated patients after about 24 hours versus the untreated control patients and we could follow their longer-term survival.

6. The ELAD system used in the two trials may have been different and affected the outcomes. This is a possibility since working with human cells is difficult and there can be differences in the way the cellular therapy is administered that could affect the outcome in ways that we could not measure. We measured all the parameters we thought could affect the cells and the way they were used. However, one of the possible issues that worried me was the pore size of the membranes in the cell cartridge. Membrane technology is considerably behind the other technologies that we were using. The pore size of the membrane that controlled which substances passed through was not possible to accurately control. We had ways of measuring this to try to ensure consistency of pore sizes but these methods were not accurate and the membranes could not be made with specific pore sizes, only a range around a mean size. If life-saving molecules could not pass through the membrane, it could have seriously affected survival.

7. Perhaps the best argument in support of the safety and efficacy of ELAD in China is the reaction of the patients and the potential clin-

ical trial patients in the China trial. They quickly figured out that ELAD was very effective and were scheming to draw a treated slot and not be an untreated control. This is exemplified by the patient who refused to participate as a control and went to our second hospital to get a treated slot, as related in Chapter 11. The FDA calls this "real world evidence" or RWE and assigns a high value to it in a clinical approval package. We had excellent RWE in the China trial.

The list of arguments as to why the US trial failed is in most cases the antithesis of the above seven points with the most important factor in my mind being the fact that it enrolled a different kind of liver failure patient than in the China Trials.

Now for the second line of reasoning. At the other end of the spectrum are "conspiracy theory" reasons such as the possibility that someone or something had influenced the control group results either accidentally or on purpose. My VC experience taught me to follow the money or the ideology as the most likely driving forces for such behavior. In other words, who stood to benefit or lose financially or culturally from the trial results? Following this line of speculation with the various groups interested in the trial yields two separate groups who stood to lose significant wealth or stature if we had succeeded and the reverse, to gain, if we failed: the short-sellers and the Chinese government. Both of these are known to be potential bad actors.

There is no information I am aware of to point to any outside interference with the trial, although my information is limited to that disclosed to the public, it should have been checked out. A thorough investigation would take several weeks and would need significant funds - it was unlikely to have been done in the 2 days between the trial results and the close-down announcement. I would still like to see it done, although with the Chinese already owning the cells and the technology, this would now be very difficult. That this was not investigated in more detail is disappointing. If ELAD comes on the market under a new name in China within a few years, that will tell us a lot.

One possible route to approval that was not pursued and does not seem to have been considered is to prepare the BLA approval document and file it with the FDA to request approval, even with the defect in the clinical trial results. We know this is possible and that the FDA has been taking a more flexible view of approval of drugs for serious and life-threatening diseases because of the well-publicized case in 2017 concerning Sarepta and its drug for treating Duchenne muscular dystrophy (DMD) in children.

Sarepta's data in their phase 3 trial for DMD was probably worse than ours. Their deficiency was in the performance of the treated group and not of the control group, as in our case. They prepared and executed a very innovative strategy to draw attention to the plight of these children who had no treatment available, including having their families attend the FDA advisory panel review of the drug filing where they made a lot of fuss and appealed to the FDA directly for approval since their children were highly deserving.

Buckling under this pressure, the FDA searched for a reason to approve the drug. They knew that they could not bend the performance of the treated group for approval and so they created a surrogate marker that they found in the trial results and used this to grant an accelerated approval - an example of post hoc analysis that we had been criticized for. To say that the whole of the biotechnology world was stunned by this approval is an understatement but many of us were pleased with the result since we felt that it was a harbinger of better days for FDA approvals which had been hard to get up to that point.

We watched this case as it developed and tucked it away for future consideration if we ended up in a similar position, which, as you now know, happened. A similar case happened in 2021 with Biogen's Aduhelm for Alzheimer's, which also was approved on a surrogate marker, again with the deficiency in the treated groups, not the controls. I submit that a deficiency in the treated group is much more serious than in the control group.

At the time that this Sarepta DMD approval happened in 2017, we reasoned that our alcoholics would not command the same kind of sympathy as young boys with genetic defects. However, we felt that there was a new attitude towards alcoholics where the disease was seen as not being their fault but the result of addictive genes. For example, they are now eligible for liver transplants instead of being ineligible for the transplant list. The average age of our trial patients was about 40 years old and we could have made them into very deserving cases and also had a similar panel hearing with actual AAH patients and the families of alcoholics who had died from or were struggling with AAH. Many of these families were very passionate about the plight of their alcohol-addicted offspring and we were sure that we could get the same kind of effect that Sarepta had so creatively used for DMD. Further, we could also point to a surrogate endpoint, either bilirubin or MELD score, for which we had good data and had already tried to get FDA to allow as an endpoint for accelerated approval, as explained in Chapter 33. Bilirubin was already known and it would not be quite such a jump for the FDA as was creating the surrogate endpoint to approve the DMD drug. It may help the reader to understand this a bit better if I include a draft memo that I wrote in 2018 to help me think things through, after I exited the CEO role and after we learned the details of the 308-trial results (the underlining is mine). Note especially the quote from the FDA's Title 21:

Proposed Strategy for FDA Approval

Basis:

1. *The trial failure is caused mainly by an unexpected result in the control curve where the control patients did not show the expected mortality of about 50% over 180 days. The mortality was about 30%.*
2. *In CFR, Title 21, sub-part E, revised 4/1/2010, FDA states:*

The purpose of this section is to establish procedures <u>designed to expedite the development, evaluation, and marketing of new therapies intended to treat persons with life-threatening and severely-debilitating illnesses, especially where no satisfactory alternative therapy exists</u>. As stated in 314.105(c) of this chapter, while the statutory standards of safety and effectiveness apply to all drugs, the many kinds of drugs that are subject to them, and the wide range of uses for those drugs, demand flexibility in applying the standards. *The Food and Drug Administration (FDA) has determined that it is appropriate to exercise the broadest flexibility in applying the statutory standards, while preserving appropriate guarantees for safety and effectiveness. These procedures reflect the recognition that physicians and patients are generally willing to accept greater risks or side effects from products that treat life-threatening and severely-debilitating illnesses, than they would accept from products that treat less serious illnesses. These procedures also reflect the recognition that the benefits of the drug need to be evaluated in light of the severity of the disease being treated. The procedure outlined in this section should be interpreted consistent with that purpose*.

1. FDA has recently shown an impressive willingness to apply this flexibility, most notably in the case of Sarepta's DMD drug. We have better data than Sarepta, an equally deserving patient group and there is no satisfactory alternative therapy.
2. ELAD qualifies on all counts.
3. In addition, ELAD is an orphan drug where FDA is already known to show flexibility.

Strategy:

1. Show that the treated curves for the 308 and the 208 ideal population are substantially similar and not statistically different
2. Show that the control curves for the studies are statistically different
3. Show that the 308-control curve is statistically different from all our prior studies and from the identical patients from the STOPAH and CANONICAL studies.
4. Work with at least 10 of our clinical sites to identify historical patients at the sites identical to the 308 enrollment criteria and with known survival outcomes. Build a data base of over 500 patients over the last 5 years and compare to the controls in 308 and 208.
5. The control curves from III and IV should clearly show that had the 308 controls performed as expected then the study end points would have been successful.

6. *If the data clearly show that the 308-control curve is an anomaly, discuss with our regulatory counsel to determine if this is a viable strategy to file a BLA and to seek approval for ELAD*
7. *This will require people who are willing to challenge FDA as Sarepta did since the initial FDA responses will be negative and highly discouraging. It will also require outstanding patient advocacy work.*
8. *If we have a good story then it will be possible to raise funds for this effort in the public markets, as Sarepta did. Shortage of cash is no excuse. Patients' lives are on the line here and we must be willing to fight for approval!*

This is self-explanatory and does not need any elaboration from me. It is obvious that ELAD qualifies and you can readily grasp the flexibility and need to approve these kinds of drugs even if the clinical data is not stellar as cited in the FDA's own regulation CFR, Title 21, sub-part E, quoted above.

In Figures 4 and 5, you can see very clearly how the control group for the last trial in 2018, VTL-308, is an aberration. Further, the ELAD treated group in VTL-308 performed as expected. If you combine the ELAD treated group from 308 with the ideal control group from 208, the result is a strongly statistically significant result with $p=0.013$. This result would have been good enough for FDA approval and ELAD would now be saving lives!

The fact that the board and the management team did not explore this route to approval with the ELAD VTL-308 phase 3 data is disappointing. Not having enough money in the bank to pursue this is not an excuse since Sarepta had the same problem and they had to raise more money in the public markets to finance the approval attempts. We could have done the same.

It seems that after I stepped down as CEO at the end of 2017, there was no one left to preach the conservative sermon of <u>not</u> spending large amounts of money on commercialization, before having results suitable for approval. This includes the BLA filing, manufacturing, QA/QC, marketing, reimbursement and sales. It seems that my goal of having at least $20 million in the bank, at the time of the results release, was dropped. The $20 million number was after paying all clinical trial expenses, allowing for severance payments on shutdown and other accounts payable. It was, of course, a stretch goal but if we had come close, there would have been enough cash to pay for a thorough review. But, apparently, after I left, the company significantly ramped up spending on these commercialization areas and ended up with only about $5 million, net of severance and payables, when the trial results were disclosed. I had set this $20 million goal to cover exactly this kind of clinical trial result where a significant amount of work was needed to learn why a particular result happened. The $5 million was not enough to support the thorough review and hence the quick shutdown. It seems that raising more money to support the review was not considered even though there was the Sarepta precedent. I do not fault the board for making the decision to shut down since, as a public company, VTL had severance agreements with all key executives and an obligation to discharge all payables.

It's likely that this low cash level influenced the decision not to take the time to investigate what went wrong with the control group because there simply was not enough money to do the work properly. This is unfortunate since the reason for the errant control group result could influence future work. For example, if the reason was benign, it could then have helped others to avoid making the same mistakes. This serious health problem of liver failure still exists, the patients are still dying because they do not have any viable therapy, except liver transplantation, and other companies are sure to continue to work on innovative solutions.

This is as far as I can take the story but I have a strong feeling that it is not over yet. We know that the Chinese, who now own the cells, the IP and the manufacturing equipment, are doing a lot of work on ELAD, which has probably been slowed down by the Covid pandemic. It may appear on the Chinese market under a different brand name and will then work its way back to the US and EU. I don't know which Chinese company owns these assets but it does not really matter since everything in China is ultimately owned by the government. We do know that the company which now owns the assets is 100% Chinese-owned.

China's xenophobia will probably ensure that the product gets speedy approval and is marketed to address hepatitis B, one of their worst health issues and fourth leading cause of death in China.

We should not ignore the possibility of interference by the short sellers. They would only have to somehow cover up the deaths of less than 10 patients to affect the control group badly enough to trash the trial and I can think of many ways that they could do that. Far-fetched and impossible you say? I would have said that about them lobbying the clinical sites with lies about the safety of ELAD and trying to shut down the trial, which happened in 2016, as described in Chapter 33. I think it's a relatively small step from this to actually interfering with the trial. Emboldened with their short selling success on the first trial in 2015, I am sure they were thirsting for more and could have easily ratcheted up their underhanded actions.

I hope you enjoyed the story even with this disastrous ending. But I do not think this is the end of the story and I expect you will be hearing more about ELAD, probably when it resurfaces with approval in China in the next few years.

Figure 1: Bridge-to-Transplant, 1999-2003

- Total of 11 patients died – 6/26 ELAD® vs. 5/15 control
  Phase I and II combined – All Patients

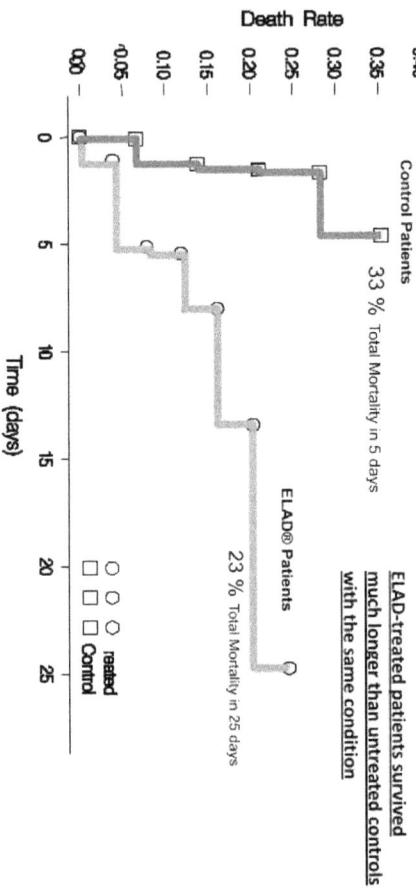

Phase 1+2, combined
FHF 1999-2003
14 sites in US/UK
44 patients, 41 evaluable
Bridge to transplant:
p=0.021

ELAD-treated patients survived much longer than untreated controls with the same condition

Figure 2
Kaplan Meier 84 day transplant free survival
VTI China Trial, 2006-7, first protocol used to file for SFDA approval

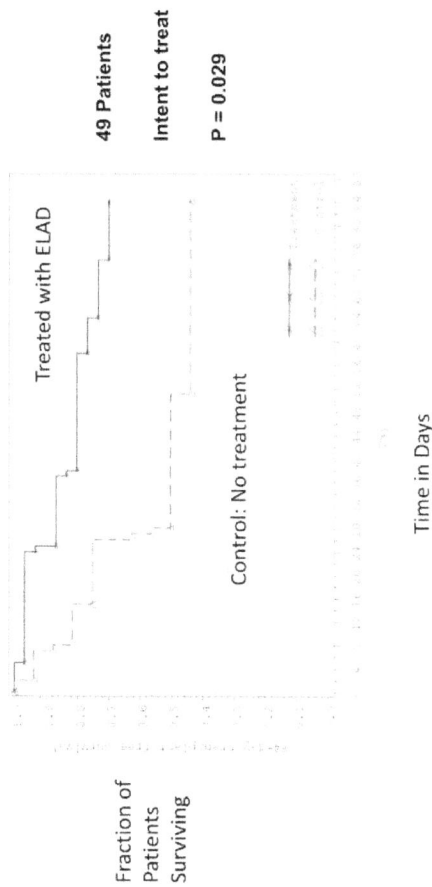

Treated with ELAD

49 Patients

Intent to treat

P = 0.029

Control: No treatment

Fraction of
Patients
Surviving

Time in Days

Figure 3: VTI-208 Phase 3 AAH Trial, 2015

- **Left: All 203 patients; primary endpoint: death/survival from any cause. No difference ELAD/Control**
- **Right: Subset 60 patients selected on pre-specified secondary end points**
- **Each curve starts with 100% alive. Each step down is one or more deaths expressed as declining % remaining alive**
- **Note:**

1. **Similarity of control curves. 45-50% controls alive at 200 days in each**
2. **P=0.006 in subset. Strongly statistically significant. 70% ELAD alive at 800 days vs. 45% controls**
3. **See text for more explanation**

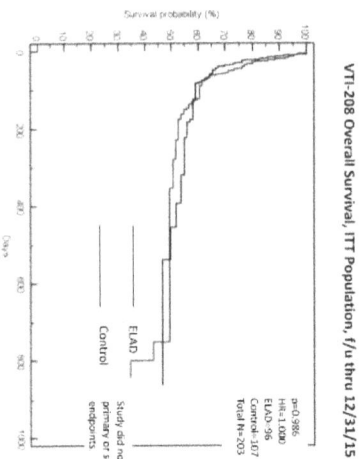

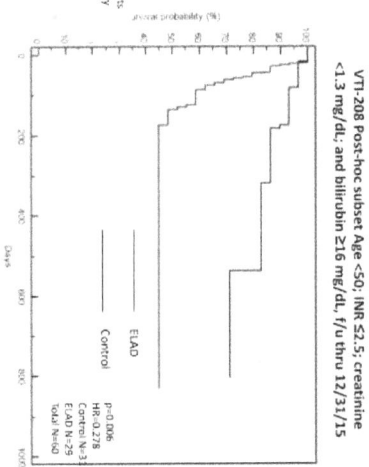

VTI-208 Overall Survival, ITT Population, f/u thru 12/31/15

ELAD
Control

Study did not meet its
primary or secondary
endpoints

p=0.986
HR=1.000
ELAD=96
Control=107
Total N=203

VTI-208 Post-hoc subset Age <50; INR ≤2.5; creatinine
<1.3 mg/dL; and bilirubin ≥16 mg/dL, f/u thru 12/31/15

ELAD
Control

p=0.006
HR=0.278
Control N=31
ELAD N=29
Total N=60

Figure 4: Control Group Comparison in AAH Trials VTL-208/308: p3 trials, 2015 and 2018

What should have been the same were statistically different 308 Trial failed due to control group higher survival.

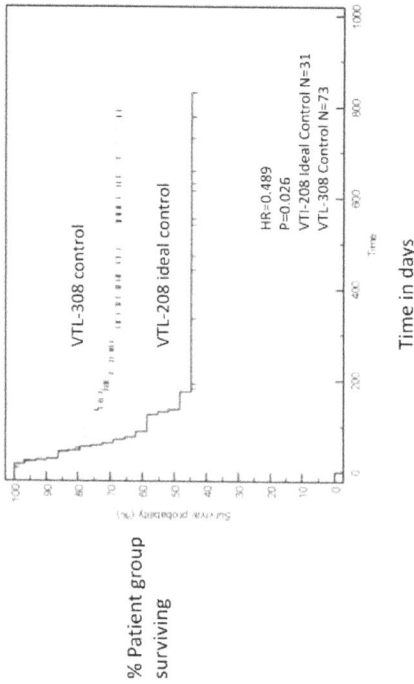

% Patient group surviving

VTL-308 control

VTL-208 ideal control

HR=0.489
P=0.026
VTl-208 Ideal Control N=31
VTL-308 Control N=73

Time in days

1. Both control groups had the same enrollment criteria
2. 70% VTL-308 control group survived at 200 days vs. 50% expected
3. Difference is statistically significant, p=0.026. means that only 2.6% chance the 2 groups are the same, 97.4% chance they are different
4. In 4 other prior trials, a similar group had always shown about 50% survival at 200 days

See Chapter 35 for more explanation

Figure 5: VTL-308 Treated vs. VTL-208 Ideal Control Groups

The VTL-308 trial result if the control group had performed as expected

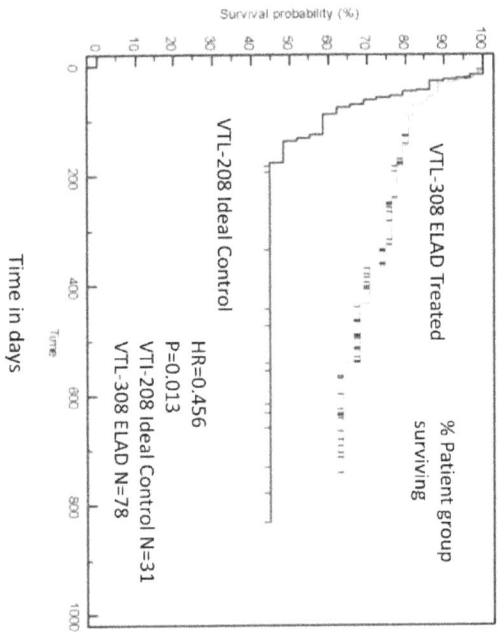

Survival probability (%)

VTL-308 ELAD Treated

% Patient group surviving

VTL-208 Ideal Control

HR=0.456
P=0.013
VTI-208 Ideal Control N=31
VTL-308 ELAD N=78

Time in days

1. VTL-308 ELAD treated group performed as expected
   - 75% survival at 200 days

2. If control group had performed as expected, then result would have been highly statistically significant, p=0.013

See Chapter 35 for more detailed explanation

EPILOGUE

"Success has many fathers, but failure is an orphan" is an old Chinese proverb and is germane to this story. When I took on this CEO job in 2003, I was aware of the high risk of the endeavor and took pains to point it out to anyone who would listen.

The complexity of liver disease makes it very difficult to design therapies for treatment. It is especially difficult to develop a therapy to improve survival from both acute and chronic liver failures. I was well aware that everything had failed before us and that it would be very difficult to overcome such a negative legacy. However, since I was at the end of my career, with no career to protect, I was prepared to take the risk, recognizing that if we succeeded, everyone associated with the therapy and the company would bask in the glory of the success.

However, if it failed, we would be just another company that should have known better. When this was balanced against the enormous upside of potentially saving thousands of lives, the risk equation became heavily weighted towards going for it. I did it with my eyes wide open and I accept the blame for the failure. My defense is to be honest and open about failing. This defense is appreciated by those who are aware of the importance of risk in our economy and culture.

This was a wonderful experience that I would not have missed for anything.

I am grateful to all who supported me and who gave up part of their lives to try to develop a revolutionary product for very deserving patients. I had a superb management team, every one of them much better than me; a supportive board, even though we sometimes disagreed; patient investors who should have made an outstanding return on their investment; and wonderful physicians to work with at the trial hospitals and on our CAB. Last but not least, the patients who battled liver failure and who readily agreed to enroll in our trials to try to advance our knowledge. Theirs is the true risk and courage. Thanks to all of you!

Finally, I would like to thank everyone who helped me with the writing of this book. There are too many to name but the management team needs special mention. Many of them reviewed it, offered really useful suggestions and helped me with my lapses of memory. They do not all agree with some of my opinions but, as always, we agree to disagree.

Thank you for reading the story. If you have questions or would like to comment, I can be reached at: chinatrials@outlook.com.

GLOSSARY

AAH: Acute Alcoholic Hepatitis. Serious liver failure caused by a succession of binge drinking events. The liver becomes inflamed and swollen and loses its function. In serious cases, the death rate is about 50% in 90 days from diagnosis. Symptoms include a yellow skin and eye color known as jaundice, a swollen belly known as ascites and weeping wounds on the skin that don't stop bleeding. The patient is capable of making a full recovery without a transplant if no further alcohol is consumed.

AASLD: American Association for the Study of Liver Disease. The leading US liver disease society.

AOCF: Acute-on chronic-liver-failure. Serious liver failure caused by an acute event such as a drug overdose, in a patient who already has chronic liver disease. The acute event causes the patient to deteriorate into serious liver failure that would not happen in a patient with a normal functioning liver.

BLA: Biologic License Application. The detailed information about the p3 pivotal trial design and results along with all the other details about the product that is filed with the CBER division of the US FDA to request approval to market the biologic product in the US. In Europe, it is known as a marketing authorization application, or MAA.

CAB: Clinical Advisory Board. A group of about 9 leading liver physicians from US and EU who were advisors to the company on clinical trial design and implementation, and all other aspects of liver disease.

CCP: Chinese Communist Party. The ruling government in China.

CIRRHOSIS: A Shrunken, Black, Fibrous Liver. Also known as chronic liver failure/disease where the hepatocytes, the main type of liver cell, are irreversibly replaced with a fibrous mass. Cirrhotic livers cannot regenerate. Caused by a decade or more of abuse to the liver by toxins, usually formed by continuous high alcohol consumption. When this progresses to liver failure, the patient cannot recover liver function and a transplant is the only therapy to save the patient's life.

EASL: European Association for the Study of the Liver. The leading EU liver disease society.

EMA: European Medical Agency. Europe's FDA.

ELAD: Extracorporeal Liver Assist Device. The name of the product that was in development by Hepatix, Vitagen and Vital Therapies for the treatment of severe acute liver failure.

FDA: Food and Drug Administration. The US government regulatory entity that is responsible for the evaluation and approval of all drugs and medical devices marketed in the US. Other countries also have similar entities usually named FDA with the country name preceding the term. US FDA is generally acknowledged to be the foremost regulatory entity in the world and many others copy its actions and procedures.

FHF: Fulminant hepatic failure. A rare form of acute liver failure caused by ingestion of some agent that is toxic to the liver. About 2,000 cases/year in both US and EU. Main cause is overdose of acetaminophen, brand name Tylenol, since the prescribed dose and the toxic dose are close together. Other causes are ingestion of poisonous mushrooms and certain other toxic natural products. Death rate is over 50% in a few weeks. Victims have priority on the liver transplant list.

IPO: Initial Public Offering. The process of selling the company's stock to the public for the first time after which the stock is freely tradeable on the public market, usually NASDAQ.

PI: Principal Investigator. The lead physician at each clinical trial site hospital responsible for treating the patients enrolled in the trial.

PRC: Peoples' Republic of China.

SARS: Severe Acute Respiratory Syndrome. A viral infectious disease that had broken out in Beijing in 2003. Careful management of the cases at our 2 Beijing clinical trial hospitals, before we became involved with them, had prevented further spreading of the infectious disease.

SFDA: State Food and Drug Administration. China's FDA.

VC: Venture Capital. Usually, private partnerships that raise money from financial institutions and invest in start-up companies in an active hands-on way. Recently, the name has come to include later stage investors such as private equity.

VTL-208 CLINICAL TRIAL: The first phase 3 clinical trial run by Vital Therapies with results disclosed in 2015. 203 patients were enrolled with a wide spectrum of serious acute alcoholic hepatitis at over 50 clinical sites in US, UK, EU, Australia and Saudi Arabia. Each patient had a 50% chance of death in 90-180 days in a randomized, controlled trial. Deaths were counted from any cause. Patients were split into 50% each treated and controls. The primary endpoint of survival/death was not met but the secondary endpoints produced much positive data that guided the design of the second phase 3 trial, VTL-308.

VTL-308 CLINICAL TRIAL: The second phase 3 clinical trial run by Vital Therapies with results disclosed in 2018. 151 patients were enrolled at over 50 clinical sites in US, UK and EU with a narrower spectrum of serious acute alcoholic liver disease based on data from the VTI-208 trial. Patients were eliminated who were:

1. Over 50 years old
2. In kidney failure
3. With serious blood clotting issues
4. With high bilirubin levels

See Chapter 35 for a detailed discussion of the results

VTL and VTI: The stock market abbreviation for the company was changed from VTI to VTL after the IPO when NASDAQ assigned the ticker symbol, VTL.

ABOUT THE AUTHOR OF CHINA TRIALS

Terry Winters was born in the midst of a German air raid in Exeter, England in 1942 where his father was sent to help prepare for D-Day, after surviving Dunkirk. After his christening in Exeter's 11th-century Norman/Gothic cathedral, he was well prepared for an eventful life. Raised in London, he attended Addey & Stanhope Grammar School, originally founded in about 1670 by John Addey and Samuel Pepys, and fell in love with science and chemistry in particular. He studied chemistry at the University of Wales in Swansea, graduating with a BSc and a PhD in 1967.

A post-doctoral fellowship at UCLA confirmed that he was not suited to academia and he went into the business side of chemistry after becoming a polymer chemist at Goodyear in Akron, Ohio and a US citizen in 1972. He sold Goodyear's technology around the world and then, after the oil shock in 1977, joined Diamond Shamrock in Cleveland. Licensing technology both out and in to be the basis of new businesses and starting his 45-year career at the commercial edge of science.

In 1981, he was fortunate to become one of a team of two running Diamond Shamrock's venture capital fund at the start of the Reagan Revolution and the nascent biotechnology business. He soon crossed into the private VC world and was a partner in 5 VC funds based in Denver and then in Phoenix. He has founded and invested in over 25 university-sourced company start-ups and sat on over 20 boards of directors.

Approaching retirement in 2003, he took on the leadership of one of the companies he helped to found, San Diego-based Vital Therapies

(VTL), thereby crossing the chasm to run a company rather than just being an investor. VTL was developing a radically new cellular therapy for liver failure and this book is the story of the wild ride that resulted in running the key clinical trials in China and a 5-year quest to gain approval for the product in China where he encountered many challenges you don't find in the US. He was a hands-on CEO and experienced these situations up close and personal.

He retired in 2018 and resides in Scottsdale, Arizona where he lives with Eileen, his wife of 42 years. He is busy playing golf, writing books and founding exciting new companies because "Old VC's never die, they only fade away……."

Vist china-trials.com for more information and a photo gallery of some of the events.

If you would like to contact the author, please email him at chinatrials@ outlook.com

www.ingramcontent.com/pod-product-compliance
Lightning Source LLC
Chambersburg PA
CBHW062123020426
42335CB00013B/1068